# THE STORY OF REO JOE

In the series

# Critical Perspectives on the Past

*edited by* Susan Porter Benson, Stephen Brier, and Roy Rosenzweig


Van Gosse and Richard Moser, eds., *The World the Sixties Made: Politics and Culture in Recent America*

Joanne Meyerowitz, ed., *History and September 11th*

John McMillian and Paul Buhle, eds., *The New Left Revisited*

David M. Scobey, *Empire City: The Making and Meaning of the New York City Landscape*

Gerda Lerner, *Fireweed: A Political Autobiography*

Allida M. Black, ed., *Modern American Queer History*

Eric Sandweiss, *St. Louis: The Evolution of an American Urban Landscape*

Sam Wineburg, *Historical Thinking and Other Unnatural Acts: Charting the Future of Teaching the Past*

Sharon Hartman Strom, *Political Woman: Florence Luscomb and the Legacy of Radical Reform*

Michael Adas, ed., *Agricultural and Pastoral Societies in Ancient and Classical History*

Jack Metzgar, *Striking Steel: Solidarity Remembered*

Janis Appier, *Policing Women: The Sexual Politics of Law Enforcement and the LAPD*

Allen Hunter, ed., *Rethinking the Cold War*

Eric Foner, ed., *The New American History: Revised and Expanded Edition*

Collette A. Hyman, *Staging Strikes: Workers' Theatre and the American Labor Movement*

Ellen M. Snyder-Grenier, *Brooklyn! An Illustrated History*


A list of additional titles in this series appears at the back of this book.

# THE STORY OF
# REO JOE

## WORK, KIN, AND

## COMMUNITY

## IN AUTOTOWN, U.S.A.

## Lisa M. Fine

Temple University Press
**PHILADELPHIA**

Temple University Press
*www.temple.edu/tempress*

⊗ The paper used in this publication meets the requirements of the
American National Standard for Information Sciences—Permanence
of Paper for Printed Library Materials, ANSI Z39.48-1992

Library of Congress Cataloging-in-Publication Data

Fine, Lisa M.
    The story of Reo Joe : work, kin, and community in Autotown,
U.S.A. / Lisa M. Fine.
        p.   cm. — (Critical perspectives on the past)
    Includes bibliographical references and index.
    ISBN 1-59213-257-X (cloth : alk. paper) — ISBN 1-59213-258-8
(pbk. : alk. paper)
        1. Automobile industry workers—Michigan—Lansing.   2. Auto-
mobile industry workers—Labor unions—Michigan—Lansing.
3. Automobile industry workers—Michigan—Lansing—Political
activity.   4. Lansing (Mich.)—Social life and customs.   I. Title.
II. Series.

HD8039.A82U6437  2004
331.7'629222'097742709041–dc22                                    2003067202


ISBN 13: 978-1-59213-258-4  (pbk.: alk. paper)

011711-P

**To Peter**

# Contents

# Acknowledgments

This book is the product of a number of collaborative efforts with members of the Lansing, Reo, Michigan State University, labor history, and archival communities. I am grateful to all of my "partners in crime" for their skilled and enthusiastic assistance and support.

The keepers of the two major collections used in this book, Fred Honhart at the Michigan State University Archives and Historical Collections, and Mike O. Smith at the Reuther Library at Wayne State University, aided and abetted my efforts for more than a decade. Jim MacLean, the head of Reference and curator of the Local History Room at the main branch of the Lansing Public Library, gave me virtually free rein over the important but underappreciated collection he oversees. Peter Berg and his staff at Special Collections at the Michigan State University Library tracked down key materials. Michael Unsworth, the history bibliographer at the Michigan State University Library, was very helpful at an early stage of the work. Archivists at the Bentley Library, the State Archives of Michigan, and the library at Central Michigan University helped as well. I would like to thank Sean Langdon Malloy for tracking down some important documents from the Jay Lovestone Papers at the Hoover Library, and my sister, Tina Fine, Ph.D., who pursued some leads for me at the New York Public Library and at the Tamiment Library at New York University. The staff of the *Lansing Labor News* graciously allowed me to read the full run of their journal in their business office.

Because the Reo Motor Car Company is still remembered and recognized as an important part of Lansing's history, many local historians and collectors were important contributors to this book. My largest debt is to the people who participated in the Reo Oral History project. My greatest regret is that I did not work quickly enough to present this book to many of these individuals before they passed away. I hope this book will be a token of my appreciation to the families of those who shared their memories. Shirley Bradley, a Lansing native and daughter of Reo workers, and I did these oral histories together. I would like to thank her for all of the fun and fascinating times we had traveling around to places like Dansville, Mulliken, Potterville, and Dimondale to interview former Reo workers. I will always be grateful for the pleasant company and the knowledge she shared with me about what is now my own community.

Three people shared with me their valuable materials on Reo. Harry Emmons, former autoworker, car enthusiast, local collector, and recent MSU graduate, shared materials from his extensive private collection. For this, and for many hours of conversation about Reo, I will be forever in his debt. I also owe a very large debt to Kenneth Germanson. After I presented my first paper on Reo, back in 1991, he introduced himself to me and asked if I would like to have the interviews he had conducted with Lester Washburn, the founder and head of the union at Reo, before he passed away. I am so grateful that Ken did these interviews and that he shared them with me. This book would have been impoverished indeed, if not impossible, without this valuable material. And I am grateful to Craig A. Whitford, of the Historical Society of Greater Lansing, for showing me his amazing collections of Lansing photos.

Michigan State University and its scholarly community provided both financial and intellectual support. During both the early and the late stages of this project, I received All-University Research Grants for release time and graduate student assistance. The College of Arts and Letters provided funds for the transcription of the oral history tapes. Graduate students contributed their skills and expertise for the directory, manuscript census, and geocoding projects. Kathleen Mapes, Mary Mapes, Kimberly Andrews, Anne Barker, and Susan Stein-Roggenbuck all painstakingly collected names of Reo workers from the 1910 and 1920 Lansing City Directories and tracked them down in the manuscript census. Susan Stein-Roggenbuck keyed this data into a computer so that we could produce demographic profiles of the Reo workforce. She and I then joined with geographer Kathleen Baker to create maps of Lansing for 1910 and 1920, which are available at www.reojoe.hst.msu.edu. I would like to thank Dean Rehberger, Ryan Scott, Joe Morgan, and Mark Kornbluh for making a beautiful web site. Using Arcview software, Kathleen plotted the Reo workers on these maps. Since I am only minimally computer literate, I am extremely grateful to both Susan and Kathleen for doing this often complicated and tedious work. They were both consummate professionals and I enjoyed working with them.

I was fortunate to receive feedback on my work, both from colleagues in my department and from the larger academic community. Individuals who have critiqued parts of the work in the form of articles, papers, or individual chapters include Patricia Cooper, Steven Meyer, Eric Guthey, Nancy Gabin, Peter Stearns, Elizabeth Faue, Roger Horowitz, Heather Thompson, Jefferson Cowie, and Joseph Heathcott. Rick Halpern, with whom I had a long talk on the way to a North American Labor History conference when I was finishing up the book, contributed enormously to my ways of thinking about workers' resistance. Kevin Boyle's insights and support have been important to me at a number of stages of this project. I would like to acknowledge the anonymous readers who reviewed the three articles related to Reo and the book itself in manuscript form. Series editors Susan Porter Benson and Roy Rosenzweig and the editor-in-chief at Temple University Press, Janet Francendese, provided skillful advice on this unruly manuscript. Lynne Frost oversaw the production of the book, for which I thank her.

Many of my colleagues at MSU are probably relieved that they do not have to listen to me go on and on about Reo anymore. Those who read parts of the work, provided me with information, or chatted with me when I reached an impasse include Peter Beattie, Lewis Siegelbaum, Leslie Moch, Richard Thomas, Sam Thomas, Susan Sleeper-Smith, Kirsten Fermaglich, Laurent Dubois, Tom Summerhill, and Keely Stauter-Halsted. Mark Kornbluh's constant friendship and support was important to me at every stage of this project. Gordon Stewart and Harold Marcus read the entire manuscript in its final stages and I am very grateful for their time and expertise. Harold Marcus, who passed away soon after he finished editing the last chapter, deserves special recognition as a colleague, friend, historian, and skillful editor.

I have some personal debts to acknowledge as well. Fred Bohm provided timely advice about publishing. Ruth Fisk and Hilaire O'Day helped me keep my mind and body in balance—*namasté*. The research, writing, and creation of this book coincided with the carrying, delivery, nursing, and early rearing of my two beautiful daughters, Zoe Ruth Berg Fine and Dana Hester Fine Berg, now thirteen and eight, respectively. My friend and colleague Leslie Moch informed me after the birth of my first child that "babies eat books," and it was a struggle to juggle all of my many responsibilities during the last dozen years. Through all of these uncharted waters, working on this book was my anchor, a psychic "room of my own" where I could retreat when babies, teaching, and departmental demands were not too pressing. None of this would have been possible without my husband and partner, Peter Iversen Berg, to whom this book is dedicated. He knows all the reasons why.

# THE STORY OF REO JOE

# Introducing Reo Joe in Lansing, Michigan

Between 1904 and 1975, on a now-polluted site on the south side of Lansing, Michigan, one could find a complex of offices and factories committed to the manufacture of motor vehicles. Over the years the names and faces of the workers, managers, and owners changed many times, but one symbol provided continuity for the events that occurred at this place: the name Reo, an acronym for the founder of the company. Ransom E. Olds, the famous automobile pioneer and inventor, began the Reo Motor Car Company after he lost his first corporate venture, Oldsmobile. If you lived in Lansing during these years and someone told you she worked at the "Reo," not only would you know exactly what this meant, you would associate the name with a place of pride.

During its first two decades of operation as a producer of automobiles and trucks, Reo and its community prospered; consumers would have found it hard to predict which of the two prosperous Lansing-based companies, Reo or Oldsmobile, would last 100 years. (Nineteen-ninety-eight saw the 100th anniversary of Oldsmobile, although the Oldsmobile line was discontinued in 2001, even as GM builds new assembly plants in Lansing.) On the eve of the Great Depression, Reo produced very popular cars and trucks, employed more than five thousand workers, and was an important and—in its technological

1

innovations, production techniques, and labor-management relations—a progressive local employer. The events of the 1930s seriously affected the company. Reo introduced expensive luxury models just as it became impossible for the vast majority of Americans to afford them. The UAW-CIO staged a successful month-long sit-down strike in the spring of 1937. The company almost failed because of poor management. A major corporate reorganization that limited production to trucks only, an infusion of capital from the Reconstruction Finance Corporation, and the first of many government military and ordnance contracts kept the company afloat.

World War II and the Korean conflict breathed new life into the company. Reo Motors successfully competed for military contracts and tentatively began to diversify its product base to consumer goods such as lawnmowers, children's toys, civilian trucks, and buses. As a leaner, smaller, locally owned corporation making products with a good reputation, Reo was vulnerable to buyouts and corporate raiding. From the mid-1950s until the company's demise, Reo was taken over several times, first by Detroit-based Bohn Aluminum, then by White Motors of Ohio; then it was combined with Diamond T of Chicago for its last incarnation as Diamond Reo, which was bought by a private entrepreneur in 1971. In 1975, the year Vietnam "fell," so did Reo, only two years after its last owner had begun selling off and gutting the plant and its inventory, depriving loyal employees of their pensions. The fire that destroyed the shell of the plant ended a representative story of twentieth-century industry.

In hindsight, the story of Reo follows a familiar script, a story of small, local entrepreneurial capitalism unable to keep up with national and international political and economic forces. In automotive history, this is the story of one of thousands of failures that brought about the oligarchic structures and global corporations of the late twentieth century. Reo's demise can also be interpreted as the failure of the union movement to pose a meaningful challenge to globalization and domestic pro-business policies. The closing of the plant in the mid-1970s foreshadowed the de-industrialization and the creation of the midwestern rust belt characteristic of the last two decades of the twentieth century. The padlocking of the plant caused unemployment, dislocation, and depression.

During the company's lowest point, in the late 1930s, J. R. Connor, writing in the AFL's *Lansing Industrial News*, described a Capra-esque everyman called Reo Joe. Connor described a scene in which "a rather spare figure . . . drifted into the grocery store, appraised the stock, picked out needed provisions, paid cash and went away—silently. He carried his modest purchase a little proudly down the street to his South Lansing home. Never had he asked for credit, never had he asked for charity, never had he spent a nickel that wasn't honestly earned."[1]

The grocer reflected,

> I remember when Joe started with Reo about 13 years ago. He was a big, strong, husky chap who took pride in his work and displayed the Reo spirit. Used to take part in the Reo entertainments. He lived for his family and the Reo. . . . I remember when the union started up. . . . Said he was getting pretty good pay but thought he ought to go along with the boys. When the sit-down came he stayed right with them loyal to the union but still proud of the Reo products. He was mighty happy when the sit-down ended and the boys went back to work.[2]

But the bad times had taken their toll on old Joe.

> Joe started to cut down on his buying, even on cigarettes. He would order cheaper grades of meat, but often I would slip over a pretty good cut on his order. He's awful proud, that Joe, but shucks, he's been a good, steady customer that I like to do him a favor. For months past there has been a blank look in his face—that terrible dread you see in men's faces when they are out of regular employment. Joe finds odd jobs here and there, but his heart is still with the Reo.[3]

The grocer hoped that the new reorganization plan would not only help old Joe but would also provide him with some return on the few shares of Reo stock he kept for sentimental reasons. He concluded with his belief that "it's people like Joe who have made America what it is today—folks who like to build cars and other things."[4]

This book is about Reo Joe and his world: a city, an industry, and ideas about work, manhood, race, and family. Reo Joe was not Joe Hill or Walter Reuther or Sidney Hillman or Eugene V. Debs or George Meany, although he may have heard of all of these men. Reo Joe was a union man, but he may also have belonged to the Masons, the Ku Klux Klan, the Republican or Democratic Party, a sportsman's club, baseball team, or a church. Much of labor history, as it has been done in the United States in the past thirty years, has represented Reo Joe as a "regular Joe," the universal white male worker. In the mid-1940s Ely Chinoy came to Lansing, which he called Autotown, to investigate "what opportunity looks and feels like to a group of automobile workers in a middle-sized midwestern city." He chose Lansing because it was a key site in the development of the automobile industry, and because "its size, location, and population composition [made] it a less complex setting for research into the problems of opportunity and aspirations than any of the other automobile cities." Locally owned manufacturing plants like Reo contributed to "greater stability and promise" for Lansing's workers.[5] Today Reo, with its overwhelmingly white, native-born, male workforce presents the perfect opportunity to reexamine working-class formation, unionization, corporate welfare, working-class leisure and consumption, and de-industrialization, with the race and gender of the overwhelmingly white male workers as self-consciously employed categories of analysis.

This book was conceived in frustration over the continued reluctance of many U.S. labor historians to acknowledge and employ gender as a category of analysis for labor history.[6] The proliferation of excellent works on women workers seemed only to reinforce the ghettoization of female workers' lives and experience within the larger labor history narrative. According to one influential labor historian, scholars whose central organizing concept is class believe that "what defines people as workers is their economic activity," while historians of women are interested in "the construction of gender ideology, the ways that ideology limits the opportunities of women, and the efforts of women to overcome the restrictions of gender role." Thus, because of their different categories of analysis, women's historians and labor historians belonged to different "tribes."[7] This unfortunate bracketing of experience misses male gender identity. Recent scholarship on working-class masculinity as a part of masculinity or men's studies has prompted a rethinking and a decentering of the male worker experience.[8]

Gender, therefore, was foremost in my mind as I began this book, but before long it became clear that race was also an important element in working-class life in Lansing. That workers in Lansing and Reo were overwhelmingly white and native-born was no accident. Racial minorities found few opportunities in Lansing. Malcolm Little (later known as Malcolm X) recalled his family's painful experiences in Lansing during the late 1920s and 1930s and the small community of African Americans in the *Autobiography of Malcolm X*:

Those Negroes were in bad shape then. . . . I don't know a town with a higher percentage of complacent and misguided so-called "middle-class" Negroes. . . . Back when I was growing up, the "successful" Lansing Negroes were such as waiters and bootblacks. To be a janitor at some downtown store was to be highly respected. The real "elite," the "big shots," the "voices of the race," were the waiters at the Lansing Country Club and the shoeshine boys at the state capitol. . . . No Negroes were hired then by Lansing's big Oldsmobile plant, or the Reo plant. (Do you remember Reo? It was manufactured in Lansing and R. E. Olds, the man after whom it was named, also lived in Lansing. When the war came along, they hired some Negro janitors.) The bulk of the Negroes were either on Welfare, or W.P.A., or they starved.[9]

Malcolm X's family experienced brutal treatment in Lansing: his father was killed, his mother was institutionalized, and the Little children were separated and put into various foster homes. To another interviewer Malcolm X articulated the other important lesson of these stories of segregation, brutality, and racism. "They didn't have too many Negro doctors or lawyers, especially where I grew up. They didn't even have any Negro firemen when I was a youth. When I was a youth, the only thing you could dream about becoming was a good waiter or a good busboy or a good shoeshine man. Back when I was a youth, that's the way it was and I didn't grow up in Mississippi either—I grew up in Michigan."[10] Malcolm X knew what historians have only recently started to assert: even if it took different forms, racism in the twentieth century could be as virulent in the North as it was in the South.[11]

Historians' recent explorations of the way whiteness operates in U.S. labor history have revealed the importance of race in working-class formation, working-class politics, and class consciousness and identity. "White racial identity," writes one historian, "serves as a token of privilege and entitlement, though sometimes unacknowledged, in American society."[12] The Reo factory and Lansing were overwhelmingly white, and Malcolm X's experience underscores the power of white hegemony in Lansing for much of the twentieth century. "Whiteness" alone, however, neither fully explains the ways Lansing's working class and the larger community understood itself nor accounts for its activities.

As I delved into the life of this company and its workers and their community, I found that religion and local identity were also extremely important. Even though they lived through significant national and international events, Reo's employees regarded politics through the lens of localism. Because of their background and orientation, some Reo workers could side with employers during the wet/dry controversy of the 1910s and the Americanization efforts of the 1920s. When they began to assert their rights and independence on the basis of class and to form their union in the 1930s, workers did not evoke a "culture of unity"[13] embracing all skill levels, ethnic and racial groups, and sexes; rather, Reo Joes made a union of their own, a union of white, Protestant, tax-paying, home-owning, respectable, male worker-citizens.

Reo's worker-citizens maintained a strong local orientation in their working-class activism and politics throughout the twentieth century.[14] Their desire for local, grassroots control of their community, company, and workplace allows us to understand seemingly disparate and inconsistent sympathies. The mainstream politics of the second Ku Klux Klan enjoyed some local support in Lansing during the gubernatorial election of 1924. During the sit-down strike of 1937, workers justified their resistance by demonstrating their restraint and respectability as tax-paying male heads of households. During the period of labor unrest during and after World War II, workers resorted to a "pure and simple syndicalism," demanding workplace justice and equity from the company, the national labor authorities, and the sometimes indifferent or resistant international union.[15] Their antipathy to outside interference from the nation-state, international unions, or radical organizations could sometimes lead them into alliances with the business class.

The local orientation of Reo's workers was rooted, in part, in their rural origins. Many Reo workers came from farm families and grew up on farms close to Lansing. Many lived on farms and commuted to Lansing. Workers returned to farms during hard times, aspired to farming as a means of independence, or worked at Reo to keep a marginal farm operating. Many more Reo workers retained their ties to the land by participating in the most popular leisure activity and the third-most important industry in Michigan: hunting. Increasingly, throughout the twentieth century, the white male automotive working class demanded access to public lands, the right to fire arms, and the right to hunt game.

Reo's employees saw themselves as part of a factory family and described the atmosphere in the plant as having a family feeling. First devised by management during the 1910s and 1920s, rhetorical and institutional expressions of the factory family tied white male auto workers to their employers through the shared values of masculinity. This paternalistic bargain, based on job security, a family wage, and fair treatment in exchange for workers' quiescence and cooperation, formed the basis for what recurred in different versions throughout the twentieth century. As it organized in the 1930s, the union appropriated this family rhetoric by casting its members as dependent sons seeking freedom from an infantilizing paternalistic bond. Evocations of the factory family waned during the disruptive World War II period but experienced a revival during the 1950s and persisted until Reo's demise. The post–World War II factory family ethic evoked the past while reflecting the new realities of women workers, geographically remote owners, and the presence of the union. As workers experienced the uncertainty and turmoil of Reo's last two decades, the memory of the factory family bound employees to each other and to Reo's past. In the era after the plant's demise, this family feeling took on a nostalgic cast, as retirees continued to recreate the factory family as a way to reconnect with a world they had lost. A 1991 article in the *Lansing State Journal* that reported on the sixth annual Reo reunion was entitled "The Family Spirit Never Leaves."[16]

These evocations of family suggest that we need to refine our understanding of how gender operates as "a primary way of signifying relationships of power."[17] For those who worked at Reo during the twentieth century, gender identity was understood through family roles. Scholars who examine paternalistic relationships between groups with unequal power, whether within the institution of slavery, an oppressive factory, or a village community, almost invariably report that understandings of family roles inform hierarchical power relationships.[18] The authors of *Like A Family: The Making of a Southern Cotton Mill World*, for example, found that "people chose a family metaphor to describe mill life." This was not simply a way to "express their dependence on a fatherly employer" but a way to explain their relationships to one another. Mill workers evoked "family, as an image and as an institution," in complicated and overlapping ways.[19]

At Reo, rhetorical and institutional expressions of family remained a powerful way not only to structure relationships of power and hierarchy but also to organize and enforce privilege. Describing and treating individuals within the community, the company, and working-class organizations as family involved the creation of clear, and sometimes cruel, distinctions between those within the family and those excluded from it. This rhetoric, therefore, was not always a benign device allowing for human connection; sometimes it created and enforced a kinship that excluded others.

*The Story of Reo Joe* is an experiment in perspective; it is labor history that is rooted in the life of a company, and it is local history that explores the impact of national and international events on a moderate-size midwestern town. Reo's workers experienced and participated in many of the important trends and events of the century, but when viewed through their eyes, these trends and events often take on a different meaning.

A great deal has been made of the sea change in party politics ushered in during the New Deal era in industrial centers. Workers "made a new deal," became Americans, and turned their gaze from their employers to the federal government to supply services and safety nets. They sacrificed local control and shop floor militancy for the legitimacy and authority of their national unions, a seat at the table as a respectable, disciplined "American" interest group, and the opportunity to participate in the fruits of the "successful restoration of the mass consumer economy"[20] during the Cold War era. Certainly the Great Depression and the New Deal had a profound effect on working-class people, labor organizations, and labor relations. Reo Joe probably voted for Franklin Delano Roosevelt in 1932 and 1936, but he may well have voted for Republican candidates both before and after these two elections.[21] During World War II and Korea, the bureaucratic requirements of the warfare state presented new opportunities and challenges to workers and their employers. In the 1950s it was to the company, not the national government, that Reo Joe and his union turned to get fringe benefits: pensions, cost-of-living adjustments, and health insurance.

Exploring Reo's history over the course of the twentieth century also challenges labor history's conventional chronology, altering our understanding of change and continuity. The factory family was not simply a product of the nonunion era at Reo, extinguished forever by the rise of the union and the turmoil of the 1940s. A new version of the factory family took shape in the 1950s, attesting to the endurance of this company culture. When examined during the period between 1904 and 1975, Reo's workers do not fit neatly into political categories of radical, syndicalist, conservative, social democratic, or liberal. The Klan had a strong base in

Lansing during the 1920s; during the 1930s Reo's rebels were not communists or socialists but virulently anticommunist and antisocialist Lovestonite sympathizers in the UAW; members of the Industrial Workers of the World made an unlikely appearance during the 1946 strike. And after 1951, the union's importance in the world of the worker diminished. Most labor histories provide little help to someone trying to understand the shifting political profile of militancy and apathy.[22]

*The Story of Reo Joe*, therefore, is an attempt to broaden our understanding of the twentieth-century working-class experience. If it could be proved that the vast majority of American workers in the twentieth century looked like Reo Joe, lived in communities like Lansing, Michigan, and worked at companies like Reo, labor historians might be tempted to fashion a new synthesis around the experiences and perspective of Reo Joe. This would be a mistake. The goal of labor historians should not be to designate any particular group as the "authentic" working class, or to depict any particular working-class experience as more politically authentic or intellectually valuable than another. Reo's Joe's story is important because it is a fresh and compelling story of working-class life that has never been told, and because it explains many recent developments in working-class politics, both locally and nationally.

If Nelson Lichtenstein is right that "from the early 1960s onward, the most legitimate ... defense of American job rights would be found not through collective initiative as codified in the Wagner Act and advanced by the trade unions, but through an individual's claim to his or her civil rights based on race, gender, age, or other attribute," then Reo Joes were forgotten workers.[23] Labor historians need to stop treating George Wallace's popularity in the North in 1968, the Reagan Democrats of the 1980s, the Ross Perot phenomenon of 1992, the so-called "angry-white-man" congressional elections of 1994, and the importance of working-class members of the National Rifle Association during the 2000 presidential election as aberrations, false consciousness, or "co-optation." The need to understand the relationship between a rural/working-class constituency in Michigan and right-wing extremism has taken on a heightened importance in the wake of the Oklahoma City bombing, when the Michigan Militia took center stage in the national media.

If we fail to understand Reo Joe and his world, we will have a hard time understanding the words and actions of Mike Green, vice chairman of

United Auto Workers Local 652, recently quoted in the *Lansing State Journal* on the occasion of the opening of new GM plants in the city. Green helped negotiate working conditions at the new Cadillac plant. "We feel it's a family operation. If it's not your brother or sister or mom or dad that's working here, it's your neighbor. You can't throw a stone without hitting somebody that you know." All of the workers interviewed for the article talked about the family atmosphere.[24] Reo and many of those who worked there no longer exist, but the desire to create family ties, even between community members unrelated by blood, continues in the workplaces of Lansing and elsewhere. If we want to understand a significant segment of the twentieth-century working class (and why GM is building new auto plants in Lansing at the start of the twenty-first century), we need to tell the story of Reo Joe.

## Reo Joes and Their Families

Workers at Reo understood their primary roles as sons, husbands, fathers, wives, mothers, and daughters in families. Generations of families had a relationship with Reo, and I would like to use the stories of four of these families to introduce the themes of this book. (See Table 1 in the Appendix.)

The Leyrer family immigrated from Germany to the Thumb area of Michigan in the 1880s and moved to Lansing at the turn of the century so that the family could find work. Before long, most of the Leyrer family was at Reo. Rudolph, Charlie, Julius, Otto, Frederick, Eugene, Robert, William, and Gustav all worked at the company. My informant for this family was Norma Grimwood, the daughter of the youngest son, Gustav Leyrer, who started at Reo in 1918 and retired in 1961. Gustav's work life was like his siblings'; he went from the assembly line to the experimental department working on navy contracts. He was in the union, even a steward at one point, but became a superintendent and a member of the steering gear club for company managers. The entire close-knit family lived in or near the original family home on the south side of Lansing. As Norma reported, "all of my uncles and aunts lived in the south end of town, which was near the plant. They walked to work. For years I remember my father [Gustav] coming home for lunch and he had an hour for lunch and my mother would have his lunch ready when he walked in . . . my uncles did the same thing."[25]

As Norma Grimwood described it, her family, the company, and the community were all intertwined. As she put it, "this was a family affair." In her memories of childhood, everyone she knew worked at the Reo, and every truck was a Reo truck. "They paid well and they had all kinds of family activities." She and her classmates left school on Fridays and walked the railroad tracks to see the free movies at the Reo clubhouse.[26] Her father was in the sit-down and active in the union during the war but dropped his membership when he joined supervision in the 1950s. She remembers Christmas parties at the clubhouse and hearing the Reo Band play. Her dad and her husband, Don Grimwood (who worked at Reo during the war but quit after the wildcat strike of 1946), both played on the baseball team. Her father and several of her uncles lived long enough to experience the company's demise and the loss of their pensions, and they were profoundly depressed by the destruction of the place where their families had spent their working lives.

Three generations of the Aves family worked at Reo, from the time the firm started until the end. The history and heritage of this close-knit family of English stock, mid-Michigan natives for several generations and proud descendants of Union veterans of the Civil War, are typical of many workers at Reo and of the region in general in representing an ongoing relationship between farm and factory. Grandfather Aves, a blacksmith in the small town of Sunfield, thirty miles west of Lansing, was brought to work at Reo by his son, who maintained a farm throughout his working life; the grandfather worked in the heat treat department and the son as a mechanic in the engineering department. Father Aves participated in the sit-down of 1937 and was at some point a union committeeman. Mother Aves began working at Reo during World War II in the bomb fuse department and after the war was transferred to the newly acquired lawnmower division, where she stayed until retirement.

The Aves sons I interviewed, Layton and Otto (called Ted) maintained ties to the land while they worked at Reo. They were as familiar with breaking up ground with a team of horses and hauling 120-pound sacks of grain as with working on the final assembly line. Both Ted and Layton began working at Reo in the 1940s and continued until the 1970s. Ted worked a variety of jobs in the plant, including constructing buses and test-driving military vehicles, until he finally left in 1972, when American Motors purchased the military engineering division. His brother, Layton, worked as a material handler in the receiving room and in export boxing, where entire trucks were torn apart, boxed, and sent overseas. In the 1960s he began working as a timekeeper and eventually became a "boss."[27] The men of the Aves family had land "up north" near Atlanta, Michigan. Ted recalled, "back in those days, we used to go with tents . . . then shortly after that we got the house trailer and put that up there and now we got a cabin and it sleeps fourteen . . . all the way through all my employment, is hunting first."[28] Both men identified hunting as their most important leisure activity.

Like the Leyrers and the Aves, Glen Green came from a Reo family. His father, Howard, began working at Reo right at the start, first on the auto and truck assembly lines and then, during World War I, as a foreman. With some interrupted service during the 1930s, Howard Green stayed at Reo until 1955, retiring from the tool processing room. He worked only part-time in the beginning, spending the remaining time on his farm in Potterville.[29]

In 1929 Howard Green, his wife, four sons, and one daughter came to Lansing. Howard found work at Reo and was joined by his son, Glen, after Glen finished the ninth grade in 1937. Glen recalled, "when I first went to work there, the first thing they did, does your dad work here? . . . I said yeah. What's his name? Howard Green. Oh, I know him and I was a member of his family, you know."[30] Glen experienced Reo's month-long sit-down strike, the Lansing Labor Holiday, during June 1937, and also recalled how he and his brother and a few other strong young workers were tapped to guard the ballot boxes during the contested union election involving Lester Washburn, the founder and president of Local 182 and the leader responsible for the general strike. Glen was laid off as the company foundered but resumed work in 1941, with a hiatus between 1942 and 1946, when he was in the air force, and retired from Reo in 1974.

Glen was a member of the union but was also a foreman and supervisor at various points before retiring. He did not see loyalty to company and loyalty to union as mutually exclusive; relations between labor and management did not have to mean class conflict. The company and its workers were dependent on each other, so the goal was figuring out a way they could work together. His was perhaps the best articulation of the values that formed the core of the paternalistic bargain at Reo. "When you got a job at Reo, you felt that you could go right through the years and you had a job. As long as you kept your nose clean, you did your job and a little bit more, you were going to be right there and they'd find a way to keep you there.... Reo seemed to be predicated on the fact that if you are loyal to us, we are loyal to you. And they showed their loyalty from the very beginning ... you got a job at Reo, raise your family, you knew."[31]

Adolph Janetzka (later this became Janetzke) immigrated from a German community in Poland (then Russia) in 1896 to join his brother on a farm in Northville, outside Detroit. Before long he made for Lansing, where he drove beer wagons. He made a delivery to a hotel where Caroline, an immigrant from a similar background, was working as a housekeeper to repay her travel debts. The two married and began their family, and Adolph took a job as a laborer at Reo, where he continued to work until he was laid off at the start of the Depression in 1930.[32] Harold Janetzke, born in 1916, one of Adolph and Caroline's seven children, began working at Reo in 1936 and moved up quickly to the timekeeping department. Because he was in a managerial department, Janetzke stayed home during the sit-down strike. Intermittently laid off throughout the late 1930s, he resumed work in timekeeping in 1941, was drafted in 1944, and then returned to Reo in 1946. He was employed in the product-design drafting room and then moved on to engineering. When the plant closed in 1975, he retired. In the early 1940s Harold met Eileen Carstensen, who was working as the secretary to Reo's secretary, Frank McKim. ("He was a wonderful person to work for," said Eileen.)[33]

As Harold and Eileen raised their family, they participated in the various activities offered by the company during the revival of the factory family after World War II. The children particularly enjoyed the Christmas parties at the clubhouse.[34] Eileen joined the Reo girls' club and Harold joined the steering gear club and was an active participant in the Reo golf club. He was also a member of TOP (technical, office, and professional workers), a union organized in 1968. Eileen remembered fondly a visit by Edgar Guest, a "humorous poet from Detroit," as she described him. He had come to Reo as a guest speaker of the steering gear club's annual ladies night banquet on March 25, 1948. Guest, a lifelong friend of Reo president Henry Hund, brought copies of his books of poems and distributed autographed copies to all those who attended the festivities.[35]

## The Poet of the People: Reo Joe's Philosopher

Edgar Guest is an appropriate chorus for *The Story of Reo Joe*. The son of a working-class English immigrant, Guest arrived in Detroit at age ten. He worked as a soda jerk and then as an office boy, and finally got a break at the *Detroit Free Press*, where he became a cub reporter before the start of the new century and stayed for the rest of his life. He began writing short verses for the paper and before long these became his stock-in-trade. He inhabited a social scene that made him intimate with automotive pioneers Charles F. Kettering, Henry Ford, and others who belonged to the Detroit Golf Club, the Masons, and other upper-class social organizations. Guest's enormous popularity was nonetheless based on his appeal to the "common man" and on certain values that recommended him as Reo Joe's philosopher.[36]

At the height of his popularity, Guest's poems and weekly column were syndicated in 300 newspapers throughout the country. While academic literary critics scorned or discounted his work—more than 10,000 poems—he was known as "the poet of the people." His most popular book of poetry, *Heap O' Livin'* (1916) went through thirty editions. Guest's work won the admiration of "millions of readers who believed that Mr. Guest spoke to them about the joys and sorrows of plain, everyday living."

Although Guest's topics were far ranging, he returned to certain themes again and again. In simple, accessible language, Guest articulated values about work, home, gender, and faith that resonated as the "apotheosis of old-fashioned Americanism."[37] One collection, *The Passing Throng* (1923), contained poems entitled "Horse and Cutter Days," "The Old-Time Lilac Bush," "Old-Fashioned Remedies," and "Old-Fashioned Dinners." In a series of gift books, beautifully illustrated small collections organized by topic (*Mother, Father, Friends, Home, Faith, You*), Guest affirmed "traditional" values in what many undoubtedly experienced as troubling and changing times.[38] He reflected on his own personal experiences as a son, husband, father, breadwinner, and Christian to explore manhood during the first half of the twentieth century. Protestant Christianity, the work ethic, loyalty to bosses, devotion to and support of family, love of wife and children, moral and upright values were Edgar Guest's themes. With the high value Guest put on manhood, family, country, and work in mind, let us now turn our focus to Lansing, Michigan, during the years when the automobile changed life forever.

# Making Reo and Reo Joe in Lansing, 1880–1929

We were settin' there an' smokin' of our pipes, discussin' things,
Like licker, votes for wimmin, an' the totterin' thrones o' kings,
When he ups an' strokes his whiskers with his hand an' says t' me:
"Changin' laws an' legislatures ain't, as fur as I can see,
Goin' to make this world much better, unless somehow we can
Find a way to make a better an' a finer sort o' man."
—Edgar Guest, excerpt from "The Need" (1922)

On December 3, 1924, faced with unemployment, a worker named Charles M. Killam of 711 Tisdale Street, Lansing, Michigan, wrote to the Lansing Chamber of Commerce. He was anxious about the personnel policies of many of the largest employers in the city and he determined, quite rightly, that the Chamber of Commerce might be able to exert some influence with these employers. His concern was not over the speed-up of the line or industry slowdowns, or runaway shops or inefficient management causing the economic troubles he saw about him; rather, it was the employment of farmers. Killam explained to Charles Davis, the secretary of the Chamber of Commerce, that while Olds and Fisher Body Co. hired all local men, "other factories here in the City hire a lot of out of town men. The Prudden Auto Body and especially the Reo Motor Car Company hire farmers and men living at Grand Ledge, Mason, Webberville." "By all means," he urged, "all the factories of Lansing should hire Lansing men only unless they cannot get what skilled

15

mechanic they need, otherwise they would have to be hired outside but cut out hiring these farmers. Let them remain on their farms instead of neglecting them to run down."[1] Killam's letter reveals much about the distinctive nature of the genesis of industrial Lansing. Narratives of the rise of the automobile industry in the Midwest do not typically begin with workers writing to the Chamber of Commerce about farmers working in factories. Lansing's story, and Reo's part of that story, offer an alternative vision of midwestern industrialization and automotive history.

Turn-of-the-century Lansing defies easy categorization. Neither a large, bustling metropolis nor a provincial rural district, Lansing was (and continues to be) a midsize city of the Midwest. Within walking distance of the state capitol were factories, residences, a vice district, churches, retail and service establishments, and farms. Farmers could send their sons, known as "buckwheats," for education and work in the city. Daughters went to town to attend school and to work as domestics, office workers, and shopgirls. If a farmer tired of the toil and uncertainty of life on the land, he might come himself and try his luck at the new opportunities for work in mills, machine shops, and stores, and perhaps own his own business one day. Or, if the smoke, noise, and crowded streets held no charm for him, or if a slow economy made jobs scarce, he might stay on or return to the farm. He would have to venture only a few miles to be back in the country again.[2]

The story of how Lansing became a premiere producer of cars, how a labor force was formed to do the work, and how the lives of workers changed there differs from the tales of places like Detroit, Chicago, and even Flint. At first glance, Lansing seemed an unlikely site for the automobile industry. It lacked the history of industrial activity and the concentration of capital that characterized Detroit.[3] It did not have the economic connections to the rich natural resources available elsewhere in the state, such as the ore mines of the upper peninsula or the lumber in the northern half of the lower peninsula. For much of the nineteenth century Lansing was a backwater, literally and figuratively. Because of the dense forests, swampy terrain, and clay soil, native people, explorers, and settlers avoided Lansing. During the warmer months, bugs and disease plagued inhabitants who decided to settle this marginal land. Southwest and southeast Michigan, by contrast, with their fertile land and waterways and some of the earliest railroads, were settled by the middle of the nineteenth century.[4]

It was by chance that Lansing, originally called the Town of Michigan, became the capital city, while the newly formed state legislature decided to use land grant funds to create an agricultural and technical college to the east, in Collegeville, later known as East Lansing. Throughout the nineteenth and early twentieth centuries, Ingham County, the county in which Lansing is located, was overwhelmingly rural. As late as 1910, 90 to 95 percent of the county was considered rural by the standards of the Census Bureau. Plank roads and eventually some basic rail connections were established by 1860. The vast majority of European-descended settlers to the region, however, initially came for farming. Clearing the land created the first industry in Lansing, saw mills, which sprang up on the whitewater sections of the Grand River.[5] Small towns and cities like Lansing and the county seat, Mason, ten miles to the south, provided the market links to the outside world as well as needed services for the hinterland communities.

The first homegrown manufacturing activities—the production and distribution of farming implements, tools, and ultimately machines—reflected both the natural resources available nearby as well as the regional market. The Bement Company, founded by Ohio-born Edwin Bement in the late 1860s, was the largest and most prosperous manufacturing establishment of its day.[6] Building on the foundry work he had done in Ohio, Bement used iron brought in on the new railroad connection, along with the plentiful local wood supply, to make plows, barrows, road scrapers, cauldron kettles, cultivators, seeders, bobsleds, and the company's most important product, stoves. By 1885 the Bement Company employed more than 700 men, and its products were reaching a national market, traveling west with the settlers of European descent. Bement and Company's success by 1890 assured Lansing a place as a leading manufacturer of agricultural implements. According to local historian Justin Kestenbaum, "An amazing number of the plows used in this extraordinary expansion of agriculture were made in Lansing, which by 1890 emerged as a world center for manufacturing plows and other agricultural implements." Until the mid-1890s, much of the city's industrial activity was concentrated around manufacturing wagon spokes, wheels, carriages, carts, and sleds from local timber.

The products of the forests and farms were processed in mills, forges, harness and blacksmith shops, and other manufacturing establishments and sold back to the hinterland.[7]

From the start, Lansing's boosters and businessmen promoted the city. "The Lansing Improvement Company, founded in 1873 by such prominent city leaders as Edward Sparrow, J. J. Bush, J. S. Tooker, and A. E. Cowles aggressively promoted Lansing as a business mecca."[8] These men continued to have a hand in Lansing's future through the next century. Promotional materials boasted of the healthy environment (a complete lie), the wonderful railroad connections (improving but certainly lacking in comparison to other Michigan cities), and ample downtown organizations and services (improving, at best.) Indeed, early pictures of Lansing depicted a spacious city with a downtown reminiscent of frontier towns surrounded by park-like residential areas.[9]

Migrants to Michigan came to Lansing with the wave of New Englanders and upstate New Yorkers who began the pilgrimage westward in search of better farmland after passage of the Northwest Ordinance.[10] Others, like the parents of Ransom E. Olds and many who would become players in Lansing's history, ventured northward from Ohio. By 1910 the city of Lansing still had only 31,229 inhabitants, barely qualifying as a city of 25,000 inhabitants or more. The population's background reflected its geographical origins. Fully 98.8 percent of Lansing's inhabitants were white, and 62.4 percent were native-born whites of native-born parents. The largest nonwhite population was listed as Negro (1.1 percent), with a handful of Chinese and Japanese. (By 1910 no Indians were listed as living in Lansing, although there had been an Indian population throughout the nineteenth century.)

The industries that emerged in Lansing during the late nineteenth and early twentieth centuries drew on a distinctively homogenous labor force, overwhelming white, rural, and native born. First-generation immigrants (foreign-born white) made up 12.7 percent of Lansing's population; second-generation immigrants, 23.7 percent. These immigrants came primarily from Canada (Ontario most certainly since they were listed as not French Canadian) and Germany (1,087 and 1,363 respectively) with a smattering from England (377), Ireland (127), Russia (200), and Turkey (153). Lansing was overwhelmingly native born in comparison to Detroit, where in 1910 only 24.7 percent of the 465,766 citizens were native whites of native parentage. Just over 40 percent of Detroit's citizens listed at least one parent as an immigrant, and a third of the city was foreign born, the largest numbers coming from Germany (44,674), Canada (again not French, 37,779), Russia (18,644), and Austria (14,160). As late as 1930, fewer than 10 percent of Lansing's 78,397 inhabitants were foreign born, with only 1.8 percent listed as Negro.

That many entering the first auto plants in Lansing came primarily from native-born, rural backgrounds affected management and working-class culture in the early factories. Michigan's upper peninsular mines attracted Finns, French Canadians, and Italians in large numbers, while to the southern lower peninsula's prosperous and diversified farmlands came primarily Yankees from New York, New England, and the Ohio Valley, as well as immigrants from Ontario (English-speaking), Germany, and Holland. Family, church, and community provided the important organizing institutions to those settled on the land. German immigrants in particular, many of them Catholics, formed close-knit insular communities, with names like Westphalia and Frankenmuth, throughout the southern tier of counties. The farmers of this region were much less involved in the cooperative or political or radical farmers' activities of the late nineteenth century than were farmers in the midwestern corn belt or the southern United States. The National Alliance and Populist Parties did not find significant strongholds in southern Michigan. The farmers' conservative and capitalistic values, the prosperity and diversification of farming in this region, and the ability of farmers to avail themselves of Michigan State Agricultural College's (later MSU's) useful extension services account for the relative tranquility of this hinterland. Only the Patrons of Industry and the Grange flourished for short periods of time, and these groups were dedicated primarily to fostering farmers' mutual aid. Both the prosperity on the land and the personnel from the land created the conditions for the start of the automobile industry in Lansing.[11]

In 1880 Pliny and Sarah Olds moved to Lansing. Having been a blacksmith, machinist, and farmer in Ohio, Pliny Olds came to Lansing after exchanging his farm for a small machine shop on River Street. He established his business with his eldest son, Wallace, while his younger boy,

Ransom, went to high school and then to a local business college to learn bookkeeping to help the family business. Olds and Son produced small steam engines primarily for farm use. Like many other automotive pioneers, Ransom Olds was schooled in the machine shop and nurtured by the promise of technology to solve the problems of the world and make him money at the same time.

Ransom Olds's story departs somewhat from the scripted narrative of the plucky young inventor who makes good.[12] Even though he became and remained a rich man, Olds did not stay with the two automobile companies he began. Olds never achieved the financial heights or national notoriety of Henry Ford, but he did make important contributions that changed the course of the industry itself. And throughout his life, a relatively quiet and uneventful one compared to Ford's, Olds continued to invent and patent new devices and processes as well as own, operate, and speculate in land and business ventures. One source of his ongoing popularity in the Lansing area was that even though he summered in the northern Michigan resort of Charlevoix, wintered in Florida, and divided the rest of his time between his more modest Lansing home and his opulent estate on Grosse Isle, down river from Detroit, Olds always called Lansing his home. The citizens of Lansing tolerated their peripatetic native son as long as he continued to return often enough to maintain the flimsiest ties. Olds's loyalty to his hometown was certainly inscribed upon many of the city's structures. In addition to the two major automotive works that bore his name, there was also the Hotel Olds, the Olds bank and office building (often called the Olds Tower) and R. E. Olds Hall, on the campus of MSU. Olds's economic connections to the city of Lansing extended beyond enterprises that bore his name, either as owner or shareholder in many smaller, auto-related companies based in Lansing.

According to most accounts, Ransom Olds first imagined powering a carriage with steam. The idea apparently came from his encounters with the railroad and steam-powered boats as well as from his dislike of horses and their effect on the urban environment. Sometime in the mid-1890s, however, Olds made the important decision to use a gasoline engine in his horseless carriages. No isolated tinkerer and dreamer, Olds had knowledge of and contact with the larger scientific and engineering world and had enough business background to know that he would need financial assistance to get a manufacturing enterprise off the ground. He most probably decided to switch to the gasoline engine after a visit to the Chicago World's Colombian Exposition, where he saw European vehicles with gasoline engines. The decision may also have been prompted by his reading of the journal *Scientific American*, which reported on innovations in the engineering of motor vehicles (including his own). In 1897 Olds delivered a paper before the Michigan Engineering Society in which he described his recent thinking and progress with this horseless carriage. When he realized that he had a marketable invention, he approached a wealthy businessman for the financial backing to begin manufacturing autos.[13]

The company started slowly, but soon news of the successful innovations convinced his financial backers of the need to move the base of operations to Detroit, which quickly became the center of automotive innovation and manufacturing. This moment at the turn of the century is crucial to our story of Reo in a number of ways. First, during this period, according to sketchy evidence, Olds experimented with what was then called progressive production. Since most of the early plants were assembly plants using parts made elsewhere, the organization of work was key in determining the rapidity and efficiency of production. According to Charles F. Kettering, an important engineer as well as writer about the automotive industry, "Olds took the first steps in modern assembly line development by an improved system of routing material in process ... applying the progressive system of assembly for quantity production."[14] Duane Yarnell, who wrote a biography of Olds that was copyrighted by Olds himself, also described how "the original assembly line was somewhat crude ... cars moved along wooden platforms, supported by rolling casters underneath."[15] Yarnell, obviously reporting an anecdote told by Olds himself, also described how "one interested observer, a tall, thin-faced man in his thirties, ... stood looking on at the progress which was being made. This young man worked from the Detroit Edison Company at an annual wage of $1,000.00. His name was Henry Ford. When R. E. saw him watching one of the curved-dash models undergo a road test, he said, 'Henry, this is going to be a great business. Why don't you get into it?'"[16]

Olds may also have preceded Ford in his desire to build a car for the masses. The curved-dash Olds was one of the first successful U.S.-made runabouts, that is, a light car made relatively inexpensively, easy to service and fix. Responses to national and trade advertising had proved successful; orders were up by early 1901 and Olds had decided to commit the company's resources to this profitable venture. Then, on March 9, 1901, a fire engulfed the Olds Motor Works factory in Detroit while Olds was away on vacation with his family. According to Yarnell, (undoubtedly quoting Olds again) "one of his loyal workers, an employee named Jim Brady, had realized the importance of saving the curved-dash model. He had remained behind, with the flames licking at his heels, and at great personal danger. But he had somehow managed to save one of the models, as well as all the drawings and specifications. The factory building was a complete loss. But in R. E.'s mind, the most important thing had been preserved."[17] Actually, according to George S. May, a more objective biographer, the specifications and plans for all the Olds models had been saved, and the plant was up and running within months. Yarnell (and Olds) wanted the world to believe that the fire had created the conditions that prompted the Lansing Business Men's Association to lure the enterprise back to Lansing with an enticing land deal. The fire was presented as momentous, cathartic, fateful; the modern Oldsmobile Corporation had arisen from its ashes.[18]

The final straw, however, and the final significant dimension of the Detroit experience, was labor unrest. In the early automobile factories, the skill and initiative of craftsmen was key to the successful creation of a car. These early workshops frequently used the labor of skilled machinists, men either from backgrounds like that of Olds himself or, in some cases, from bicycle shops.[19] These workers had, by the turn of the century, long experience with trade unionism, and despite the newness of the automotive industry, they did not see their experiences as fundamentally different from that of their brothers in other machine shops. When the first automobile factories were getting started in Detroit and elsewhere after the depression of the 1890s, these machinists were beginning to flex their muscles.[20]

Ransom Olds had already sparred with organized labor in Lansing in early 1898. After a shop superintendent dismissed Wallace Olds (Ransom's brother) because of his sympathies with the machinist union getting organized in the shop, Olds replaced his brother with Richard Scott, a Canadian recruited from a shop in Toledo. Scott, who remained with Olds throughout the 1920s, when he ran the Reo Motor Car Company, had a reputation for imposing strict moral and industrial discipline among his workers. According to one worker, Scott began to speed up production as soon as he arrived on the scene, insisting "that one of the men run two machines." This action precipitated a walkout of thirty workers.[21]

Ransom Olds, who treated his workers fairly and employed union and nonunion men alike, saw this strike as an opportunity to change the rules of the game. He told a reporter that he "was not sorry for a change in the working force" and added, "we have men who have worked for us 12 years and somehow they got in a rut. By a long continuance in one's employ, they come to think they ought to run the business."[22] Olds pledged to hire men who presumably would be better suited to the new workplace he had in mind. After just a few weeks, however, the workers blinked, perhaps realizing that Ransom was not going to reinstate his brother after Wallace left Lansing and sold his stock in the Olds Gasoline Engine Works.[23]

Olds reorganized, recapitalized, and renamed his manufacturing activities Olds Motor Works and moved it all to Detroit,[24] where once again workers, acting as good machinists in honoring a call for a nationwide strike for the nine-hour day, challenged his managerial prerogative.[25] Faced with the potential strike of 700 workers, twenty of Detroit's largest employers of machinists met to pledge their opposition to the nine-hour demand. Both sides assumed their own moral, righteous, manly stance, assuring opponents that they had no grievance with individuals, just groups. Superintendent Calder of the Detroit Shipbuilding Company, one of the twenty employers opposing the union, said, "We have no disagreement with the men, but we cannot and will not sign that agreement." Taking their lead from the international union, the machinists of Detroit were resolved to stand on their own, "opposed to sympathetic strikes. We are going to win this battle on manly lines," said business agent Gore.

When the strike entered its second week, violence erupted at the Olds Motor Works. According to the *Detroit Free Press*, a "lively riot" occurred at 5:15 P.M., when a dozen strikers were joined by "500 men, comprised principally of workingmen of different shops," prompting the intervention of twenty-five patrolmen. The crowd stormed the factory and pulled out nonunion workers. "Three . . . received badly swollen and black eyes and suffered with bloody noses. . . . 'There was a colored man there,' said one of the officers, 'and he informed me the men tried to get at him. Yet, he told me, that they would not let him join the union when he applied.'" Armed with gas pipes for protection, police escorted the nonunion men out of the plant at quitting time.

Olds acted quickly. He had sought an injunction against the union to stop members from picketing at the plant and threatened that he was going to use University of Michigan engineering students and graduates to replace striking workers. As the unusually hot summer dragged on and the machinists made significant gains in cities throughout the country, the manufacturers' group, including Olds, resisted the machinists. By August 1901 Olds had decided to move the plant to Lansing.[26] This episode revealed Olds's shrewd calculation that Lansing's skilled workers would be cheaper and less militant than their counterparts in Detroit.[27]

The Olds Motor Works had reestablished its main assembly plant in Lansing by the end of 1901. Workers' barracks were erected to ease the housing problems caused by the move. Within a year Olds had built a new home for his family and returned to live in Lansing (see Illustration 1). Just as Olds and his invention were beginning to receive national publicity and some financial success, Olds extricated himself from the company he had begun. Disagreements with his financial backers over administration and production prompted Olds to divest himself of his stock in the company and to resign from the board of directors.[28]

Ransom did not remain idle for long. He traveled a bit and used the money he had made in the sale of the stock for some speculative ventures. Before long, other men of means from Lansing approached Olds to begin a new motor vehicle company, capitalizing on his name recognition, expertise, and experience in the field. Drawing on longstanding connections, Olds recruited many of his former employees. As a result of earlier stock deals and the holdings of new financial backers, construction of the factory began on a site in south Lansing. New Reos were rolling out of the factory by the end of 1904. In addition to the buggy-like curved-dash runabouts, Reo produced vehicles that reflected Olds's belief that successful automobiles needed to be sturdy and heavy enough to withstand the demands of country roads. The models were well reviewed at automobile shows and in test drives and competitions, and the Reo became one of the most popular and successful cars on the road until 1920. Clever publicity

ILLUSTRATION 1. The Olds family home in Lansing. Photo courtesy of Library of Congress, Prints and Photographs Division, Historic American Buildings Survey, Reproduction Number HABS, MICH, 33-LAN, 3-3.

stunts, such as the manufacture and display of the Baby Reo (1906) and the chauffeuring of President Theodore Roosevelt during his visit to Lansing in 1907, helped make the Reo Motor Car Company more successful than its hometown competitor, Olds Motor Works.[29]

Olds began to change the nature of the industry itself by integrating vertically. In 1906 he organized and headed the National Company, the Michigan Screw Company, the Atlas Drop Forge, and the Capital National Bank, all in Lansing and all supplying his Reo Motor Car Company with parts and services. In 1908 the Reo Motor Car Company of Canada opened for business, and in 1910, in a move with both practical and symbolic value, Ransom Olds purchased the old Bement and Sons plant, long bankrupt, to begin producing trucks, notably the popular and ultimately lifesaving addition to the line, the Reo Speedwagon. Lansing's transformation into a premier producer of automobiles had begun.[30]

## "The City Is . . . Like a Family"
## (Lansing Chamber of Commerce, 1912)

Lansing's businessmen were very well organized and influential, and Lansing's Chamber of Commerce had a significant influence on Lansing's industrial development. In the late nineteenth century businessmen formed the Lansing Improvement Company, which in 1901 became the Lansing Businessmen's Association and finally, in 1912, the Chamber of Commerce. The Chamber of Commerce attempted to lure new businesses to the city, publicizing its charms to capitalists, workers, and tourists alike. It provided the umbrella for a number of what were essentially trade associations, groups organized by their economic activity such as farmers, retail establishments, and, most important for our story, a group called the Manufacturers' and Jobbers' Club, a collection of the important industrialists and manufacturers in the city.

The Lansing Chamber of Commerce promoted an ethos about the city that contained class conflict. Class warfare was a serious and menacing specter during the first two decades of the twentieth century, and Lansing's business elite sought to preempt any problems. Using the metaphor of family, the business elite quelled dissent while preserving their authority as the heads of the community. The Chamber of Commerce proclaimed that "the city is more or less like a family and in a great many families, the children are very different, some being leaders and others not."[31] By controlling the types of industry allowed into the city and the types of immigrants and migrants attracted to the city for work, the Chamber of Commerce attempted to transform this rhetoric into reality. They stated baldly, "the question may arise as to why Lansing has never made serious effort to bring other industries to the city. . . . Lansing has not invited a large influx of population on account of the many problems which follow in its wake. . . . It brings a large floating population, which is not a desirable class. It results in labor troubles and industrial unrest, particularly during dull business periods."[32] Throughout the first three decades of the twentieth century, the Lansing Chamber of Commerce committed itself to an industrial program that attracted the kind of industries that would pay a family wage, so that a male worker and the occasional female head of household or daughter could support the family.[33]

These mostly white Anglo-Saxon Protestant business, civic, and political leaders of the community shared and embodied a set of values that acknowledged and faced the technological, spatial, and population changes brought about by the start of the new century. Consummate pragmatists, they sought ways to accommodate what they considered core values— religion, loyalty and pride of country, the work ethnic, traditional family roles, home ownership, "respectable" leisure, and an intense localism—to changed conditions brought on by urbanization, immigration, and mass society.

The more heavy-handed efforts to preempt class conflict involved stifling any organized labor activity, supporting Prohibition, and limiting the immigration into the city of undesirable immigrants (and converting to "Americanism" those already there). Although Lansing's labor history dates back to the late nineteenth century, it always had a reputation as a tough town for unions. The Michigan Federation of Labor, at its annual convention in Lansing in 1915, included barbers, bookbinders, carpenters, cigar makers, pattern makers, pressmen, press assistants, streetcar men, musicians, stage hands, and a typographical local affiliated with the Lansing Trades and Labor Council; but it also reported that "there is an excellent field in Lansing in the following crafts—plumbers, molders, machinists, painters, and decorators."[34]

When the molders went on strike on May 18, 1912, to form a union, the Manufacturers' and Jobbers' Club went to work. Molders were primarily employed in the forges and machine and engine shops throughout Lansing, supplying parts to the automotive industry. Aware that union recognition was the issue, the Manufacturers' and Jobbers' Club set out to infiltrate and destroy the incipient movement.[35] Three weeks into the strike, the club officially stated that it would appoint a "disinterested committee" to investigate the causes of the unrest and report to the people of Lansing. One of the companies affected, Seager Engine Works, pursued an injunction against the union that resulted in the arrest of five union members.[36] With no solution in sight, the Lansing Iron Molder Union 225, 153 strong, took to the streets on July 11 in a peaceful march, an American flag and fourteen-piece band leading the way, with banners proclaiming, "a traitor to his trade is worse than a traitor to his country," "higher wages we demand so we can prosper," "the most powerful weapon of the workingman is to be unified," and "short hours means more education."[37]

By late July the manufacturers' patience had run out. Buoyed by the sentencing of one of the striking molders arrested for violating the injunction[38], seven of the affected companies issued an ultimatum in the local newspapers stating that they would begin employing replacements (scabs).[39] The Manufacturers' and Jobbers' Club set out "to immediately break the Molders' strike and prevent possible walk-outs in other departments." Each member was supplied with the names of striking molders "to enable him to prevent their employment in his factory."[40] During this period, as a machinists' union was forming in the Seager Engine Works, C. A. Henry, its general superintendent, provided the Chamber of Commerce with a list of those attending the union meeting. In addition to the names of 200 men in a number of enterprises, Henry also identified three men—Leland, Stewart, and Metzger—whom Henry had sent in as infiltrators.[41]

Although systematic documentation is lacking, there is evidence that management gathered intelligence, infiltrated unions, and took other forms of direct action until the 1920s and beyond. In 1913, for example, the Manufacturers' and Jobbers' Club established a card file that they called the Free Employment Bureau but that actually kept track of Lansing workers' union activities. By 1919 the Lansing Chamber of Commerce was receiving weekly reports from the Corporation Auxiliary Company in Detroit on the "union activities for the central district of Michigan,"[42] and also probably maintained a blacklist of union members in the city.[43] When a worker at Reo spoke about the machinists' union in 1918, a foreman reported him to personnel director Cy Rath, who instructed the factory superintendent to have the foreman "watch the man closely and send him a dismissal slip on the very first infraction of the Reo rules."[44]

When the United Automobile, Aircraft, and Vehicle Workers of America (UAAVW) came to Lansing to organize in the summer of 1919, its representatives met with unusual opposition. Organizer Charles E. Dickerson reported that "the situation here is absolutely funny; can you imagine a Chamber of Commerce fighting labor's battle?" Charles Davis, the secretary of the Chamber of Commerce, alleged that the UAAVW of America was in Lansing to "break up the unions already established, then to leave them disrupted; that this organization was backed by manufacturers to accomplish this purpose."[45] Although Dickerson did all he could to disabuse Davis of this misconception, the union found it impossible to find a hall in which to hold its meetings. Again and again an arrangement would be made only to have Lansing police tell the organizers that the hall's owner had changed his mind. At the biennial convention the following year Dickerson described the failed efforts in Lansing and added that efforts to establish a local at this time had been abandoned.[46] Although unions were not exactly thriving during this period, either in general or in the automotive industry specifically, the UAAVW of America had limited success in cities like Buffalo, Toledo, Cleveland, Chicago, Flint, Detroit, and even Grand Rapids. But it decided to abandon Lansing in the face of the stiff resistance of the local Chamber of Commerce.

Lansing's elites were also concerned about alcohol use among workers. "Wets" and "drys" battled between 1910 and 1918, the years preceding Prohibition. Six months before the general vote on local option, the Lansing Chamber of Commerce declared itself "opposed to the opening of any saloons as heretofore existed in the city," and pledged "to oppose any measure which attempts to legalize the 'open saloon' . . . a menace to the moral and social welfare and a detriment to the business prosperity of our city."[47] Reo's management was involved in these efforts. Richard H. Scott, the superintendent of the Reo factory, was chairman of the Ingham County Local Option Committee[48] and president of the Anti-Saloon League of Michigan.[49] Dry rallies took place in the Reo plant. Horace E. Thomas, chief engineer at Reo, stated at one of these that the return of booze "would be the worst thing that could happen to the large industries of Lansing." A reporter sympathetic to the dry cause, Miss Aleta Estes Munger, opined that "To me a dead town at 11:00 P.M. means a town in bed and asleep—a decidedly 'live town' at 6 or 7 o'clock in the morning, when the men and women set out for their day's tasks." A town without liquor meant "bright eyes" in offices and stores, "steady hands" at the machines and factories, "happy children and joyous mothers."[50]

Throughout this period, Lansing was fairly split on the issue of alcohol. Although the Michigan Federation of Labor opposed Prohibition, the rank and file of Lansing did not unanimously agree. The successful mobilization of the most prominent elite in the capital city and the state, and the coerced or willing compliance of many workers, meant that there were many "dry" years before the passage of state and national prohibition laws.[51]

Prohibition went hand in hand with the business elites' efforts to encourage certain types of industries and the immigrants they brought. The Lansing Chamber of Commerce also tried to control the types of religious denominations in the city. Industrial cities elsewhere had religious institutions that catered to a multiethnic, religiously diverse population, but Lansing's offerings were comparatively meager. In 1923, when an African American appealed to the Chamber of Commerce for help in raising funds for a new Baptist Church, the Chamber declined, claiming that the city's four "colored" churches sufficed. One year later, when a Mr. Goldberg requested the Chamber's endorsement of a new Jewish temple, it also demurred, though it ruminated that the "Jewish organization is somewhat different from the numerous other requests for new churches, especially among colored people."[52] Workers and their employers sometimes agreed about the consequences of greater diversity in their community. When the Michigan Federation of Labor met in Detroit in September 1907, delegates noted that more than 1 million immigrants from Italy, Russia, and Austro-Hungary, "with their low standard of living, their prejudices, their disposition toward violence, their contempt of law and order," had been unloaded on the country. This "alien industrial menace" needed to be restricted or abolished altogether, and the Michigan Federation of Labor resolved to ask the American Federation of Labor to prepare a bill to accomplish this end.[53] At least regarding Lansing's population growth, the overwhelmingly white Anglo-Saxon Protestant workers and business elites could agree: they all wanted the city peopled by more of their own.

## Making Common Ground

The homogeneity of Lansing's population abetted the hegemony of the business class. Fraternal societies, religious institutions, civic associations, and urban residential space itself allowed for ample interaction between the workers and the owners and managers during these early years. That workers and members of the business class met together at their fraternal societies, in church, at civic groups, on the street, or at their children's schools does not necessarily mean that bonds between the classes existed; but for some members of the working class, the elite's willingness to fraternize, to participate in common spiritual and civic activities, and even to live in the same neighborhoods must have been powerful examples of shared values. The weakness of Lansing's labor movement may have resulted as much from these interactions as from outright repression.

Turn-of-the-century Lansing was a hotbed of organizational activities, but not of self-described working-class organizations. While the city's anemic labor movement, consisting of a city central, the Lansing Trades and Labor Council, and small affiliated trade unions, struggled, thousands of white, primarily Protestant men belonged to lodges, secret societies, and a variety of civic organizations. The nineteenth century had seen the proliferation of "secret societies" made up of men of many different class backgrounds and even different races and religions, which have been recently understood as manifestations of distinctively masculine white middle-class culture.[54]

During the early twentieth century, despite its relatively small size, Lansing was a vital site of this type of masculine culture. According to a publicity handbook published by the *Lansing Journal* in 1906, Lansing was a "secret and fraternal society town," with twenty-nine organizations with sixty-two lodges. These organizations, many with multiple lodges in the city, included the Masons, Knights of Pythias, Odd Fellows, Elks, Grand Army of the Republic, Modern Woodmen of America, Knights of the Templar, and Knights of Columbus, as well as the more obscure and vividly named Knights of the Grip, Knights and Ladies of Security, Loyal American Assembly, K.O.T. Maccabees, Knights of Honor, and the Deutchen Order of Harugari, to name only a few.[55] The Masons, one of the largest groups, had eight lodges in the city in 1909 and listed more than 2,000 members in its directory.[56] Lansing directories reflected the proliferation of these fraternal and secret societies through much of the teens; in 1912, the last year in which these societies were listed, Lansing had twenty-three separate organizations with sixty-one locals.[57] In a population of fewer than 25,000, this meant that the average white adult citizen of Lansing maintained an active organizational life. The Lansing Elks Lodge, founded in 1891, drew its members from "all sections, from all denominations, and from all political parties."[58]

Fraternal societies may have provided an important outlet for working-class organizational activities during this period of hostility toward other forms of working-class organization.[59] In 1904, during its annual convention in Jackson, Michigan, the Michigan Federation of Labor passed a resolution urging all friends of labor to request that the secret and fraternal organizations patronize the union label of the Cigar Makers International Union of America. This request was apparently prompted by the "large number of the members of labor organizations who have joined the secret and fraternal organizations of the state."[60] When the federation convened in Lansing ten years later (in the Chamber of Commerce Hall), the Lansing Loyal Order of the Moose, "also a laboring man's organization," invited those in attendance to avail themselves of the order's headquarters while in the city.[61] The vigor of the city's fraternal organizations suggests that white male citizens of different classes shared common ground.

The business elite's participation in religious, educational, and civic organizations also created opportunities for social control, again through the appearance, and often the reality, of mutual interests. Ransom E. Olds and Richard Scott were among the founding members of the YMCA. An important part of the Y's program was promoting industrial harmony. The Y offered an industrial program with a basketball league, vocational classes, shop meetings, an employment department and naturalization program, and a foreman's club.[62] The Y also sponsored entertainment designed to bring workers and management together, including industrial "stunt" nights. It was not uncommon, the local paper reported, "for bosses to take off their coats and compete with men in relay races, pillow fights, cageball games, and other sports."[63] Lansing's YWCA was an important outlet for the wives of Reo's supervisors as well. Both Mrs. Ransom Olds and Mrs. Richard Scott joined the board of directors as soon as the organization became affiliated with the national board in 1906. Both women were instrumental in establishing a residence home for girls and a camp at a nearby lake. Foreign community clubs and nationality clubs targeted mothers and daughters of certain ethnic groups for "Americanization work."[64] Richard Scott was a trustee of the downtown Central United Methodist Church, which had 820 members in 1915. In 1921 the Scotts provided funds for both a Temple House and a small chapel, the former so that the church could "serve with a seven day a week service and not operate only on Sunday, in order to build the physical and social life of the community as well as [the] moral and spiritual."[65]

Men of the business class also actively participated in the delivery of public education in Lansing. According to the historian of the Lansing schools, during the late nineteenth and early twentieth centuries, "one would find in the composition of [the Lansing School Board] a cross cut section of the best and most substantial elements of the city's life.... Industry has furnished such well known leaders as Schuyer Seager, the Bement Brothers, R. E. Olds, Eric Teel, Christian Breisch, and C. C. Carlton."[66] During these early years, the children of working-class and business-class families went to school together.

The arrangement of Lansing's neighborhoods provided additional sites for interclass contact. One of the most striking features of early twentieth-century Lansing was the relatively undifferentiated urban space and minimal residential segregation by class. Even today, a drive through the downtown neighborhoods of Lansing reveals a promiscuous mix of retail, manufacturing, and residential space of varying value. In the first decades of the century, the proximity may have functioned to both reflect and forge the mutual interests of the different economic classes.

In 1910, when Reo had 1,024 employees, 426, belonging to 367 families, were located in the manuscript census.[67] The demographic characteristics of these employees mirrored those of the city itself. The overwhelming majority of the 250 Reo workers who were heads of their households were white, married, and in their late thirties; 195 had been born in the United States (139 in Michigan), and 112 either owned or were paying off a mortgage on their home. Of the 55 foreign born, 33 were already naturalized U.S. citizens, and the majority came from either Germany (22) or English-speaking Canada (17). Only 10 of these men's wives listed any occupation other than housewife, and their jobs ranged from schoolteacher to laundress. Even those classified as boarders, presumably a younger and more transient group of workers, conformed to this basic demographic profile.

Although a wide variety of kin relationships might tie a Reo worker to a head of household, the single most numerically important relationship to head of household was that of son.[68] The Leyrer family, featured in the introduction, are a good example. In a rented and undoubtedly crowded home on Sparrow Street, lived sixty-two-year-old Julius, the head of the Leyrer family, a naturalized citizen from Germany (immigrated in 1883) who was married to Gertrude, a sixty-year-old housewife also originally from Germany. In addition to Julius, who was a laborer at Reo, three single sons, Fred, 24, William, 22, and Robert, 17, all worked at Reo as laborers or machinists. A forth son, Eugene, 18, and a boarder, Adolph Rorler, 21, also worked in the automotive industry.

The Reo households were distributed throughout the city. Despite the clustering of the largest boarding houses around the plants, there was virtually no residential segregation on the basis of class. The 367 households examined for spatial orientation within the city's boundaries of 1910 did not cluster in working-class districts. (There was, however, residential segregation by race. There were certain clearly circumscribed neighborhoods in which the small number of African Americans, Mexican Americans, and Jews could live.)[69] When the white-collar, managerial, technical, and supervisory employees are separated out, there is no discernible clustering by class. Similarly, there is no discernible clustering based on whether a worker was native or nonnative, based on ethnicity in major nonnative groups or based on forms of home ownership. (See maps for 1910 at www.reojoe.hst.msu.edu.)

Workers from all parts of the Reo plant lived in Ransom E. Olds's neighborhood. Olds lived at 720 South Washington at the corner of Main Street, within walking distance of his plant. Nearby was Mae Smith, a stenographer at Reo, who lived with a solidly middle-class family. One block away, at 620 South Washington, lived the Gardner family. Forty-five-year-old Charles Gardner was a laborer who did odd jobs at Reo. Also about one block away, at 214 East Street, was the Gill family. John Gill, the fifty-seven-year-old head of the family, originally from English-speaking Canada, was an illiterate factory laborer at Reo who owned his own home. In this household lived his wife, Mary, and five children, ranging in age from eleven to twenty-nine, all working except for the two youngest. The Gills also had six young male boarders, at least one of whom worked at Reo as well.

Mildred Bayes Alspaugh's family lived four blocks away from the Olds home. When Mildred's family moved to Lansing from their farm in Gratiot County in 1911, to improve the educational opportunities of the children, her father, Richard, got a job as a day worker at Reo. Mildred recalled learning arithmetic by tallying up her father's piece-rate slips and that they had a nice, affordable house in a good neighborhood. Her mother made all of the clothing for the five children, and during the slow times at the plant her father mowed lawns in the neighborhood. "He was just a plain old farmer. Now that's all he was," says Mildred of her father.[70] The Alspaughs, Gills, Gardners, and Smiths all lived in the same neighborhood as their boss. It was no different in the neighborhoods of Reo's managers, Richard Scott, Horace Thomas, and Donald Bates (the maps on the web site indicate with O, S, T, and B where these men lived). Most of the managerial elite at Reo who lived within the city limits probably lived in neighborhoods with the workers they supervised.

Even as the company and the community grew during the 1910s, these demographic and residential characteristics remained basically unaltered. As other industrial centers either began or continued to experience immigration from Europe and migrations from the southern United States, Lansing remained a white city. The 2,115 Reo workers located in the manuscript census for 1920 (of 4,711 employed that year) resembled those employed in 1910.[71] The significant majority of Reo workers were male heads of households (67.2 percent, or 1,422), with a median age of thirty-eight years. Almost 17 percent (239) were foreign born, although the vast majority (185) were either naturalized or had taken out papers. The largest number of foreign-born male heads of household who worked at Reo were English-speaking Canadians (67), Germans (47), or English (41). Of the 1,182 male heads of household born in the United States, 71 percent (839) were born in Michigan. Only thirteen of the 1,422 male heads of household in the sample were listed as nonwhite. Boarders, again, were no more likely than homeowners to be foreign born.

In 1920 only a small number of women (132 out of 2,115) worked in the plant. Twenty of these women were heads of their own households and all were white, either divorced or widowed. Only three were foreign born. The rest were related in some way to a head of household. Women working at Reo held a narrow range of jobs, reflecting their class and educational backgrounds. In the factory, women were found in either the trimming, sewing machine, or punch press departments. Women were also employed in the clubhouse cafeteria and in a range of clerical jobs. A smaller number of women were inspectors, timekeepers, or forewomen in the female departments, or nurses in the factory clinic.

In 1920 the 1,375 Reo households identified were distributed throughout the city. While there was some clustering of higher-level employees
on the west side, a healthy array of skilled and unskilled workers lived
throughout the city. The elites that ruled Reo still lived in neighborhoods
that included all the class and skill gradations of the plant. (See web site
for maps for 1920.) Even though both Ransom Olds's and Richard Scott's
neighborhoods contained expensive homes and prominent people, workers from the Reo plant lived within a few blocks. Donald Bates, the secretary treasurer at Reo (who would become company president during the
turbulence of the late 1930s), H. Thomas, vice president and head engineer, Cy Rath, director of personnel, and Harry Teel, the factory superintendent, all lived on the same blocks as plant workers.[72] For example,
Donald Bates lived across the street from the Pohl family. Joseph Pohl, a
fifty-six-year-old German-born widower, worked as a drill press operator
at an engine factory (probably not Reo), and his youngest son, nineteen-
year-old Roman, worked as a toolmaker at Reo. As in 1910, 1920 maps of
Reo workers based on ethnicity or on type of home ownership do not
reveal any significant clustering based on class or ethnicity.

While census material can provide information about residential patterns, it provides no insight into patterns of interaction and sociability.
Nevertheless, the arrangement of Lansing's residential housing is consistent with the goal of the city's business elite to create an environment in
which class difference and class conflict would be contained, both by acts
of covert repression and by overt cooperation and mutualism. That the
sidewalks of Lansing provided common ground for the working and business classes during the early years explains the type of company culture
developed during these years in the Reo plant.

Between 1904, the year Reo was founded, and 1929, both Lansing and
Reo grew. Lansing residents quickly came to see Reo as an important local
industrial enterprise. The industrial business elite of Lansing had made a
good start in creating a "family-like" community, free of the diversity and
conflict so often associated with rapid industrial growth and development.
Even organized labor could share some of management's goals for the
future. In 1919 Carl Young, president of the Michigan Federation of Labor,
addressed his organization with cautious optimism. Although Lansing's
labor leaders complained about blacklists and unfair treatment by putting

"up a manly struggle" and fighting "in a manly way, … the prospect is none too bright," said Young. Nevertheless, he articulated three principles that he believed would spell success for labor's future. First, "a square deal for all, and [that] includes the employer as well as it includes the employee." Second, "that every man, woman and child is guaranteed at least a comfortable living, a wage that carries with it sufficient of food, clothing and shelter for the worker to live in comfort, something to lay aside for the rainy day that comes in the lives of all and something for recreation." And, finally, that "the American labor movement stands first of all for one country, one people and one class." Young denounced "the charge of one big union, I.W.W., Bolshevism, and kindred evils that are antagonistic to the organized American labor movement."[73] Reo's managers could not have said it better themselves. As we shall see in Chapter 2, the square deal, the living wage, and antiradical Americanism were three significant features of what I will call Reo's company ethos or culture, nurtured in Lansing's institutions and neighborhoods and forged in the factory by workers and management alike during the 1910s and 1920s.

# 2

# Reo Joe and His Big
# Factory Family, 1904–1929

The hissing of steam would drive me mad
If hissing steam was all I heard;
But there's a boy who calls me dad
Who daily keeps my courage spurred;
And there's a girl who waits
Each night for all that I may bring,
And I'm the guardian of their fates,
Which makes this job a wholesome thing.

Beyond the dust and dirt and steam
I see a college where he'll go;
And where I shall fulfill my dream,
More than his father he will know;
And she shall be a woman fair,
Fit for the world to love and trust—
I'll give my land a glorious pair
Out of this place of dirt and dust.

—Edgar A. Guest, "The Workman's Dream" (1922)

rom its founding in 1904 until the late 1920s, the Reo Motor Car Company was an excellent example of Antonio Gramsci's observation that "hegemony . . . is born in the factory and requires for its exercise only a minute quantity of professional political and ideological intermediaries."[1] The concurrent developments of Americanism and Fordism during this period amounted to the

Portions of this chapter are reprinted from "'Our Big Factory Family': Masculinity and Paternalism at the Reo Motor Car Company of Lansing, Michigan," *Labor History* 34, no. 2–3 (spring–summer 1993): 274–91.

"biggest collective effort to date to create, with unprecedented speed, and with a consciousness of purpose unmatched in history, a new type of worker and a new type of man."[2] During the 1910s and 1920s, Reo's management did attempt to mold a new type of industrial man—a white male Protestant worker-citizen, and this effort was coordinated with community, civic, and private initiatives of the industrial and commercial elites of the city. Kenneth Park, the editor of the company journal, the *Reo Spirit*, conveyed Reo Joe's qualities in a folksy anecdote. He described how he had witnessed a solitary man in the cafeteria who said grace before eating his "canned beans and flea-bitten hot dog and coffee." Park, like many in the cafeteria, "felt drawn to the young fellow … admired his manhood and his staunch and uncompromising adherence to a principle. The boy was not ashamed of his religion." His behavior was all the more admirable, Park wrote, because in this "jazz generation of thoughtless, irresponsible, cynical unbelievers, it takes courage, and a pile of it—to be a real Christian."[3] Self-reliant, moral, steadfast, almost ascetic—these were the qualities of the perfect working-class man. And "Reo Joe" was not just a company creation; workers, by participating in the factory family, helped to forge a new definition of working-class masculinity.

## Creating Workers' Utopias

To Reo's founder and managers, Reo was not just a way to make money. As members of the business elite they also acted as leaders and role models within the Lansing community. Olds and his family always called Lansing home, but they were not provincial. Olds's personal papers reveal a well-traveled individual with wide-ranging business and personal contacts. Reflecting on his life, Ransom Olds told his biographer, "I could have retired years ago, but the joy I get in business is to furnish a livelihood for men who want to help themselves honestly. My greatest satisfaction has been that my plants have furnished employment to thousands of men who are buying homes, educating their children, and enjoying the ordinary comforts of life along with the rest of us."[4] Through his leadership of the company and in the community, Olds sought to instill certain values by pursuing his vision of a workers' utopia.

Olds's social and civic activities reflected his values and beliefs. Olds belonged to a variety of fraternal orders, including the Knights Templar and the Rotary, provided financial support to Republican candidates (though he flirted with endorsing Theodore Roosevelt and the Progressive Party in 1912),[5] contributed to the YWCA and a variety of religious institutions both locally and nationally, and supported women's suffrage and temperance. In a letter to the mayor of Lansing in 1912, Olds urged the passage of an ordinance prohibiting Sunday theaters. "Their moral effect on the young people is bad, it reflects upon the good name of the Capital City and there is no valid reason why the Sunday theater should be tolerated. Your action in suppressing them," Olds continued, "will receive the hearty approval of all citizens who wish to see Lansing a clean, wholesome home city."[6]

Olds used his company to extend his reach into the community. The Reo Motor Car Company took the lead in organizing industrial sports leagues throughout Lansing.[7] Reo started the first radio station in the Lansing area, WREO, and was involved in residential land development. In 1916 an Olds staff member wrote to Laurence Veiller, the secretary director of the National Housing Association, to inquire about the best housing for workers in Lansing. Instead of large apartment buildings accommodating twenty-five to fifty families, Veiller suggested building single-family dwellings, an idea Olds supported.[8] In the mid-1920s Richard Scott and Donald Bates ran the Sagamore Hill Land Company, a subdivision of single-family homes just south of the plant.[9]

Olds deplored any outside interference from unions, state authorities, or radicals. When the Men and Religion Forward Movement supported the idea of the closed shop, Olds wrote an angry letter to the organization's president, James B. Cannon. Encouraging unionism in this way would mean "a reproduction of the Lawrence affair in nearly every city which will produce more anarchist[s] than any religion can offset," Olds warned. "It is a mistake for the Religious Movement to take up the club against the class that has been supporting the churches." Endorsing the closed shop would "bar out the independent worker."

In this revealing letter, Olds also decried child labor laws, regulations to provide for safer working conditions, and equal pay for women and men. Child labor laws prohibited minors from assisting the family, Olds wrote, and he expressed his admiration for "the young girl who seeks employment and earns an honest living rather than running the streets and going the bad way." Equal wages for men and women would "put the women out of business as the men would have preference when the wages are the same." Compensation for injured workingmen would be a hardship on the employer, who "as a rule has done everything possible to guard against accident." Most accidents were due to the carelessness of the workman, he claimed.[10] The obligation to improve workers' lives rested with the employer, not with interfering outside agencies, and Olds welcomed this responsibility.

One of Olds's more utopian and ill-fated projects was the attempt to create a planned working-class community near Tampa, Florida.[11] Starting in 1912, Olds and his representatives began to survey 37,541 acres on the east side of the isthmus between Tampa Bay and the Gulf of Mexico in Pinellas and Hillsborough Counties. They purchased the land, and in 1916 and 1917 the site was platted, roads were laid, a hotel was built, and construction began on some homes.[12] "Oldsmar" was to be a workers' utopia in the sun. The bungalows were modest and reasonably affordable. The community offered a variety of residences (farm or village sites of varying prices) and contained schools, a church, a power plant, a bank, a variety of options for employment (a tractor factory, a saw mill, a turpentine factory, to name a few), cleared land for farming, and livestock (available from the Olds estate at Grosse Isle, Michigan). An extensive publicity brochure advertised an array of "amusements. . . . Golf, tennis, baseball, and other games will be enjoyed . . . on large tracts of land set aside for athletes. The Oldsmar Fishing and Hunting club—Quail and rabbits are found in an hour's walk. Uncleared districts have wild turkey, deer, duck, alligators, and catamount."[13]

Olds advertised around Michigan, particularly in Detroit, with brochures that extolled the virtues of the weather and fertility of the land, but the enterprise failed.[14] The vision that inspired Oldsmar, however, persisted: creating the right sort of community, with "the right kind of people whom you will find to be good neighbors, among whom you will make friendships which are worthwhile." Perhaps his vision for the American working class could be fulfilled back home in Lansing.

## Creating the Big Factory Family

During the 1910s and 1920s, Reo's management team created a popular array of welfare capitalist programs that formed the basis of an enduring company culture at Reo.[15] Recent historical works on labor-management relations during the first four decades of the twentieth century have significantly revised standard conceptions of "lean" and "turbulent" eras.[16] Gerald Zahavi's account of the "negotiated loyalties" of shoe workers at Endicott Johnson, New York, and Lizabeth Cohen's discussion of the "contested loyalties" of the workers in Chicago's large industrial plants suggest that those involved in welfare capitalist programs were not simply co-opted or oppressed; they took a self-conscious and active role, using these program to their own advantage.[17] How workers responded to these programs and their employers during the 1920s helps explain their attitudes during the Great Depression, when these programs ended and workers turned to the federal government and their national unions (particularly the CIO) for assistance.[18]

Welfare capitalism at Reo created a company culture in which employees saw themselves as part of a "big factory family." While other workplaces employed similar rhetorical and programmatic devices to tie workers to a firm, the manner in which it was done at Reo, and the power and endurance of the culture there, was unusual.[19] Certainly, the coordination between community and factory elites in perpetuating this type of discourse served to enhance its power. The family metaphor was ubiquitous throughout the teens and twenties. It appeared in the *Reo Spirit,* the company magazine, in management materials, in literature generated by Lansing's business community, and in the language of the workers themselves. Evoking the Reo family meant calling upon a series of values and expectations about how men should behave and be treated at work, how workers should use their leisure time, and how worker-citizens fulfilled their duties to their community and nation. The Reo man was loyal to company and country, sober and straightforward; he demonstrated his manliness by his service to his public families—the community and the company—and his private family, the wife and children he supported at home. He demonstrated manliness not through autonomy on the shop floor or through his trade union, but through his cooperation and skill on the line and on the baseball field, not through his participation in an alternative working-class culture, but in his compliance with middle-class decorum. Through the benevolence and paternalism of the company, the male worker provided his family with security, independence, and a place in the emerging consumer culture.

Through personnel policies and a wide range of programs and services, Reo's management clearly articulated its vision of a new type of working-class man. The services and activities available included citywide sports competitions, clubs for hobbies ranging from shooting to rabbit breeding (usually mixed by class but not by sex), clubs for different sexes and ranks in the company, apprenticeship classes, Americanization classes (for the small number of foreign-born workers) and mutual-benefit associations and cooperative stores. Reo workers and their families could listen to the Reo Band and edifying religious programming (from Protestant churches) on WREO,[20] enjoy various types of entertainment at the Reo clubhouse (including the extremely popular movie screenings), and read about all these offerings in the *Reo Spirit*.

Complementing these services were personnel policies, enforced by Reo's labor department and employment division, designed to give the workers a "square deal." In return for their hard work and loyalty, management promised workers fair pay and job security with a personal touch.[21]

As in most auto factories, the organization of labor at Reo was undergoing significant changes during the late 1910s and 1920s. Reo had more unskilled and semiskilled than highly skilled workers, a large plant and workforce with a large output, a labor management plan that stressed efficiency and rational methods, and a bureaucratized organizational structure—all of the hallmarks of a "Taylorized" or progressive labor process.[22] Reo not only manufactured all of its own parts and equipment and maintained labor crews for all of the various needs of the plant; it also expanded its product base, sales division, and the range of its markets during the 1920s.[23] Times were good for Reo during this decade, perhaps the company's most successful (see Table 2 in the Appendix).

During the first three decades of the twentieth century, the degradation of skill, governmental repression of union activity, and the efforts of the middle and upper classes to clean up the unsavory features of working-class culture, such as drinking, rowdy holiday celebrations, and street life, all contributed to rob craftsmen of the "moral imperative of a manly bearing," in David Montgomery's words.[24] Nineteenth-century craftsmen's sense of manhood was bound up with the dignity they derived from their skill and autonomy at work, the resistance they could muster to maintain

"just" hours and good working conditions, their fraternal and trades iden-
tifications, and their ability to earn a living wage. The rationalization of
work and managerial paternalism and repression of the early twentieth century threatened the culture of nineteenth-century craftsmanship and the
masculine imperatives that went with it—control, independence, and fraternity. During these years of explosive growth at Reo, new qualities of
working-class manhood took shape.

Although Reo was in every sense a "modern" factory, the de-skilling of
the labor force was uneven. In Reo's first year of operation, two-thirds of
the workers were semiskilled or unskilled.[25] By the early 1920s, Cy Rath,
the director of the employment division, had begun to use the designa-
tions "skilled," "semi-skilled," and "unskilled" to describe "mechanics,"
his term for the workers in the factory. Of the total number of mechanics
working for Reo in April 1922, 48.7 percent were listed as semiskilled,
35.3 percent as unskilled, and 16 percent as skilled.[26] Because Reo maintained its own staff of skilled workers for a variety of tasks, pockets of male
workers could still claim pride of craft (see Illustration 2).

## Forging Bonds of Manhood at Work

The Reo plant did not distinguish itself as an exemplary workplace in the
standard ways: the wages, hours, and conditions of work were probably
comparable to those of other shops in the industry and were high relative
to other industries. In an industrial environment of great volatility and
uncertainty, Reo promised security and seniority. One of management's
major concerns, and perhaps the impetus for the creation of the employment division, was high turnover. A major goal of the welfare capitalist programs was to tie workers to the company so as to lower turnover rates.[27]
This effort to encourage a long-term commitment to the company both
reinforced and was strengthened by the rhetoric of family. Even if there
were troubles or hard times, even if you did not always get what you
wanted, you did not abandon your family. You did the best you could for
your family and your family did the best they could for you.

Personnel policies favored the retention of the existing workforce and
supported the family wage. Even during the contractions of the labor force
during the early 1920s and 1930s, management attempted to keep as many

ILLUSTRATION 2. The Reo factory around 1905—the blacksmith shop. Photo courtesy of Craig A. Whitford, Lansing.

workers as possible by reducing hours and spreading work more thinly among employees. When one foreman gave preference to single men while laying off married men with families who were just as capable, workers complained to Cy Rath. In a letter to the factory superintendent, Rath wrote "if these complaints are justified, Mr. Hale [the errant foreman] is wrong in his attitude. . . . All other things being equal, a man with a family, who is buying a home, paying taxes and who has given the Reo good loyal service for a number of years, should be given the preference over a man who has no dependents, or who would not feel the sting of unemployment as keenly as the former."[28] As Reo PR materials put it, "with the factor of stabilized employment firmly established in their minds, . . . the workers . . . can feel free to plan their lives without the menace of sudden shut-downs or lay-offs."[29]

This was all part of the "square deal" Reo management promised its workers. The company welfare department distributed to new workers a handbook that read, "friendly relations should exist between employer and employees . . . [but] if you think you have a grievance and believe your own hands are clean in the matter, the Welfare Department will be glad to investigate the case and seek a Square Deal."[30] In 1918 the newly formed Reo labor department reiterated its intention to talk to the men, from foremen on down, to clear up any dissatisfactions or complaints. Established so that it might "be helpful to the Family as a whole," the department and its director functioned as the final arbitrator, "the court of last appeal." To give workers a stake in the productive process, the labor department also proposed shop meetings at which employees could make suggestions.[31] Richard Scott claimed, "I trust Reo men. . . . If any man of you has a grievance tell it out to us. . . . Every one of you will have an audience and we shall do our best to be absolutely fair to all."[32] Reo management accepted that, as in all families, there were disagreements, but these were handled through negotiation, man to man, not through an organized grievance procedure between representatives of labor and management.

The "family" valued its older members as people who could help instill loyalty and minimize turnover. The *Reo Spirit* printed lists of workers who had been with the company for years, and articles frequently honored those with the longest tenure and deepest company loyalty.[33] The *Reo Spirit* of January 1921 featured a picture of seven gray, grizzled master mechanics to demonstrate "their importance in the factory and to the company and the influence which they have had on the lives and success of the men younger than they." The writer of the article, H. C. Teel (an old-timer himself, Richard Scott's brother-in-law and the factory superintendent), encouraged those "of this younger generation," who might not be fully aware of "their long years of training," skill, and wisdom, to "turn to them for a bit of advice, or a little talk to steady you when things get snarled." Evoking a powerful nostalgia for the early days of Reo, Teel recollected, "Back in my apprentice days it was not the president of the company or the superintendent, but a couple of mechanics who were masters of their trade, who held the greatest influence over me, causing me to become their equal—a master mechanic."[34]

The many stories in the *Reo Spirit* highlighting "old-timers" served a number of functions. The evocation of the "old days" tied the ranks of the company together, provided the lure of upward mobility, and also asserted values that had more to do with contemporary concerns. In 1920, for example, the Lansing Chamber of Commerce sponsored a dinner to honor old-timers from a number of plants. As the story in the *Reo Spirit* described it, "The main idea was to give the old-timers the growing city had scattered, the opportunity to shake hands and recall some of the seriousness and much of the fun of ye olde times in Lansing's industrial life a generation ago." Even the "eats" were "old fashioned corned beef and cabbage, . . . that hearty and filling combination that every old time boarding house served 30 years ago when hard working folks started the meal with prayer rather than illegal cocktails and radio music."[35] Alongside the "feed" were a cob pipe and a sack of tobacco for the pleasure of the guests. Ransom Olds, who could not attend, sent a letter congratulating the attendees who had started at the River Street plant. Edifying speeches concluded the evening, including one by A. B. C. Hardy, the general manager of the Olds Works, who exclaimed, "it's your kind of men, the boys who stick and are not carried off their feet by wild theories and the wanderlust to try new pastures, who are the leaven of Lansing's loaf. You represent the stable and reliable citizenship upon which a community must depend in good and bad weather. Lansing is 98½ per cent American. Let's keep it so against Bolshevism, communism, red radicalism, and other crazy 'isms.'"

By honoring the old-timers of all ranks, the company forged interclass bonds as well. George Rosa, for example, who began as an apprentice at Reo in the tool and jig room in 1906 and was a superintendent by 1920, was honored in the same "Old Timers Section" of the *Reo Spirit* as Charles Cook, who began in the shipping room in 1906 but who, after filling a number of positions, ended up in final assembly by 1920.[36] Even though their clothing gave away their economic class, the old-timers featured in company photos were grouped together regardless of class or position, a clear statement that all of these men were important to the company (see Illustration 3).

The company also supported and nurtured its young by starting an apprentice training program. In one of his many meticulous reports on worker turnover, Cy Rath described the purpose of the program. "Because of the specialized nature of modern industry, the old time mechanic who could design and make every part of a manufactured product, assemble

**They Have Been Reoites Since December 31, 1907**

All of the Reoites in this group were in the employ of the Reo Motor Car Co., on Dec. 31, 1907, and have been with the Reo since its organization in 1904, others came during 1905, 1906, and 1907. The names of those in the picture are as follows:

Top row, left to right: Harry McFadden, Leon Royce, Stanford Spurrell, Carl Giersbrook. Dorland Hayes, Chas. Southwell, Thomas Nelson, Thomas Pickworth, John Spayd, Myron Beal, Paul Theodore, Sam Rowe, Chas. Schalla, Gust Semrau, R. E. Olds.

Second row: Harry Lewis, John Fillingham, A. A. Sinclair, Henry Nourse, Chas. Burroughs, Wm. Jordan, Edward Seibly, Chas. W. Stro-

bel, Rudolph Leyrer, G. R. Albaugh, Carl Ferris, Wm. Matthey.

Third row: Jess Stanley, Geo. Steeds, Dan Barlow, Edwin Noyes, Wm. Anderson, Bert French, Wm. Steinman, James Hall, August Schlaack, Henry F. Clark, H. C. Teel.

Fourth row: Peter Bergh, Arthur Sprayman, C. L. White, Herman Hoyt, James Freeland, August Bishop, Geo. Manning, Dewitt Byram, H. T. Thomas, Geo. Smith, D. E. Bates.

Front row: Wm. Schultz, Fred Radford, Geo. Rosa, Jake Siegrist, Dean Parsons, Floyd Greenamyer, R. H. Scott, Andrew Restau, Helen Hall.

ILLUSTRATION 3. Old-timers honored at Reo. *Reo Spirit*, January 1923, pp. 12–13, Reo Papers, box 53, folder 3, Michigan State University Archives and Historical Collections. Photo courtesy of Michigan State University Archives and Historical Collections.

the various parts and make all necessary tools, jigs and fixtures, has almost disappeared," Rath acknowledged. But skilled workers of a different sort were needed just the same. "The 'all around man' is more necessary today than ever before. High grade inspectors, toolmakers, foremen and superintendents must be found." Because of the shortage of men for these positions and the high turnover in this job category, "the Reo Motor Car Company decided that the best way to get these men is to train them, and therefore introduced an extensive training school known as the apprentice department."

Unlike other apprenticeship programs that focused more on company propaganda than real training, Reo's program was legitimate.[37] A well-screened pool of two to three dozen students (no smoking, drinking, or immoral behavior) entered this school and spent two to three years training in mechanics. Upon satisfactory completion of the course each student received a certificate and diploma signed by the factory manager. Significantly, while training, students received monthly wages as high as $125. Graduates were promoted up the line and received substantial raises. Rath explained the advantages of the program.

> During his training period he becomes acquainted with the policies of the company, knows the quality of work demanded, is made to feel that the company desires that he stay with them after he finishes, and has an additional incentive in seeing that promotions are made from the ranks of those holding certificates. With all this knowledge on his part he is anxious to continue his employment indefinitely thus relieving the serious situation of a shortage of skilled labor and preventing a high labor turnover among skilled workman.[38]

The apprenticeship program, along with management's real commitment to promote within the ranks and to lower turnover rates, helped to ensure a supply of workers committed to taking advantage of upward mobility in the plant. Movement through the ranks was in fact common, and labor turnover diminished as a result. The graduates of the apprentice program testified to its success and became models for other workers in the plant.[39]

Reo's management identified loyalty and dedication to the company family as essential attributes of Reo workers regardless of their rank. The company boasted in PR materials that "the factory proper is run under military system and discipline," but also that their men were not mere machines. "On the contrary, we want our men to stay men . . . intelligent, loyal men they are, and respond to square treatment by giving the best they have."[40] Reo's annual report for 1921 reminded investors that Reo was not an assembly plant but a manufacturing plant, where "practically everything . . . motor, transmission, clutch, axles, steering gear, radiator—is designed by Reo engineers and built in the Reo plant. Their quality and workmanship are absolutely assured." In fact, "Reo has a corps of employees who are both loyal and capable—real craftsmen."[41] Two years later the company reported that "manufacturing capacity has been increased just as rapidly as its supply of skilled workmen could be increased. . . . Reo prefers to instill the knowledge rather than take it for granted, realizing that a thoroughly trained force of workers is an asset, and an inexperienced organization is a liability."[42]

## Men at Play

The arms of the Reo family reached into the realm of leisure as well. The focal point of the company's commitment to leisure was the Reo club-house, built in 1917 (see Illustration 4). Workers and their families called this commodious, multipurpose building their "Temple of Leisure." It was equipped with a large auditorium for movies, dancing, and concerts by the Reo band, "creating harmony," a cafeteria for inexpensive meals, bowling alleys, a reading/smoking room, and pool tables. The movie show-ings were extremely popular, particularly with children, throughout the life of the clubhouse.[43] The company also sponsored noontime religious obser-vances in the clubhouse.

Starting in 1918 and continuing through the 1920s, the company orga-nized a large annual company picnic in August, featuring the culinary skill of women, the sporting acumen of the men, and the green thumbs of both. For the company, the popularity and success of the fair was a testament to the wise use of leisure among its workers. "The Reo Family . . . does not doze away its spare moments . . . the family is evidently not joy riding after the whistle blows."[44] The annual picnic was only the largest and most elaborate social event for most Reo employees; other company social groups formed and met throughout the year. In 1919 the accelerator club, dedicated to providing a social outlet for the superintendents and key men of the company, started with 43 members.[45] The accelerator, radia-tor, apprentice, die and tool room, and welfare and payroll department clubs all held their own outings and picnics throughout the 1920s.[46]

Probably the most obvious way the Reo Motor Car Company attempted to forge bonds among men—workers and management alike—was through athletics. Sports were a pleasurable outlet for many workers, who sponta-neously participated in a variety of games on the Reo field,[47] but man-agement believed that organized team sports taught valuable lessons about competition, fair play, sacrificing for the good of the group, and teamwork. Article 2 of the constitution and bylaws of the Reo bowling league stated that "the object of the league shall be to unite its members in the closest bonds of fellowship: to get a better understanding of each other and thereby insure fair play in keen competition."[48] Baseball teams could also teach important lessons about modern industry. One reporter in the *Reo*

ILLUSTRATION 4. The clubhouse. Photo courtesy of Library of Congress, Prints and Photographs Division, Historic American Engineering Record, Reproduction Number HAER, MICH, 33-LAN, 1-1.

*Spirit* noted that one team's performance improved after the star left. "The same principle applies to modern industry. It is frequently necessary to divorce from an organization, men of rare talent because it is impossible to keep things running smoothly with them on the job. Their imaginary grievances are many, and they're constantly trying to stir up their co-workers into a rebellious mood."[49] The lesson was plain; rebelliousness was no good on the field or in the factory, and the man who could not go along might have to be "divorced" from the family. Cooperation with the team, in work as in play, was the hallmark of the good working man.

Sports also provided a safer arena in which to work out tensions between management and workers. Bowling in particular was a sport in which "factory executive and factory sweeper bowl side by side with many times the sweeper rolling the best score."[50] Teams were often made up of workers from similar shops and of similar status, but members of the Reo bowling league came from all ranks.[51] Jocular taunting was common during sporting events, often between managers and foremen and workers, as in this poem about Cy Rath, director of the labor department and a member of one of Reo's baseball teams: "The only thing that Cy could hit was his club upon the ground. / So if Cy can't hit or Cy can't pitch, or Cy can't steal a base, / Perhaps if they play another game, they'll put a boy in Cy's place."[52]

Athletic competition not only leveled the playing field between the different classes but also allowed different ranks to socialize together. Every year the Reo bowling league held its banquet in the Reo clubhouse. At the 1923 banquet, Reo's factory superintendent, A. A. Lauzun, spoke on "Bowling as an Aid to Shop Morale."[53]

## Policing White Working-Class Manhood

The company never let workers forget that they were citizens in a larger community and Americans, a status that required certain behavior at work and at home. Particularly between 1918 and 1925, Americanization and good citizenship programs forged bonds between native-born males in management and the factory. The workforce at Reo was unlike the ethnically and racially diverse laborers at many large Michigan auto factories. As we have seen, the Reo workforce was predominantly native-born white. In 1925 only about 12 percent of Reo's workers were foreign, while the automobile industry workforce in Michigan as a whole was 36 percent foreign in 1920 and 30 percent in 1930. During the same period, the percentage of foreign-born workers at Reo actually fell slightly. Reo's labor force was not simply native born, it was homegrown: 65.5 percent were white men from Michigan, with 11 percent from Ingham County. When management enlisted the workers in a variety of campaigns for what it called Americanism, the cry fell on more receptive ears than at other automobile plants.[54]

During the late teens and early twenties, Americanization at Reo meant naturalizing foreign workers in the plant, stifling any activity with a taint of radicalism, and campaigning to make Lansing a dry town. The relatively small number of foreigners in the Reo plant could participate in English and citizenship courses. Reo started classes in Americanization in 1919 and its own school for Americanization in 1920.[55] Cy Rath, in a letter distributed throughout the plant, explained, "the Reo Motor Car Company is going to do all this for you, free of charge. All we ask is that you give two to three hours a week in attending the school."[56]

The company made it clear that acquiring U.S. citizenship was only the first step in a process that was cultural as well as legal. Immigrants needed to adopt American customs and values. One *Reo Spirit* editorial told of a

Syrian employee who had built a house and rented the upper floor to eighteen of his countrymen. In response to complaints from neighbors, the director of the Reo welfare department warned Lansing's Syrians, "This hiving business is neither sanitary nor moral. Nor is it in keeping with the principles of civilized countries. If you don't intend to be Americans then don't expect the same treatment accorded to good citizens."[57]

Bolshevism or any other "ism" was also not tolerated. The years immediately following the 1917 Russian Revolution saw a great deal of anti-Bolshevik and antiradical rhetoric in company publications. Bolsheviks embodied the opposite of the cherished qualities of the American working man. A Bolshevik was a slacker, a complainer, a man who wanted something for nothing, and worse. A poem reprinted in the *Reo Spirit* entitled "Practical Bolshevism" represented Bolshevism as a menace to the integrity of the American family. If Bolsheviks were to gain power, they would require that the worker hand over everything he owned. The poem ended,

> Is your wife a matron stately?
> Who does rule your home sedately?
> Do you love your daughter greatly?
> Hand THEM over!!!

Management encouraged workers to expose radicals within their ranks. Rath urged workers to report any un-American activities and assured them that their reports would be treated confidentially.[58] Foreigners, radicals, and Bolsheviks lacked the work ethic and traditional concept of family, and they did not cooperate with their fellow workers and employers. They were bad workers, bad Americans, and bad men (see Illustration 5).

Reo management always equated sobriety with good work habits. During the local option battles between "wets" and "drys" in the teens, the company actively campaigned for Prohibition. Dry rallies were staged in the Reo plant under the guise of providing election information. An article in the *Reo Spirit* made it clear where the company stood, urging workers to "vote yes for state wide prohibition" and "vote no against home rule or the open saloon possibility."[59] In one of its more heavy-handed editorials, the paper contended that Reo needed "100% Americans, not a rout of law breaking, riot fomenting, grog-guzzling foreigners."[60]

JULY, 1919     WHOLE NUMBER, 44

## DOG DAYS

ILLUSTRATION 5. "All Dogs should be Muzzled." Cover of *Reo Spirit*, July 1919, Reo Papers, box 53, folder 1, Michigan State University Archives and Historical Collections. Photo courtesy of Michigan State University Archives and Historical Collections.

While the company devised an array of welfare capitalism programs to forge a new identity for native-born working-class males, it also took a position on women and non-Protestant nonwhites. In general, Reo's management endorsed a paternalistic and respectful stance toward women summed up in the word "chivalry." "Chivalry toward women is an evidence of decent breeding." When a woman passing the Reo shops was subjected to whistles and "fresh remarks," she reported it to her father, the superintendent of the shop, Harry Teel. He ranted, "any man who will deliberately insult or embarrass . . . any woman is not only a pretty cheap specimen of manhood, but needs a few good man-handlings to teach him decency. . . . Americans, that is real Americans, have always been noted for the manner in which they protect and regard their women. By Americans is meant manly Americans, not cheap bums, fresh flirts, or half baked cute Alecs."[61]

Women were most often included in the life of the company as the wives and daughters of workers. Home life supported and expressed the values of working-class manhood. Reo workers were encouraged to save, buy their own homes, become involved in community activities, keep the Sabbath, tend a garden, and be good husbands and fathers. Needless to say, wives also had clear roles to play. To prevent accidents and other problems at work, wives were to "encourage their husbands to be industrious, ambitious, sober, and careful; to make their homes tidy, clean, comfortable and cheerful; to make good food; to send their husbands to work with a smile and a word of cheer; to make the husband think of her while he is at work."[62] In August 1928 the *Reo Spirit* began including a new column called "For Women Only," which featured fashion news and recipes.

As we saw in Chapter 1, women made up only a very small percentage of the labor force at Reo before World War II, and their activities were limited. Reo employed women as stenographers and other types of office staff as well as in the upholstery and wiring workrooms (see Illustration 6).[63] Women's work in the Reo factory was limited to areas where women's skills were considered "natural" and transferable from work done at home. For example, thirty women worked in the national coil assembly room, assembling "delicate parts of the car's electrical equipment." The company boasted that "while winding spools of wire may come naturally to them, they are also very proficient in handling drill presses used in the finer work of the department."[64] Women employees also worked different hours from men and were paid lower wages.[65]

ILLUSTRATION 6. The Reo factory around 1905—the upholstery shop. Photo courtesy of Craig A. Whitford, Lansing.

It was the company's policy that women should inhabit separate public spaces in both the factory and the clubhouse. While opportunities for women did increase over time, sports teams were segregated by sex and many fewer of these and other leisure activities were available to women.[66] In addition to family-oriented activities at the clubhouse, women's major social outlet was the Estes Fidelis Club. Designed to include all women in the Reo family—office and factory workers alike—the club provided a way for women of different classes to forge their own bonds. When it started in 1919, with 125 girls from three departments, it set forth its goals to "promote a feeling of better understanding and closer cooperation, to give aid in time of distress; to be loyal and faithful to the employers; to encourage social gatherings and entertainments." Within a year, however, the Estes Fidelis Club became affiliated with the City Club Council of Business Girls' Clubs and met at the local YWCA. The banquet at the Y, at which the different clubs performed their own "stunts" (in the case of Estes Fidelis, a mock wedding), speaks to the dominance of middle-class women within this organization.[67] Management was more comfortable with chivalry than with equality.

African Americans, Mexican Americans, and any other groups considered nonwhite were excluded from the plant. The treatment of foreigners in Lansing and at Reo reveals the extent to which workers and employers could come together to enforce their narrow concept of Americanism. This is less apparent in the case of groups that could never gain a foothold in the plant, though it was probably no less true of them. While there is virtually no mention of nonwhites other than the Syrians, an anecdote about a Jewish worker is revealing. A 1924 *Reo Spirit* column entitled "Noon Hour Gossip" described an apparently humorous episode involving Milton "Abie" Kositchek, "a well known young Reoite who has lots of conversation and plenty of smiles for most everyone in the shop. . . . He made a mistake recently which has probably never been made before by a person with Abie's kind of nose," when he returned to one Roger Adams a $50 bill instead of a $5 bill. Adams enjoyed seeing Kositchek "fret away eight pounds and nine years off his life," but finally gave him the difference. The gossip column ended, "oh, *oy, oy,* what a thanksgiving."[68] The majority of the plant, owners and workers alike, could get a laugh from their shared stereotypes and anti-Semitism.

A snapshot of the Reo factory in the first half of 1927 demonstrates the success of the company's programs and the level of compliance of the workforce. Cy Rath reported with pride that the average age of the 5,877 factory workers was 37.52 years. Forty percent of these workers had worked continuously for the company for five years or longer (before some recent hires, the figure was 53.7 percent). Rath calculated that 63.83 percent of the married employees (4,389, or 74.7 percent of all factory workers) either owned or were in the process of buying their own homes. Only 4.7 percent of Reo factory workers had been born in non-English-speaking countries, and 70 percent of the foreign born were already naturalized and buying their own homes.[69] The company's paternalistic bargain was not without its appeal.

## Our Big Factory Family

Not all Reo workers adopted these values uncritically. There is sketchy evidence of some opposition as management began to put these programs into place. Between 1916 and 1918 skilled workers tried to organize. A rare critical letter in the *Reo Spirit* from a plant worker assailed Reo's paternalism. Describing the workers as contented wage slaves, Ed Koster urged them to "assert your manhood, join the organization of your craft. Secure for you and your family a larger share of the product of the labor." The company allowed this letter to be printed, but as time went on management was more careful to nip such troublemaking in the bud. Foremen watched carefully for any sign of union organizing, and were advised to use any minor infraction of company rules to dismiss those suspected of it.[70] When skilled workers trying to organize a machinists' union challenged the company's "dry" position, general manager Richard Scott addressed the workers in the *Reo Spirit*, insisting that the company was not coercing its men.[71] Objections to company paternalism waned until 1918, when they ceased altogether, drowned out by the rhetoric of the factory family.[72]

Direct opposition was not the only way in which workers responded to the changing conditions of work and leisure at Reo. Workers from rural backgrounds who had no previous experience with labor organizations experienced and responded to these developments in their own way. In 1924 a Reo worker contributed a poem called "The Blues" to the *Reo Spirit* and dedicated it to his foreman. The poem concluded,

> There's somethin' keeps callin' and tuggin' my heart,
> An' my eyes get so dim I can't see,
> There's a lump in my throat—I am just an old fool
> But by jing, it's the country fer me.
> I'm sartin when Nora brought me to town,
> She didn't mean one bit of harm,
> But I'm homesick fer neighbors an' horses an' cows,
> An' I'm going straight back to the farm.[73]

Because many of Reo's workers came from farming backgrounds, many thought nothing of absenting themselves from factory work for the harvest and hunting seasons, or for a long weekend to help on the farm (see Table 2 in the Appendix). Reo's managers may not have been happy with this absenteeism, but they accepted it. Indeed, they often shared, and certainly benefited by, these attitudes and values.

Workers used Reo's social spaces, groups, and activities to create their own big factory family. Even though management provided highly organized and structured sports teams and tournaments, workers continued to use company playing fields for their own pickup games and fun. As the reporter in the *Reo Spirit* put it, "sometimes we organize and go to great pains for some particular program, clubs or otherwise, and yet, regardless of all the work, fuss . . . the things falls flat. The fun somehow isn't there." "Real fun," the writer maintained, "generally originates spontaneously," and he went on to describe an event at the clubhouse instigated by the workers themselves that had become "a genuinely Reo institution: the Friday noon dance." One Friday, when one of the religious speakers scheduled for the noon hour failed to show up, "somebody started a barn dance." With John Nelson "hollering" and Tom Vrie fiddling, "the fun was on." This was Reo, however, and "the dance is strictly a stag affair . . . although the Reo girls do not fail to sit and watch the fun. The 'ladies' who participate are now dressing in the latest styles, but where they borrow the duds, nobody knows."[74] Girls who worked at Reo danced with each other, too. A 1920 issue of *Reo Spirit* featured a picture of female employees dancing during their noon break, with the men looking on wistfully, left out of the merriment (see Illustration 7). Workers both acquiesced in and revised Reo's practices and values as they danced away their precious hour of freedom at lunchtime.

The persistence of the rhetoric of the factory family until the company's demise, the comparatively low turnover rate, and the popularity of these programs suggest that workers were generally positive and supportive of these welfare capitalist programs. When the *Reo Spirit* reported in 1919 that the labor turnover percentage at Reo was the lowest of any company in the automobile world except for one company in Detroit, it indicated both the company's desire for and success in fostering workers' loyalty.[75] The scores of employees who participated in the various groups and teams, the subscriptions to the various welfare and benefit programs, and the large number of activities in the clubhouse suggest that thousands took part in this vibrant company culture.[76]

# Our Own "No Man's Land"

ILLUSTRATION 7. Women dancing at the clubhouse. *Reo Spirit*, April 1920, p. 8, Reo Papers, box 53, folder 2, Michigan State University Archives and Historical Collections. Photo courtesy of Michigan State University Archives and Historical Collections.

## The Wages of White Manhood

The informal, stolen moments of fun ended in 1929, but the factory family forged in the early years endured. In February 1933, in the middle of a dark Depression winter, Cy Rath, who had just laid off more than half of the Reo workforce and discontinued many of its social programs, began to think about planning the sixteenth annual Reo bowling league banquet. Perhaps he imagined that the banquet might revive feelings of the good old days, when workers and management shared cigars, sumptuous meals, ribbing, and ribaldry. Perhaps he racked his brain trying to think of a way to accomplish this in diminished circumstances. Perhaps this is why he wrote a letter to H. H. Jackson, the warden of the Michigan state prison in Jackson, inquiring about hiring the "prison quartet, the colored dancers, and any other suitable entertainments, along with a master-of-ceremonies to take charge of the program." On April 6, 1933, 300 of Reo's keglers crowded the Reo clubhouse auditorium to see "the famous prison entertainers of Jackson, namely the Harmony Kings, the four fast stepping Brownies, a talented pianist and a fiddler."[77] As Reo's native-born white male bowlers, drawn from all ranks of the plant, joined together to watch African American men dance, sing, and play music, they embodied the success of welfare capitalism and the enduring company culture at Reo.

# 3

# Reo Joe's New Deal, 1924-1939

Men are of two kinds, and he
Was of the kind I'd like to be.
No door at which he ever knocked
Against this manly form was locked.
If ever man on earth was free
And independent, it was he.
No broken pledge lost him respect,
He met all men with head erect,
And when he passed I think there went
A soul to yonder firmament
So white, so splendid and so fine
It came to almost God's design.
—Edgar A. Guest, "A Real Man" (1916)

**"The White Race Cannot Survive without Dairy Products"**
—Herbert Hoover, quoted in an ad for Arctic Dairy Products, Inc.,
*Lansing State Journal* (January 1, 1931)

September 1, 1924, Labor Day, was a day of mass celebration in Lansing. Representatives from every county in the state of Michigan descended on the capital city, many camping in an empty lot called the circus fairground just east of the capitol building. Large white tents and festive banners flowed as 50,000 men, women, and children watched a huge parade, with floats, music, and uplifting speeches by local and national leaders. The city provided police protection, but there was no need for the supervision except to coordinate the huge volume of traffic flowing into the city for the festivities. There were many booths, some for women and children and others with information from the various constituencies represented in the parade. Organizers provided medical services and the sheriff's department staffed a tent for public relations. The day's events came off without a hitch, apart from a storm that blew in and curtailed the evening's activities. Lansing shopkeepers took advantage of the influx of revelers and stayed open. Many displayed two flags—one commemorating working people on their national holiday, the other representing the organizational sponsor of the event, the Ku Klux Klan.[1]

Thirteen years later, on June 7, 1937, Lansing experienced another disruptive mass event, a general strike that came to be known as the Lansing Labor Holiday. This demonstration was the culmination of a season of unrest: winter sit-downs in Detroit, Flint, and Lansing, strikes at Oldsmobile, a month-long sit-down strike at Reo, and finally a strike at the Capital City Wrecking Company, which provoked the June event.[2] How does a working-class community like Lansing host a major Klonvocation and then thirteen years later witness class conflict profound enough to incite a general strike? What does the appearance and popularity of the Ku Klux Klan in the 1920s portend about the ways in which Reo Joes understood and responded to the changes and challenges of the 1930s?

Recent works on working-class militancy in the 1930s tell the story of how workers—embittered, betrayed, and impoverished—turned from voluntary organizations and their employers to their unions and the state for assistance. In the process, they united behind the Democratic Party, the New Deal, and the CIO's "culture of unity," a labor movement uniting all sexes, races, and ethnicities.[3] The mass mobilizations of the 1930s were important, if brief, moments of possibility and they make a chronological divide between the days of low wages, long hours, poor working conditions, and repression, on the one hand, and collective bargaining, closed shops, equal pay for equal work, grievance procedures, cost-of-living indexes, and pension plans, on the other. Rank-and-file militancy, particularly on behalf of previously under-organized groups—women, white ethnics, and ethnic and racial minorities—flourished until union discipline and bureaucracy stifled this grassroots progressive activism.[4]

Automobile workers were important in the organizing efforts of the 1930s, but they had only just started to experience widespread success. Automobile factories remained relatively untouched by unions between 1900 and 1929. Certain craft unions, like the machinists', made short-lived forays into shops, making modest and spotty gains. Relief came when the national government ensured the rights of the workers to organize. Because of the changing nature of the labor process in the plants, the increased reliance on semi-skilled and unskilled workers, the structure of the production process, and the size of the enterprises themselves, successful unionization campaigns occurred only after the widespread adoption of industrial unions. Unionization required a seasoned cadre of leaders who had spent time in the ranks and understood the conditions and demands of autoworkers.[5] National Industrial Recovery Act (NIRA) provision 7A, and then the Wagner Act, sparked the creation of new industrial unions at automotive plants. The birth of the CIO set in motion several years of internal battles between AFL and CIO auto unions, as well as profound, wrenching conflicts about the role of the left in the auto unions, conflicts exacerbated by the charged context of the emerging popular front. The UAW-CIO prevailed, but a UAW-AFL persisted until 1955.[6]

The conditions that prevailed in Lansing challenge this picture of labor in the 1920s and 1930s. Few labor histories consider how conservative white native-born Protestant working-class men, men who had been enlisted in a powerful civic and company paternalism, encountered the Depression, the New Deal, and the new unionism.[7] Former Reo worker Layton Aves reported that members of the Ku Klux Klan organized the UAW-CIO in Lansing and participated in the sit-down strike at Reo. Aves, featured in the introduction, recalled that his father was in the engineering department when the Klan organized the union at Reo, and that "in order to join the union you had to be a member of the KKK, Ku Klux Klan ... the KKK and the unions were together."[8] After the strike, Aves's father brought home "a time bomb ... and a sword with the KKK emblem on it." The popularity of the Ku Klux Klan in Lansing during the 1920s challenges us to rethink how Reo Joe responded to the events of the 1930s and made a union and a new deal of his own.

## Fellow Travelers on the Right

The Klan enjoyed support in Ingham County during the 1920s, but a more general "reactionary populism"[9] more accurately describes the political terrain of Lansing. The intense program of Americanization undertaken both within the Reo plant and in the community at large was part of a general climate that was racist and ethnocentric in both obvious and subtle ways. The Ku Klux Klan was the most extreme exponent of a set of beliefs popularly and powerfully endorsed throughout the city and county. Even if individuals felt the need to distance themselves from the negative associations of the KKK, particularly its violent vigilantism, they may have had few objections to the basic tenets of the organization. Tactics (and perhaps the exclusivity and secret rituals), not ideology, separated those who formally belonged or identified from those who did not. Those who subscribed to the Klan's basic ideas without actually joining were "fellow travelers on the right." Although it is impossible to document Klan membership for any of the early unionists at Reo in the late 1930s, it is probably safe to say that Klan members worked in the plant during the 1920s and even 1930s.

The Ku Klux Klan does not usually figure in histories of Michigan in the 1920s, and stories of the Klan's revival do not identify Michigan as a key site. The most prominent scholar of the Klan in Michigan, Calvin Enders, estimates that during the 1920s Klan membership in Michigan was higher than in any southern state.[10] The second Ku Klux Klan made its appearance in Lansing in the early 1920s. In July 1922 a *Lansing State Journal* reporter was allowed to witness an initiation ceremony of the Lansing Klan. After hooking up with various carloads of Klansmen, the blindfolded reporter ended up in the woods north of Lansing, where the ceremony was held. The oath taken by those in attendance revealed the ideological and programmatic priorities of the organization: Christianity, white supremacy, protecting womanhood, just laws and liberty, upholding the Constitution, states' rights, separation of church and state, a closer relationship between capital and labor, preventing the causes of mob violence and lynchings, and limiting foreign immigrants. As the initiates were accepted into the organization, the group began to chant, "God give us men, God give us men, God give us men."[11]

By 1923 the Klan was enough of a presence to burn a cross across the Grand River from a park where hundreds of people were listening to an open-air concert one late summer night.[12] Later that fall, the local Klan began to meet in the Prudden Auditorium, a meeting place controlled by the Chamber of Commerce. The first meeting of Lansing's Women of the

Ku Klux Klan, early in 1924, "the largest in Michigan outside of Detroit," ushered in the Lansing Klan's busiest year.[13] Emboldened by their increasing numbers and acceptance, the Klan appeared in public many times during the year—at churches, in meeting halls, at concerts, and at rallies. In June 1924 the Klan circulated petitions in factories seeking support of its opposition to Michigan State College's football match with (Catholic) Notre Dame. On June 20, 1924, the Klan held an open public initiation ceremony at which another cross was burned; this was the first time Klan members had appeared in regalia (but without masks) in an open-air meeting within the city limits. Three hundred new members were welcomed into the organization while a crowd of 1,000 watched.[14]

These activities were consistent with efforts by the Klan—in Lansing and elsewhere—to make the organization appear more mainstream. In addition to organizations for women and young men, the Klan began to appeal to its members to patronize its institutions. If you wanted to spend your vacation with like-minded individuals, there was Klan Kamp at Woodward Lake, seven miles north of Ionia (about half an hour from Lansing), owned and operated by the KKK Realm of Michigan. On Labor Day, 1928, a large celebration was scheduled there with both men and women of the KKK enjoying a basket dinner, bathing, boating, and fishing. The Klan sponsored a Kigy Camp for the kiddies, and Senator J. Thomas Heflin was the invited speaker.[15] The *Michigan Kourier* contained advertisements for Klan businesses in various cities and readers were encouraged to patronize them. For example, for Klan shoe repairs in Lansing, one could patronize "the American opposite the Reo Truck Plant."[16]

For many in Lansing and Ingham County, the appearance of the Klan was not a controversial or even unpleasant development. The articles in local papers on the 1924 Labor Day celebration described a celebratory, bucolic, "normal" atmosphere.[17] At the evening ceremonies a series of speeches highlighted the major issues and concerns of the Michigan Klan, with a great deal of attention devoted to the upcoming primaries and November election. From the festive atmosphere and the talk of "Americanism," patriotism, and the rights of the workingman, the event might have passed for an Independence Day celebration. In addition to the huge crowd that had streamed into Lansing for the event, local enthusiasts cheered the motorcade as it passed through the neighborhoods of Lansing.[18] The Ing-

Mon. Sept.-1        1924
Labor-Day-Parade

Nick's car (Reo)

Presented by
Men of K.K.K.

ILLUSTRATION 8. Reo sedan presented to Ingham County Ku Klux
Klan leader, Lansing, September
1924, with inscription from back of
photo. Klan vertical file, Special Collections, Michigan State University
Library. Photo courtesy of Special
Collections, Michigan State University Libraries.

ham County Kleagle (the county's Klan leader), who had organized the
event, even allowed the *Lansing State Journal* to print his name in its report
on the brand-new Reo sedan he received in appreciation for all of his hard
work (see Illustration 8). As recorded in the Lansing City Directory for
1924, Kleagle Lawrence H. Nichols (the "Nick" referred to in the illustration) boarded in a house on North Pennsylvania Avenue and worked at
another popular (but smaller) automotive employer, Motor Wheel.

The popularity of the Klan in mid-Michigan reflected fear less of blacks
and Jews than of Catholics. One man, named Fred, who lived in North
Lansing recalled, "We lived in a nest of them [Klan members]". Fred's
father was opposed to the Klan and Fred remembered his father being
threatened by neighbors, "They'll get you. You'll join." Against his father's
wishes, Fred witnessed a number of Klan events in and around the city,
including the cross burning at the Labor Day rally.[19] As Fred recollected,
"the order of priority was first the Catholics, because the Klan feared the
Pope was trying to take over the country; second were the Jews . . . then
came blacks."[20]

The 1924 Klonvocation had two purposes. The huge Labor Day event
was a fund-raiser for the organization. Michigan Klan officials had

designated Lansing as the potential future site of the first Klavern, or convention hall, which would accommodate 12,000 to 15,000 people. "Thousands of small bricks stamped with the words, 'I bought a brick in Lansing Klavern' . . . will be given in return for any donation, the funds going into the local building fund,"[21] read an article in the *Lansing State Journal*, as would revenues from the concessions and booths (in the end, the hall was never built).

The second and more important reason for the rally was political and revealed the Klan's concern over parochial schools, and the number of "fellow travelers" within the general population. The major speaker was Judge C. J. Orbison of Indiana, who identified the major issue uniting his listeners—that "all children should come under the guidance of the public schools in receiving their education."[22] A prominent emblem of the event was the little red school house, which represented the Klan's support of a state constitutional amendment that would require all school-age children in the state of Michigan to attend public school. The Klan urged all adults to vote in the Republican Party primary for gubernatorial candidate James Hamilton, who supported this amendment.

The school amendment first appeared on the ballot in the 1920 election and was defeated; Hamilton, however, organized a group called Public School Defense, which worked, with Klan support, to get the amendment on the ballot in 1924.[23] Some were more inclined to support Reverend Frederick Perry, a minister and field organizer for the Klan from Lenawee County (an hour south of Lansing and home to the city of Adrian). Attempts to iron out differences and unite behind one candidate in the Republican primary were unsuccessful.[24] The three leaders in the Republican primary were Alex Groesbeck, who won with 348,955, Hamilton, who came in second with 129,244, and Perry, who was third with 79,225. Candidates with Klan affiliation or sympathies garnered 208,469 of the vote.[25]

Perry won in Ingham County, one of his few victories, demonstrating that Ingham County and Lansing were important strongholds of the Klan in Michigan.[26] Perry had been a pastor and served as president of the Michigan Conference of Methodist Protestant Churches in Lansing from at least 1910 until 1912, when he was called to the Plymouth Methodist Protestant Church in Adrian, Michigan. In 1920 he left his pastorate to pursue work he described as "the Americanization of the foreign element now causing so much trouble in our country with their Bolshevik teaching."[27] He first surfaced in connection with the governor's race on March 1, 1924, when a newspaper reported the speech he had delivered before the Ku Klux Klan.[28] He admitted that he had spent the summer of 1924 lecturing for the Michigan Klan for a fee but insisted that he was not a member of the Klan and was not the Klan candidate for governor.[29]

Perry may have won in Ingham County because he had special ties to Lansing. He asserted that, without his knowledge or consent, a Perry-for-Governor club had formed in Lansing to draft him as a candidate. The organization was incorporated by "Lansing businessmen who formerly were members of his Sunday school class while he was pastor of a Lansing church . . . and had maintained a life contact with him, holding weekly meetings for that purpose during the time he was abroad as a missionary many years ago."[30] The Lansing businessmen were not identified, but there is evidence that Ransom E. Olds had supported Perry's ministry financially during his time as a minister in Lansing.[31] Perry spoke before 1,500 workers at the Reo plant just a few days before the Labor Day rally. Before the "crowd of Reo workmen [who] appeared to be favorably impressed," Perry proclaimed, "we must think of the home and keep it sacred; we must keep close to the church as long as it is a Christian church, for it too is sacred; We must maintain our schools—our public schools— and build up and add strength to our government by representation and not by a concentration of power."[32]

Groesbeck's victory in the primary and the defeat of the school amendment in November (760,571 to 421,472) were setbacks for the Klan, but not for what it represented. Ingham County voters were evenly split over the school amendment in 1924; 17,839 voters were in favor and 17,675 against.[33] It is unlikely that there were more than 17,000 Klan members in Ingham County, so it is probably safe to conclude that a considerable number of "fellow travelers on the right" voted in favor of the amendment.

The Ku Klux Klan was not the only organization promoting "Americanism." The elaborately garbed members of the Knights Templar formed themselves into enormous "passion crosses" while marching for their conclaves, and Templars frequently wore hooded robes. One of the largest of the Templars' gatherings took place on Memorial Day, 1921, when the local order hosted a state conclave. On May 30 and 31, 5,000 renewed their commitment to "patriotism, republican ideals, and love of fellows." The class nature of the organization is suggested by the participation of Reo's Donald Bates, who served as the general chairman of the event, and Charles Davis, secretary of the Lansing Chamber of Commerce, who transported attendees. The elite social status of the Templars was also suggested by the types of activities the wives of Templars organized: an open house at the Lansing Women's Clubhouse during the day and entertainment at the Lansing Country Club at night.[34] At this particular conclave, the Reo Motor Car Company Band played while the platoons marched through downtown Lansing in their passion cross formation.[35]

In 1927 the *Lansing State Journal* published the findings of an industrial commission appointed by the mayor that documented the ways in which citizens understood Lansing's advantages.[36] "Lansing rates high in native born whites," read the article, "and the colored population is negligible." Lansing boasted a high marriage rate, and a population that came primarily from northwest European countries. "The city has no 'little Italy,' or 'little Germany,' so disconcerting to community development. . . . Industrial organizations down to the very foreman, are always eager to play their part in the community Americanization program." Schools, government, and industry coordinated "citizenship work" to encourage workers to "take pride in their job . . . and feel that they individually are units in the big industrial machine" so that "the factory can be depended on to stand behind workers in the many questions that arise outside of working hours and quite beyond the actual walls of the factory." Lansing's workers were "free, cooperating directly with their employer for the general advancement of themselves, of their trade, and with the business with which they are allied. They do not bow their heads before the dictation of outside forces. . . . Lansing is an Open Shop City."[37]

The "community family" and the "factory family" were intertwined and committed to an Americanism defined by the pervasive ideologies of the right. Reo and its city reaped the fruits of its elites' population policy. The native-born Protestant white males of all classes sustained this arrangement during the flush times of the 1920s, and all reaped the benefits. The stock market crash and the Depression challenged workers and employers to retain this independence, localism, and family feeling in the midst of trouble and intrusions from afar.

## The Depression in Lansing

The Great Depression seeped into Lansing, the local economy bottoming out in November 1932.[38] Many automakers had experienced lowered sales and rising inventories before the crash, and local factories laid off workers in response, which contributed to the deflationary spiral characteristic of this economic calamity. Automotive employers in Lansing generally cut their labor force by half by the early 1930s, creating a serious unemployment problem and straining the ill-prepared social welfare services, both private and public, in the city, county, and state. Perhaps the scope of the cataclysm was tempered by the ability of Lansing's white male labor force to fall back on the land. Although Michigan's agricultural sector was also affected by the Depression, the state was no dustbowl; fields, orchards, and livestock still needed tending, and some unemployed workers returned to the farms.

Lansing resident Sadie Smith recalled,

> My husband didn't have work in the shops. Reo wasn't doing much. But he went out and worked for a farmer south of Williamston [about ten miles from Lansing]. The farmer had a lot of trees he wanted cut down. He took our oldest son and they went out and cut trees. We had an old Studebaker car and they took the back seat out and they filled it up with wood and made enough to buy gas and have a little left over. He worked for different farmers for threshing time. One farmer gave him a bushel of wheat. He took it to the milling company in Lansing and had it ground up for flour, so we had bread. Another farmer gave him a bag of beans, so we had beans.[39]

Ransom E. Olds himself saw the return to the land as the solution to the nation's problems. Speaking before a Junior Chamber of Commerce dinner in his honor, he suggested a "back to the land" plan to give every unemployed family ten acres of land and a ready-made house. The land would be tax exempt for five years, and instead of paying for welfare, the localities would provide seeds.[40]

The Reo Motor Car Company, like other automotive employers, reduced the number of workers on its payroll and cut many of its programs. In 1927, at its peak economic performance, Reo had employed 6,141 people, set a new sales record, and completed a year-long "modernization" program.[41] The average monthly factory labor force of 5,621 workers produced 47,009 units and made an average of $1,530.53 per year.[42] By 1932 a factory workforce of 2,556 made only 7,030 units and earned an average annual wage of $714.86. Non-factory workers also experienced significant layoffs, shorter hours, and pay cuts.[43] The programs long associated with the Reo Motor Car Company, its extensive array of welfare capitalist services and activities, also suffered as a result of hard times. By 1931 the company had to cut back its services to a few sports teams, some activities in the clubhouse, and the *Reo Spirit* magazine, or roughly the level of services that existed in 1916. As the Depression deepened, so did cuts to programs.[44]

Ideas about the importance of the city's independence and the dangers of outside interference died hard, as desperation forced many to seek help from the programs of the New Deal. Lansing took relief reluctantly and city leaders mediated the nature of the relief through their own local institutions. Local governments distributed temporary relief unevenly to individuals who needed food, fuel, or shelter to tide them over between jobs. Lansing's unemployed looked to a variety of public works projects to build a new urban infrastructure of sewers, roads, parks, post offices, and school buildings. Although Lansing and Ingham County received more than their fair share of relief from federal programs, the assistance never provoked the kind of radical critiques of the capitalist system typical of other cities. Detroit, Flint, and even Grand Rapids witnessed significant mobilizations of the unemployed organized by communists, but Lansing did not. What labor organizing there was, among both the employed and the unemployed, revealed few leftist tendencies.[45]

In late May 1931, Lansing experienced its first and virtually only communist rally, when several hundred unemployed people marched to the capitol building. The *Lansing State Journal* reported that the participants, most of them outsiders, had slept in the bleachers at the municipal ballpark the night before and turned out in full force, listening to four hours of speakers at the capitol square. Once the demonstration was over, the police began to disburse the group and ordered them to "turn their backs on the city and keep going." Participants in the demonstration, according to the police, were outsiders, diseased and contagious and "not typical of the average American workingmen such as to be found in the average industrial plant." The *Lansing State Journal* reported that the vigilance of the police prevented any scattering of the marchers. Police chief Alfred Seymour proclaimed, "never again as long as I am chief of police will a crowd like this be allowed to come into Lansing. If they want to see the Governor they will have to meet him someplace else."[46] The same evening, Republican governor Wilber Brucker spoke at the meeting of the Masons in Battle Creek. The title of his talk was "Radicalism Is Banned."[47]

## A Union for Reo Joe

Because auto union membership was ethnically, racially, religiously, and politically diverse, auto unions had different political orientations and forms of activism. Reo's union resembled Peter Friedlander's description of Local 229 in Detroit: "The working class was not so much influenced by the Left, as the U.A.W. was influenced by the church, the political machine, several kinds of rural Protestant conservatism, and a variety of local subcultures."[48] The union that developed at Reo reflected Reo's and Lansing's history.

It took the actions of the federal government to finally break the long impasse in the history of auto union organizing in Lansing. As a result of the creation of industry "codes" through the NIRA, the AFL renewed its efforts to organize workers in the automobile shops, "simply trying to aid the workers to realize the goals of the N.I.R.A.," with "no intention of fomenting strife," in the words of historian Sidney Fine.[49] Starting in 1933 as a result of the federal labor union drive through the AFL, the first union organizations appeared in the auto shops of Lansing. Their arrival coincided with the short-lived appearance of socialists in Lansing.[50] At the start of the New Deal, the Federation of Automotive Workers tried to organize auto workers for the AFL, and Reo's management responded with the familiar tactics of paternalism and repression.

On July 13, 1933, several hundred workers attended a membership meeting at which Reo management planted a spy who reported on the proceedings. Most of the workers came from Motor Wheel, some from Olds, and a few from Reo, plus a smattering of unemployed and some socialists and communists. The Reo spy reported that the workers "admitted that conditions in Lansing were better than Detroit. In mentioning Reo, one of the speakers brought out the point that when the organization got going it would then be necessary for Mr. Scott to deal with the organization and the men." Only fifty Reo workers signed on, an indication that the company's tactics had the desired effect. There is evidence that company spies reported on the organizing efforts until the recognition of the UAW in 1937.[51]

Organizing a union at Reo was also difficult because of the history and power of company paternalism. In June 1934, when the union brought claims of the discriminatory layoff of five men to Cy Rath, the claims were handled in the old-fashioned way. According to Rath's report, these cases were given individual attention. Each of the employees was interviewed, "the specific demerit charged against them was made known and frankly discussed." The men were referred to the foreman "for a mutual understanding before being returned to work." Four employees with less seniority were laid off instead.[52] Labor relations according to the principles of the "square deal" persisted into the 1930s.

How the fledgling Reo Federal Labor Union developed into a strong and successful organization that won its recognition through a month-long sit-down strike can be explained in part by focusing on Lester Washburn, who was responsible for building the union. Washburn was born on May 28, 1906, in the northern Michigan city of Pellston[53] and by 1916 was in Lansing, where he finished tenth grade. Washburn's father, a carpenter, taught him the trade and took his son to work as a helper. Lester also held printing and clerk positions in Lansing, but the pay did not match what he could make working with his father.

In 1927 Lester and his father were hired as carpenters at Reo.[54] "My father-in-law was also a carpenter. We went to work in the carpenter crew of [sixty] maintenance carpenters. Reo was a company that never farmed out any, never contracted out any building. They wanted to build ... a building, they built it themselves. They had the whole set-up." Not long after the three arrived at Reo, "things got worse. They started cuttin' down on the carpenters and they gave me a job puttin' doors on the assembly line." Lester lost his job in 1930 when the plant shut down temporarily (it continued to shut down intermittently throughout the Depression). In 1933 Lester was rehired in the export shipping department, where workers made the crates and boxes and packing information that went with disassembled vehicles that were shipped all over the world.[55] "In addition to nailing, packing, and this type of thing, I was given a job of stenciling all these boxes as to what was in 'em, and of course I had the serial number and the model number, model, and everything else of every unit that went in, see."

Because Washburn's working-class family was hostile to unions and because Lansing in the 1920s was not a union town, Washburn claimed that "it was just an accident that I got in [the union], knowing nothing about it." Initially hostile to unions himself, he balked at the thought of going to a union meeting.

> In export shipping . . . was a group piecework type of a deal, and in this group was a man that used to work in the woods with my dad while the lumbering was going on in Michigan. He worked in there and one time he came to me and he said, kid, what are you doing tomorrow night? I says nothing . . . he says, I want you to go to a meeting. . . . I says, what kind of meeting? He says a union meeting and I says nothing. . . . I'm not going to pay a dollar a month to pay somebody to sit with his feet on the desk smokin' cigars, not with my money. I didn't know the first thing about a union. All I knew about a union was what I'd maybe read in the newspaper and I didn't do much of that. Those days I read the funnies and the sports page.[56]

Washburn recalled being elected recording secretary of the union at his first meeting, but it is more likely that he attended some meetings (they occurred almost weekly) after the union formed in September 1933 and was elected to office on September 4, 1934.[57] He was an active union member for the rest of his life, first in the Reo local and the Lansing UAW, then serving on the UAW executive board and becoming a regional organizer and international president of the UAW-AFL. Between 1933 when unionization started and 1937 when both the Reo sit-down strike and the Lansing Labor Holiday occurred (Washburn is always given credit for the sit-down at Reo and the Lansing Labor Holiday), Washburn and the Reo Joes he represented became auto union men.

According to Washburn, the working conditions of the 1920s had nothing to do with his decision to get involved in organizing the union. In fact, he claimed, "[Reo] wasn't a bad company. They used to be better, see." Reo had a good apprenticeship program, one that provided skills and advancement, "they had a clubhouse, a big clubhouse that showed movies to the families and everything. . . . The company was considered to be a good company and basically they were but they got in a hard space, you know, they had to refinance and as the things started to slow down, you know."[58] Washburn's participation in the union was based on his interpretation of the events of the 1930s. His analysis of the Depression and the source of his life-long commitment to unions is worth quoting at length.

> In the first place, probably one of the reasons that I got into the union during the Depression, all you had to do was go to the employment office and sit around there and see if you could get a job, and we used to talk to the guys, you know, used to talk 'bout, you know, just had a good period through the late '20s. . . . So we said, what happened to all the money? Why should there be a Depression? Didn't anybody throw it in the ocean. Didn't anybody burn it up, see. So what happened? This is the type of discussion that you get into, see, with people that are unemployed trying to find a job. . . . Well my conclusion is that these things are planned. You set the stage, you made all you could during that particular period of prosperity, see, then you have a Depression and all the weak ones get, go down the drain, well, workers, jobs and small businesses . . . and then those that's got the money, I mean, they can buy up these businesses after they go bankrupt for, what, ten cents on a dollar, probably, or whatever. Then you have another period of prosperity and if it don't come around, there's always a war. See?[59]

Washburn obviously had a structural analysis for the causes of the Depression and of inequality and injustice (one also somewhat driven by conspiracy theories), but he was clearly neither a communist nor a socialist. In fact, the interviews of Washburn are full of anticommunist and anti-socialist sentiment. He heaped scorn equally on the socialists and communists in the labor movement and on the spies and company stooges from the Corporation Auxiliary at work in the Olds and Fisher Body plants. Washburn conceded that a communist or socialist might be "a damn good union man,"[60] but he tended to see communist beliefs and good unionism as mutually exclusive. He described a meeting in 1934 that had been suggested by a fellow union member. "It was a socialist meeting and they had one of their top speakers . . . and so I went there and, of course, I was strictly a greenhorn, you know, so when the meeting was over, why, it was left open to questions." Washburn asked the speaker, "lots of the things you say . . . corresponds with the labor program. Why can't this all be put together, you know, in the union, so instead of having two organizations fighting for the same thing?" Because the meeting broke up after that question, Washburn was accused of disrupting the event. In 1936, when Washburn asked Norman Thomas and Jay Lovestone a similar question on the issue of communism versus socialism, the meeting did not break up. As far as Washburn was concerned, there was no difference between communism and socialism. He asked what would happen to the labor movement if either party took over, and Lovestone replied (according to Washburn), "'there's no more need for the labor movement. It will be a working-class government' and so forth . . . that helped me a lot. Whenever somebody would get up and start spoutin' and sounding like a commie . . . I'd tell 'em that story and that guy never opened his mouth again."[61]

## Most Uncommon Lovestonite

Washburn is a largely unknown figure in the formation of the auto unions, even though when he was elected to the eleven-member executive board at the UAW convention in South Bend, Indiana, in April 1936, he was identified as a progressive force.[62] A short biography of Washburn that appeared in the pages of the *United Automobile Worker* reported that Washburn, the recording secretary of his small but stable local union, was active in the Lansing District Auto Council and in the national South Bend Convention. At the age of thirty-three, he was a promising young union man.[63] The socialist *News of Lansing* described Washburn as the "typical auto worker. Washburn represents the new type of union leader that is arising in the ranks of the labor movement with the organization of the mass-production industries of auto, steel, and rubber." Described as "sincere . . . a scrapper and a spark-plug," Washburn was popular among the men and "largely responsible for the rapid growth of the Reo local." He was quoted as saying that "every auto worker should be a member of the U.A.W. A worker's education begins when he joins a union. He can learn more in the labor movement than he ever could out of books . . . why they lose their homes, why they're laid off and forced to go on relief, why they can't afford the things that are supposed to be a part of the American standard of living."[64]

Just three years later, after being ousted from the UAW-CIO, Washburn was discredited as a member of "Jay Lovestone's wrecking crew."[65] A former leader in the Communist Party of the United States, Jay Lovestone, a shady figure in auto union politics during the late 1930s, aided and abetted UAW president Homer Martin's efforts to rid the UAW of all communist influences. Lovestonites were anti-Stalinists and were unsympathetic to the Popular Front at home. Even though a range of individuals, from Black Legionnaires in the Midwest to former communists in the East, were linked to Lovestone's Communist Party Opposition (CPO) or the Independent Communist Labor League (ICLL), which published the *Workers Age*, the typical Lovestonite was an East Coast intellectual who, while militant rhetorically, tended to be conciliatory when dealing with management.[66] Many layers of internal conflict between 1937 and 1939 exacerbated this nefarious effort, including the competition between the AFL and the CIO for the UAW, revelations of Homer Martin's shady dealings with insurance schemes in his negotiations with GM, and, finally, allegations of collusion between Martin and Harry Bennett of the Ford Motor Company regarding union organizing at Ford. Break-ins at the offices of a number of parties involved resulted in a dramatic court case that exposed Lovestone's influence in the highest ranks of the UAW.[67]

Even though many anti-Lovestonites identified Washburn as part of the opposing camp, it is more difficult to find positive proof from the Lovestonites themselves. Bill Munger, a graduate of Michigan State College and a Lovestonite who headed Local 182 before the sit-down strike, was the closest link between Washburn and the Lovestonites.[68] More damning was the allegation of Stuart Strachan, a Martin partisan, that Washburn was involved with the Lovestonites.[69] News and information about Washburn and his activities appeared regularly in the Lovestone papers pertaining to auto unions and in the *Workers Age*.[70]

All of this evidence is circumstantial, however, and gets us no closer to the truth about what was going on in Washburn's mind. If Washburn was a Lovestonite, he was a most uncommon one. He was a militant unionist who was open-minded, progressive, intelligent, and well liked by his men. He saw himself as fighting for an independent labor movement responsive to the needs of the rank and file. Because he believed that the communist and socialist project in the unions was misguided, Washburn felt that had no choice but to ally himself with anti-leftist efforts. While he had no affection for Homer Martin, whom he saw as a brilliant orator but a poor administrator, he was adamantly against any faction that allowed communists and socialists. (He spoke no more fondly of Walter Reuther, whom he considered a better politician than a union man.) A troubled Washburn recalled,

You had the vice president, Mortimer [Wyndam Mortimer], who was an avowed Communist. There wasn't any question about that. And then you had the socialists in there workin' with them and it was just a continued turmoil all the time until it came to the point that ... when issues come up, I mean, it would be one side or the other. It'd be just like the Democrats and the Republicans voting the party line, see, in a sense. It got that bad ... until it broke.[71]

Washburn believed he was "forced into a camp," even though CIO men made attempts to recruit him to their side and the national union continued to challenge his control.[72] We need to understand historical figures like Washburn as more than simply anticommunists, company stooges, business unionists, or victims of "false consciousness." We need to ask what they stood *for*, not simply what they believed they were forced to position themselves against. Washburn may have rejected left-wing interpretations of class conflict and its remedies, but his ideas about the goals and tactics of an independent labor movement were deeply rooted in the conditions and constituencies of Lansing, Michigan.

Washburn's unionism was informed first and foremost by the need to listen to the rank and file and to respond freely and creatively to their needs and desires. He believed in localism and disdained outside influence, politics, and bureaucracy. When asked about the value of small, independent unions, he reflected, "if it remains a good union ... good principles and all that, I'm not so sure that there is anything wrong with that. Now if they just become a dead organization for the purpose of collecting dues ... that's something else. But if it's a good, live, progressive union, then who knows. It serves a certain purpose, see ... big is not always better."[73] Washburn's intense localism and his responsiveness to the concerns of the rank and file go a long way toward explaining how he could be anticommunist and antisocialist while believing that the remote forces of capitalism had planned the Depression. International communists and socialists were just as threatening as international capitalists. It was this intense localism and loyalty to the rank and file that makes me question whether Washburn's alliance with Lovestonites was genuine or merely tactical.

Washburn's effort to bring unions to the auto plants during the 1930s was also a response to the paternalistic class relations that prevailed during the teens and twenties. Those who participated in creating the union and helped to implement union programs employed the rhetoric of family, so ubiquitous in this firm and community, for their own ends. By creating an alternative community centered on the unions but also including an array of progressive programs and popular entertainments, auto union men proclaimed their coming of age and broke free from the paternalism of their employers. They were not making a new deal with the federal government or joining in solidarity with their international union; they were claiming the authority to stand on their own, supported by an organization of white, primarily native-born working-class men like themselves.

## Respectable Labor Militancy

From his first foray into the Reo local in 1933 until the Lansing Labor Holiday in 1937, Washburn adopted a stance of respectable labor militancy. Throughout all of his various tussles with company and public officials, Washburn, and those for whom he spoke, stressed the lawfulness, justice, and legitimacy of the workers' cause, evoked the qualities of Americanism and masculine independence, and boasted of the sobriety and discipline of their ranks. These qualities help to explain Washburn's success—although, as we shall see, historical circumstances both at home and abroad conspired to stifle this success.

The year after Washburn became secretary treasurer of the Reo local, the union began to take on its own character and direction, even amid great turmoil and confusion. At first affiliated with the AFL and then, by 1936, with the CIO, the local had to contend with a popular company union called the Reo Employees' Association. While the labor papers periodically reported on its demise, there is evidence that this organization survived until the Reo sit-down in the spring of 1937.[74] Nevertheless, in May 1935 the local union successfully bargained with Reo management for an increase in piecework rates.[75] Between the UAW conventions of 1935 and 1936 it was already becoming clear that local auto unionists were leaning toward the CIO rather than the AFL, which "seems to insist that every organization it builds up shall be a tower of Babel with the workers on one level not understanding those on the next."[76] In 1936 Washburn, who helped create an amalgamated union of all autoworkers in Lansing Local 182, was sent to represent the local at the UAW convention at South Bend, Indiana.[77] At the same convention that elected Homer Martin UAW president (ousting F. J. Dillon), Lester Washburn, along with Walter Reuther and eleven others, was elected to the international union's executive board.[78] Later that year Washburn became a paid organizer for the union because of his hard work and popularity among the men.[79]

He also became shop steward for Reo's export shipping department. Export shipping was to become the battleground for union attacks on Reo's longstanding personnel policies. After halving the workforce after the first shock of the Depression, there was a brief rise in the number employed, but after 1935 the numbers fell again, while the average age of workers began to increase. Whereas in 1917 the average age of the 4,365 employees was 33.67 years, by the end of 1935 the average age of the 2,277 employees was 42.17, a trend that continued until 1940.[80] Reo was so seriously stressed by poor profits, shifting and inefficient management, and stockholder battles that it decided to cease producing cars, which had long been unprofitable, and devote itself entirely to truck production by the spring of 1936 (this was actually accomplished by the fall of 1936). To make its operations even more efficient, the company began to lay off more workers.[81]

When six men were laid off in Washburn's department in late August 1936, the men in export shipping responded collectively. They recognized that the foreman had singled out the most inefficient men and they pledged to divide "the work among all the men [so that] no one [would] be laid off."[82] Washburn requested organizing assistance from Adolph Germer of the CIO, and the city's auto men began planning for an action at Reo.[83] Six union men in export shipping protested the layoffs and promptly got laid off themselves. All told, the company locked out forty men. Charging a violation of the Wagner Act and a breach of the company's own agreement on seniority, the union appealed to "all workers and fair-minded citizens of Lansing" to "fight to the finish."[84] In October the company and union began talks; the discharged men were reinstated within a month.[85]

After this positive outcome, the union experienced remarkable growth. Union leaders attributed this to a "growing union consciousness and a feeling that it is only through union organization can they hope to receive a security of income and independence. The sharp rise in the cost of living and profits of the large auto corporations far beyond corresponding increases in wages also tend to waken the economic consciousness of the auto worker."[86] If the company could no longer deliver on the promise of a family wage and masculine autonomy, the union would. The Reo local presented its demands to the company: a 10 percent pay increase with no speed-up in production; time-and-a-half for overtime and double time for Sunday; adjustments for all wages out of line; job security through a strict seniority agreement with no loopholes; and replacement according to strict seniority of all workers laid off or locked out.[87] The widespread defection from the company union, the Reo Employees' Association, prompted the company to raise the question of amalgamation with Local 182. The labor papers triumphantly reported that "another company union is turning against Papa Management at the Reo Plant in this city." Lester Washburn was confident that all the workers would join the union.[88]

Despite agreements with the company over seniority rights and hours of labor, work sharing, leave policies, overtime pay, the retention of the Reo Benefit Association, union/management committees' meeting times, and some preliminary piece rates during the winter of 1936–1937, negotiations dragged on and on.[89] The union wondered, "Why is the committee the Reo officials have appointed to bargain with the United, like a young girl on her first date? Answer. Because the official's committee is very coy and shy about meeting with the union committee. Finds excuses and always manages to have some members missing so that the meeting must be postponed."[90] As the union cast its opposition as effeminate, it also formulated a familiar masculine identity for the good union man. In the pages of the *Lansing Industrial News*, the Lansing Automobile Council called on local auto men to fall in.

> You felt you wanted a union not dominated by the A.F. of L. so they gave you your International. Have you made any effort to build it through your own individual effort? . . . No? Then you've been bending over and asking for the corporation to give you a kick. And don't think they won't if they see you can't stand shoulder to shoulder with your fellow-man on the assembly lines. Fire you? They won't fire you—not unless you do something foolish like signing up men on company property or announced to the cocked-eyed world that you are a Communist out to plow under some capitalists. They'll respect you for meeting them across the conference table like a man.[91]

"A Union Man," the *Lansing Auto Worker* editorialized, "has respect for himself and for his family. As an American citizen he knows he has certain Constitutional Rights which he is determined to fight to retain. He believes that his family and his children have a RIGHT to a DECENT STANDARD OF LIVING, an education, and some of the things that make life worth living!"[92] Reverend C. M. Winters, the assistant pastor of the Church of the Resurrection, concurred. "A cornerstone in the program of Social Justice is the LIVING WAGE. Now a living wage means that the man who labors has a God-given right to such an annual income from his toil as will suffice to provide support for himself, his wife, and their children according to the prevailing standard of living."[93] In a powerful symbolic gesture, the Reo workers even asked why they could not have their union meetings at the Reo clubhouse, the space that best represented the paternalism of the company itself.[94]

The company's decision to fire fifteen men and reduce wages in a number of departments (apparently export and domestic shipping were hard hit) was the final straw. Even though there were concrete workplace issues at stake, the arbitrary actions of the company demonstrated that the union needed formal recognition. Washburn recalled,

> They wouldn't deal so we decided we'd have a sit-down strike and we decided that we would start it then, while we were in negotiations on a certain day. We have been fooling around for two, three weeks with them. So about three or four o'clock in the afternoon, before quittin' time, we just went to the phone in the main office and called the contacts, and then you could just hear the noise of the factory just slow down till it stopped.[95]

On March 10, 1937, between 1,500 and 2,000 men, approximately 90 percent of those employed at the Reo factory, shut down their machines and sat down. Donald Bates, now the president of the newly reorganized company, initially said in anger and frustration, "the boys can have the plant for all I care. We haven't made anything out of it in the past eight years anyway!"[96] Bates issued a formal statement that "friendly relations had always been maintained with the A.F.L. and the Reo Employees' Association independent group which joined the U.A.W. recently," and that the CIO represented only a minority of the workers.[97]

The broad community support for the sit-down strike and its ultimate success were a strong rebuttal to Bates's assertions about labor relations at Reo. During the month-long occupation, there were no violent or illegal incidents either within or outside the factory. As Washburn recalled, "the watchmen were in the union, the plant guard, and that was an interesting sit-down. . . . They continued their work during the strike, watching to see if everything was right. Nobody was wandering around the plant getting into trouble and there wasn't no problem, no problems."[98] There was never a hint of menace in any of the accounts of this sit-down; in fact, union leaders and the participants created a labor culture of unimpeachable respectability. Children of Reo workers who later became Reo workers themselves remembered going to the windows to chat with and pass food to their striking fathers.[99] Within hours of the strike's beginning, the ladies auxiliary went into action, coordinating the preparation and distribution of food to the strikers.[100] The various labor papers reported on the contributions to the strike of the Ingham County Farmers' Union, and more than forty local merchants featured sample menus of the meals eaten inside the plant. The workers prided themselves on their discipline and their wholesome pastimes. The papers printed the songs they sang (locally revised versions of labor standards) and reported that the men "made up a little orchestra of their own and called it the Reo Ramblers and they entertained themselves." Strikers organized boxing, exercising, and checkers matches.[101] As the *Lansing Auto Worker* proclaimed in a headline of its "Reo Extra" during the strike, "Reo Strike Is Nation's Model Demonstration."[102]

The peaceful sit-down not only prompted a reinterpretation of the decades of paternalism endured by the workers at Reo but also demonstrated the respectability and discipline of the strikers. "The thirty-three years of peace were also . . . thirty-three years of industrial oppression such as had never been seen in American industry outside a 'company town.'" A writer in the *Lansing Auto Worker* claimed that a new and modern Reo Spirit had come to the Reo Family. "Memories of the days when the management told the workers what to eat and drink and what to think and vote inspires the workers to a declaration of independence." These workers, the writer continued,

are different from other workers. They are older, more settled, more thoughtful than the mass of employees in the mass production industries. They are sound citizens. They own their own homes—or at least they always tried to. They did not rush into the union movement. They did not strike without thought. Slowly, almost prayerfully they considered their grievances and saw that only through the co-operative effort that comes in a union could they win their rights as men and workers.[103]

Like their leader, Lester Washburn, they cited the Depression itself as the catalyst for the rebellion after years of poor treatment. "When the depression came, they were left out in the cold . . . and when employment returned, they were asked to accept wage cuts while others received raises. No wonder they rebelled."[104] This sounds more like an apologia than a justification for rebellion. Mindful of their position in the community and the values shared over many decades, those participating in Lansing's first serious industrial strike needed to justify their actions to those who might judge them harshly. By reminding readers of their legacy of civic responsibility, commitment to family, temperance, and "prayerfulness," they represented themselves as respectable, responsible male worker-citizens.

A small group of workers, however, did not share these sentiments or join the sit-down. As soon as the strike began, forty-one Reo workers wrote to their mayor, Max Templeton, objecting to the union, the action, and the negative representation of Reo. These workers were all former members of the defunct Reo Employees' Association (the company union) and long-time veterans of the plant.[105] Many of these men claimed that conditions at Reo were as good as if not better than those at other plants and that Reo's management was receptive to sorting out problems and grievances on an individual basis, which suited them just fine.

They were good members of the Lansing community family, too. J. E. Graham, employed for eighteen years by Reo, a tax-paying resident of Lansing since 1891, did not join the union or the strike because he did "not approve of their conduct." Sidney Brummet, who worked at Reo for twenty-four years, wrote the mayor, "I am paying for a house and I think they [the sit-downers] are trying to sink the ship that carried us through the Depreshion [sic]." Claiming that the strikers did not represent the majority of workers in the plant, these loyalists invoked the same qualities the strikers did to justify their actions. H. E. Nickels claimed that many workers had been as loyal to Reo as the company had been to them. "Most of us have too, been loyal to the City of Lansing. We have put our labor into building up the town. We have established homes, paid our taxes, patronized Lansing businesses and have . . . conducted ourselves in such a manner that . . . we may be considered . . . good citizens."[106] These loyalists were not ready to end their paternalistic bargain with the company. They wished to remain in the Reo community family that had dominated the first three decades of the century.

In late March Mayor Templeton convened meetings between union and management committees, and although these were helpful, real progress did not occur until Governor Frank Murphy brought the parties together.[107] By the second week of April, a month after the sit-down began, workers returned to the Reo plant. Lester Washburn, who participated in all of the efforts to bring the sit-down to a successful conclusion for the union, regarded the new stature of the union as the major outcome of the action.[108] The strike also united a community just emerging from the paralysis of the Depression, and strikers thanked their supporters, the merchants, businessmen, and fellow unionists at Olds, Fisher, and smaller shops. They even thanked the management at Reo "for their non-intervention with us in our line of duty protectin' our jobs and makin' it possible for us to give our kiddies a little more of the common necessities of life."[109] As a fitting end to the carnival-like atmosphere of this sit-down, after the agreement was signed and the men came out of the shop, six thousand people marched in a victory parade through the streets of Lansing, and some of the men went to the river and gleefully jumped in.[110] Washburn was now in charge of all of Lansing's roughly 15,000 newly energized automobile workers through Amalgamated UAW Local 182, which included Reo, Olds, Fisher Body, and a number of smaller workplaces.

Meanwhile, business began to pick up. Even a small company like the Capital City Wrecking Company, struggling since 1928, doubled its business and its labor force.[111] On April 25, 1937, nineteen of Capital City's twenty-five workers walked into the union hall and asked to be organized. The men elected officers that very night, and the next day the company fired all of the officers and refused to negotiate with the union.[112] Several weeks of futile attempts to get a contract and have the fired workers reinstated resulted in a strike. Lansing's workers did their stints on the picket line. The building and lumber firms joined in support of the Capital City Wrecking workers, while the company began to appeal to the courts and law enforcement for an injunction against the strikers and picketers. Washburn paid no attention to the injunction after it was served on him and twenty-five militant picketers. The injunction deadline passed and the pickets continued, with no response from law enforcement for several days.

At 2:00 A.M. on Monday, June 7, 1937, Sheriff Allan MacDonald, a former Reo worker, first cut the phone lines and then knocked on the door of the Washburn household armed with warrants for the arrest of Lester Washburn, who was not home, and his wife.[113] The sheriff took Mrs. Washburn to jail, leaving three children unattended, while his deputies dispersed throughout the city to round up seven other picketers. When Lester Washburn got home at around 2:30 A.M. and discovered what had happened, he called his union representatives to meet at the union hall as soon as possible. As Washburn tells the story,

> So we got on the phone and got [Homer] Martin out of bed, told him what was happening. Told him what we proposed to do and he agreed with it. So then we called the plant managers of all the plants and told 'em ... what happened and told 'em what we was gonna do about it. Then we sent these plant chairmen out to their plants to meet the night shift coming off, the day shift comin' on, and told 'em the story and then they all start flooding to this little plant. It was a dead end street.[114]

Although Washburn was upset by the events of the evening, he also recognized it as an opportunity. Imprisoning women (another striker's wife was arrested as well) and leaving children unattended in the middle of the night were not actions likely to win much public sympathy, and Washburn undoubtedly recognized the value of this story for bolstering the union cause. The official UAW Local 182 statement described the Lansing Labor Holiday as a "celebration of Sheriff MacDonald's knavery." His "dragging a harmless and innocent woman out of bed in the middle of the night and in terrorizing and leaving alone in the house her three young children and throwing her into a filthy jail that even a self-respecting reptile would not wallow in, met and will continue to meet with the undying resentment of every worker and decent citizen."[115]

The Lansing Labor Holiday was also a spontaneous mass event that provoked almost no violence or disorder (see Illustration 9). In all, 2,000 to 5,000 union members and sympathizers poured into the downtown streets, forcing the closing of many shops, factories, theaters, and businesses of all kinds. Washburn described workers walking away from workplaces, including the *Lansing State Journal* office, where there had been ongoing disputes regarding representation or a closed shop, suggesting that this "spontaneous" uprising tapped into ongoing disputes.[116] Armed with clubs, sticks, and two-by-fours, workers paraded down the streets of the city singing labor songs, while Washburn and other union representatives successfully negotiated the release of those imprisoned. By nightfall the holiday was over and the picketers were released. Just a few days later, Capital City

ILLUSTRATION 9.  Lansing Labor Holiday—in front of Capitol. General Photo Collection, State Archives of Michigan. Photo courtesy of State Archives of Michigan.

Wrecking negotiated with the union, and all seemed resolved. Unionists of Lansing saw the event as a "show of power to the bosses."[117]

The meaning of this Labor Holiday is more complicated, however. Four days before the crisis erupted, on June 3, the very day the injunction had been served on Washburn and the picketers, preparations for another celebration, scheduled for Tuesday, June 8, began. June 8 was to be the day for a huge conclave of the Knights Templar. By Thursday, June 3, the work of decorating the downtown streets was well underway. By the weekend, June 5 and 6, the 4,000 Knights began to pour into the city for a variety of activities, including meetings and banquets at the Masonic Temple. The conclave culminated in a huge passion cross on Tuesday, June 8, at 4:30 P.M. "The parade [was] led by dignitaries of the lodge, mounted, followed by the masses bands and masses colors," with other marchers, "forming a mammoth 'Passion Cross,'" to the tune "Onward Christian Soldiers." The march was well attended by the people of Lansing.

What went through the minds of those carrying clubs and closing down businesses downtown as they gazed up and saw the flags of the Knights Templar, which featured the Celtic cross, flapping in the wind? Did they imagine that they had made a final break with the paternalism gripping their world for so many decades (see Illustration 10)? Were they asserting their own class-based declaration of independence by taking to the streets at this particular moment? We know how those participating in the conclave and the business elites of the city felt. The commandery immediately adopted a resolution against "atheism, communism, and any effort on the part of any organization to disrupt or tear down principles of the constitution, property rights, and those institutions which protect the home, prevent mob rule, and maintain law and order and Christian religion." The Lansing Labor Holiday, they declared, stirred law-abiding citizens to

ILLUSTRATION 10.  Lansing Labor Holiday. Banner of UAW Local 182 on right, flags of Knights Templar on left. Photo courtesy of Craig A. Whitford, Lansing.

mobilize to pursue these goals.[118] By the end of June 1937, Lansing had its very own Law and Order League, started by Dwight Rich, the local commander of an American Legion Post and the principal of one of Lansing's high schools. Washburn blasted Rich and his efforts and reasserted the workers' need for their unions.[119]

The newly empowered UAW Local 182 engaged in a flurry of activities after the Lansing Labor Holiday, many of them designed to replace the paternalistic programs formerly provided by their employers and to create a broad-based grassroots working-class culture in Lansing. The union proclaimed its commitment to "real democracy," announcing that it welcomed differences of opinion and would reject the "practice of 'hero worship'" in favor of the "free unfettered constructive criticism of the leadership."[120] The union began to sponsor educational classes in parliamentary law, public speaking, and the history of the labor movement. It showed movies related to the labor movement at the union hall. The various branches of the union, the women's auxiliary, and the "flying squadron" hosted parties. The union also organized a variety of sports programs, including boxing and baseball leagues.[121] Local 182 sponsored professional boxing and wrestling matches at the Prudden auditorium on Friday nights.[122]

The welfare program was particularly important; advice and help for the unemployed was available daily at the union hall. Subcommittees took care of rent, auto financing, furniture financing, foreclosures, and clothing for the needy.[123] UAW Local 182 and Washburn in particular became active in influencing the dispensation of local relief through the union's welfare department. The union repeatedly objected to any cuts in appropriations to the Works Progress Administration (WPA) or any welfare programs earmarked for the unemployed of Lansing. On March 5, 1938, in the aftermath of fresh evictions of the unemployed, 1,500 people gathered in front of city hall to call for the end of such evictions. UAW Local 182 was an important presence at the demonstration, which was also held to protest delays in obtaining WPA projects and adequate relief in Lansing.

Washburn and his union articulated a political position that reflected local conditions and concerns. First, they held that additional relief was justified in an economy in which corporations were making profits. Second, Washburn advocated that relief expenditures for rent be used for payments on mortgages, a position reflecting the high percentage of homeowners in the workforce at Reo and other auto shops in Lansing. Third, Washburn challenged the redirection of relief to military preparedness, proclaiming, "We want homes, not battleships. And we want to get them right away— by proper legislation."[124] Finally, the union appealed to the governor over mistreatment or unfairness in the local dispensation of relief. In one dramatic case, UAW Local 182 protested that the Ingham County Relief Agency was apparently withholding funds from pregnant women unless they agreed to be sterilized after the birth of the child. The union declared, "this is undemocratic and against all principles of Americanism."[125]

This was a brief moment in Lansing's automotive union history. Washburn's continued commitment to respectable labor militancy, the rank and file, and local control proved to be his undoing in Lansing. Not only was he arrested for his participation in the picketing during the Capital City Wrecking strike (he was found guilty and fined as a result),[126] but his boss, Homer Martin, denounced his efforts in the Lansing Labor Holiday. Speaking in Lansing at the Prudden Auditorium on July 8, 1937, Martin proclaimed, "the labor holiday was a mistake made by a young and growing organization. . . . From now on, we are going to have a clean organization from top to bottom. It will be democratic, honest, and righteous." The menace that Washburn and his union posed to the establishment was clear. Martin had to caution "the vigilantes [to] put away their guns. We aren't out to do any one any harm and we are going to abide by the law. We aren't armed and we aren't going to arm."[127]

After the contentious UAW National Convention in Milwaukee in 1937, at which the conflict between Unity and Progressive forces dominated union politics, Washburn reasserted his leadership of UAW Local 182 and his commitment to local authority and control. The Unity faction endorsed the use of outside organizers (including Victor Reuther) and "all *forces* at work in the C.I.O. movement today seeking to solve our economic problems." Washburn responded angrily, "since the word 'forces' means anything that might be at work in the movement, this would mean recognition of the L.I.D. [League for Industrial Democracy], Workers' Alliance [the radical organization of the unemployed] Conference for the Protection of Civil Rights, Renters and Consumers League and every other *parasite* that seeks to utilize the strength and resources of the union which the automobile workers have struggled to build and to hold." The union, Washburn believed, could adequately handle all of these matters but had "been hampered because of *outside* interference." Casting all of those "who would *take the business of a local union and air it in the capitalist press and on the radio,* where manufacturers and those who are the avowed enemies of labor can get it . . . *a Traitor to this organization,*" Washburn pledged that "NOTHING but STRAIGHT UNIONISM" would be carried on within the union hall.[128]

Despite all that had been accomplished in the aftermath of the Reo sit-down strike and the Lansing Labor Holiday, by 1938 the UAW's internal conflicts had split the local in Lansing. At the 1939 UAW-CIO convention, Martin, Washburn, and a number of others were expelled from the union, and the CIO prevailed. Meeting at the International Organization of Odd Fellows Hall, representatives from all of Lansing's autoworker local unions convened to hear the UAW-CIO leaders explain the issues. According to the reporter for the *United Automobile Worker,* after the meeting "a large group announced that they were through with company unionism and wanted to go to the C.I.O."[129] Writing in the *Lansing Auto Worker* as the head of Local 182, UAW-AFL, Washburn wrote, "Somewhere, somehow we know that all automobile workers will be together. Therefore our first concern at this time must be the solidarity of the individual locals, wherever they may be, in order that the day of unity may not find our local disintegrated and weakened, washed out." And so Washburn, pledging himself to the rule of the majority in local union governance, disappeared from the standard narrative of automotive unionism in the United States.[130]

Replacing Washburn was Guy Hack, who had been a steward at Reo with Washburn back in 1935. He was elected as the labor member to the board of directors of the newly reconstituted Reo Motors. The labor press praised the appointment as a step toward industrial democracy, and Hack himself declared that "much misunderstanding would be eliminated if corporations would follow Reo and let their employees elect their own representatives to the Board."[131] The first action of the newly designated bargaining unit for the Reo shop, Local 650, was to assure the labor-management committee that "labor relations were most harmonious in the plant and that employees would cooperate to their fullest extent in helping resume operations." They pledged to meet weekly on company time in Cy Rath's office.[132] Until the company's reorganization in 1939, labor relations at Reo involved meetings to update the workers' representatives on a loan taken from the Reconstruction Finance Corporation. By the end of 1939 rumors were afoot that Reo would resume production. By December nearly 500 men were back at Reo, as the courts approved the reorganization plan.[133] At the start of the new decade, Colonel Fred Glover was named the new company president and proceeded, without objection from the union, to subject all factory employees to physical exams, including blood tests.[134] In May 1940 the workers at Reo signed the first union shop contract in the UAW-CIO with Reo Motors, a cause for real celebration.[135]

Some of the old ways persisted nonetheless. That same month, the first new line of Reo trucks pulled off the assembly line. The *Lansing Industrial News* proclaimed that "the old time Reo spirit was exemplified at the Reo christening party." The workers and management of Reo, the mayor of Lansing, and the president of the Lansing Chamber of Commerce all came together once again with "pride of achievement."[136] There were still only 800 employees at Reo; for many, the good days would never return. But after the past thirteen years, perhaps there was some comfort in reuniting the big factory family one more time before its white male members faced another great change.

# 4

## Reo Rebellions, 1939–1951

*Wars, Women, and Wobblies*

The turmoil of the late 1930s began a twelve-year period of profound change, challenges, and labor unrest at Reo. In 1936 Reo's board of directors decided to bow to competitive pressure and focus production on trucks and other commercial vehicles, while workers continued to organize in the shop. The disarray in the company provoked conflicts among stockholder groups at the very time that internecine union battles divided workers in the UAW.[1] The successful month-long sit-down strike of the spring of 1937 had brought the UAW to the shop, but this must have seemed like a Pyrrhic victory to many workers, for the management continued to bicker and the company continued to falter. In 1938 Reo filed for reorganization under national bankruptcy laws. At various points during the next four years the plant would shut down, and workers, whose numbers had been diminishing since the sit-down, were laid off without any knowledge of when they might be called back. Out of the maelstrom of bankruptcy and reorganization, Reo Motors, Inc., was born.

Reo's story might have ended at this point had it not been for two related developments: the increasing hostilities in Europe and a loan from the Reconstruction Finance Corporation (RFC) to begin retooling to produce trucks for the military and for Lend Lease. The $2 million RFC loan was contingent on a number of reorganization provisions that modified manu-

94

facturing, management, and personnel practices. In *Labor's War at Home: The CIO in World War II*, Nelson Lichtenstein states that labor leaders had "their eyes focused on Washington."[2] So did management. Labor and management awaited the results of this infusion of capital, only vaguely aware of the implications of the new rules of the game.

For the remainder of its corporate existence, Reo depended on the federal bureaucracy for cash, contracts, and the conditions of production. Both workers and employers had to contend with outside interference, bureaucratic initiatives, and requirements from governmental and private-sector organizations in their day-to-day affairs. The company had to disclose the salaries of all managers and report any increases to the authorities.[3] It had to conform to the requirements of the Fair Labor Standards Act as it rehired its workforce.[4] The union worked with the company to set wage rates, develop a grievance procedure, and monitor the orderly rehiring of workers according to seniority.[5] Reo's management understood that the company's livelihood was tied to its ability to procure government contracts and that there would be strings attached. Union leaders and workers understood that security and relatively good pay, if not safe conditions, could be had, but they had to remain disciplined unionists, maintain the no-strike pledge, and submit to nationally and regionally imposed limits on their ability to bargain with employers for wages, hours, and conditions of work. Both local unionists and management understood that there were other parties at the table now.

To suggest that Reo's management resented outside interference while the union welcomed it, or that the company was able to use wartime instruments of the state to their own ends at the expense of workers, would be to misrepresent the more complicated ways in which the state affected how Reo and its workers functioned during World War II and the Korean conflict. As they had done throughout the 1930s, workers and managers at Reo responded to national events in ways that reflected local conditions and history. The story of how the warfare, welfare, and regulatory state intruded on a small independent producer and its workers shifts our gaze from the halls of power in Washington to the board room, the shop floor, and the negotiating table.[6]

Mobilization for war changed Lansing in significant ways. Business and building both geared up; young men enlisted or answered the call of the

draft, and migrants flooded into the city for work, creating serious housing shortages.[7] African Americans and Hispanics began to enter Lansing
in significant numbers for the first time.[8] Until late 1942 or early 1943,
when the flood of contracts and new workers began to pour in, a détente
had existed between workers and management, both operating in their
own worlds but often with similar goals in mind.

## Adjusting to the Warfare State

With the company struggling financially, Reo's management sought war
work as soon as possible.[9] Within a year of assuming the presidency of Reo
Motors (and before Pearl Harbor), Henry Hund wrote to Andrew Stevenson of the Office of Production Management asking for an improved quota
on restricted materials and more defense work. Hund described a largely
idle plant with good facilities and workers whose preliminary defense work
was deemed "satisfactory for use in the military service" by a War Department performance report at Camp Holabird. Reo could produce tactical
units, trucks for shipment to foreign countries under the Lend Lease Act,
and trucks and coaches for highway transportation.[10]

Procuring defense contracts was a joint labor-management effort. As
early as September 1940 Richard Reisinger, the head of the truck division
of the UAW-CIO, spoke on Reo's behalf in a variety of defense venues and
also informed local unionists about how to proceed in getting government
contracts.[11] After the Japanese attack on Pearl Harbor, W. O. Scholz, the
president of Local 650, and Allen S. Haywood, the director of organization for the CIO in Washington, wrote Morris Cooke of the National
Defense Committee and the Office of Production Management to press
for defense contracts for Reo. Scholz pledged the union's willingness to
"cooperate 100% in any program for defense." The problem, he continued, was that the company employed 1,556 men, many with seniority and
skills, and made one of the "best trucks on the market but to date we have
only built about 350 trucks for the Government." Reo workers wondered
why "work has been placed all over the country, new factories being built,
work allotted to companies that are working overtime on their own work
and we are sitting here with no work, plenty of men, and plenty of empty
floor space." Allen Haywood stressed that Reo was 100 percent organized
with the UAW-CIO.[12]

Reo received its first defense contract in 1940 in conjunction with the RFC loan.[13] This order, for large dump trucks, continued the tradition of truck production started in 1912.[14] In 1941 the Navy Department, Bureau of Ordnance, awarded Reo a contract to make projectile or bomb fuses. This order led to the creation of a naval division at Reo that oversaw a large and vital part of the company's defense work and remained a feature of Reo through the early 1970s.[15] The first shipment was just over 3,000 units, but by the last quarter of 1942 Reo was producing more than 100,000 units per quarter.[16]

Reo also received a number of orders for vehicles for defense-related activities that required Reo's engineers to innovate in design while conforming to military specifications. When Reo redesigned its standard 4 × 4, 4 × 6, and 6 × 6 trucks, it positioned itself for future military orders. Reo also serviced more than twenty companies as a subcontractor.[17] In September 1941 approximately 9 percent of underutilized production was oriented directly to defense, 18 percent to customers with defense orders (subcontract work), and about 10 percent to shipment overseas (many for Lend Lease). By 1942, 50 percent of production was for defense, and this percentage increased during the remainder of the war years.[18]

To take advantage of government work, Reo established a permanent presence in Washington, D.C. John T. Clark and, later, John Tooker[19] filled their days with social events with military personnel and tours of military camps and proving grounds to maintain Reo's competitiveness.[20] In a confidential memo sent to Tooker back at Lansing, Clark described a discussion with Lt. Commander J. N. Kelty of the Ordnance Bureau about why Reo had not received the coveted "E" rating given to productive and efficient defense plants.[21] Kelty reportedly stressed that Reo needed to improve its relationship with the Detroit Naval Office. Clark wrote, "it seems to be the clash of personalities or just lack of acquaintance and he [Kelty] stated that it was the Detroit office ... which was holding off the 'E' for us." Clark's prescription was for Reo men, "to get personally acquainted with them. If they be dimwits," he added, "and an evening spent with them occasionally is lost from a personal standpoint, this is no different than a lot of evenings with our other customers."[22] Such were the sacrifices of wartime.

Reo slowly increased its truck production and share of defense work.[23] At the start of 1943 the company produced hundreds of thousands of bomb fuses, and tank transports for the Ordnance Bureau, and acted as a subcontractor by machining and treating aircraft and truck parts for other companies.[24] By the end of 1943 additional orders for a variety of trucks trickled in; these orders increased in 1944 when Reo also began to manufacture rocket fuses.[25]

The welcome resumption of nearly full production and the explosive increase in the number of Reo factory workers brought significant changes and challenges for labor and management. Capital and contracts came from governmental, not civilian, sources, which altered all aspects of planning and production. For example, representatives from Reo participated in trade association meetings that were key in allocating production quotas and disseminating information about scarce national resources needed for production. Starting in August 1942, the chief of ordnance for the War Department mandated procedures for industry integration committees. These committees were to "make commonly available to each manufacturer, the benefit of the production experience and techniques of all manufacturers in the group, and so to integrate the facilities of the group as to attain maximum production in the shortest possible time."[26] Reo would participate in three industry integration committees, one for companies producing motor trucks,[27] one for companies producing bomb fuses,[28] and one for companies producing rocket fuses.[29]

War work brought with it an endless amount of bureaucratic red tape. Whether it was a basic machine tool or an office chair, Reo could not make a purchase without clearance from the military bureaucracy.[30] As a prime contractor at the end of the production line, Reo had to contend with delays and the capriciousness of vendors.[31] Finally, and probably most demoralizing of all, prices for all products were determined in large measure by the Office of Price Administration.[32]

The engineers at Reo were often on the front lines of the government military bureaucracy, and they relieved their frustrations with departmental memos that rivaled Joseph Heller's *Catch-22* in their biting satire of the irrationality of the "order" of war. Take, for example, the following memo regarding purchase-order procedures.

> Suppose our company completes the fabrication of an airplane. Just as we are about to push it out of the door, a workman discovers that the engineering department, in designing the plane, failed to provide two nuts needed to hold the tail wheelband in place. It now becomes necessary to acquire these nuts.

So what does the workman do? After lunch he notifies his leader, the leader notifies the supervisor, the supervisor notifies the department clerk, the department clerk notifies the department superintendent, the department superintendent notifies planning and scheduling, planning and scheduling notifies the standards department, and the standards department notifies cost control, which issues a shop order (S.O.).

This shop order is issued in quadruplicate. One copy goes to the General Manager, one goes to the shop, one goes to follow-up. The fourth copy is thrown away. Now we have a shop order.

After traveling about the plant for a day or two, the shop order arrives at the Purchasing Department. To it, however, has been attached various papers, including 16 blueprints and an authority card. The authority card is of no special importance and can be ignored in the discussion. Its principal use is to have something to which the shop order and blueprints can be pinned while in transit.

These papers arrive at our Department at 8:00 A.M. and are mailed at 10:30 A.M. Promptly at 11:30 the next morning, 17 engineering orders #426849-326-1 arrive. By adding the last five figures together, we know at a glance that these are 17 engineering orders and should be attached to the 16 blueprints on the nut order. What happens is that after the shop order is issued, someone discovers that the only tool available at the tail station is a hexagon wrench, a situation not provided for in the blueprints.

Now we are ready to get bids. Bid requests are sent out to three nut factories in accordance with GOVERNMENT REGULATION. Only one bid comes back, so we decide to order the nuts from a factory not previously contacted.

The next step is to issue the actual Purchase Order. This operation is started by a group of persons in the write-up department, who, working together, produce a paper known as a requisition. On this paper, the writer places various marks, signs, figures and initials. This is done by passing the paper back and forth until it is filled up. The requisition is then turned over to Agnes, who discovers 67 errors. She sends it back, 49 of the errors are corrected, 18 missed, and 7 new errors are made in making the corrections.

The purchase order is now ready for the ditto machine. On this machine, 82 copies of the order are produced. The first copy, though, is usually spoiled and is known as the first copy. This is sent to the vender along with a rule book, 17 acknowledgments and a greeting card from our president. The copies are distributed to the Army, Navy, Marines, Gerald L. K. Smith, Hitler, the FBI, our supervisor, his secretary, her boy friend, and the various departments. Sixteen copies are filled [filed] in files scattered around our office. The purpose of this is obvious. Suppose you want to find a copy of an old order. Instead of trying to hunt for it, or guess what file it is in, you just run around in a circle. The first file [cabinet] you fall over, just pull open a drawer and there it is. Forty-one copies of the order go to a small group of men known as follow-up men. These are furtive looking fellows who occasionally sneak in and out of the office. . . .

As soon as the follow-uppers get wind a new purchase order has been issued and placed, they fly into action. The unfortunate vendor who received the order becomes the subject of persuasion, threats and intimidation in an attempt to get his signature on a paper known as a delivery schedule. God help the vendor who signs that paper! From then on at any hour of the day or night, he will be confronted with follow-uppers demanding, "Where are those nuts?"

Months go by, but in the meantime someone in the tail section finds two nuts that fit the tail gadget. Without authorization from the salvage department, he applies the nuts that fit the tail gadget and finishes the job.

The plane is pushed out of the factory (Again) onto the loading dock, disassembled, crated, boxed and shipped to British South Africa, where it is now on the dock waiting for an American engineer to show the natives how to put it together again.

So what do we do now? We cancel the order for the two nuts.

Now to issue the cancellation——OH HELL, what's the use? Let's all go nuts. BUY MORE BONDS. WE NEED THE DOUGH.[33]

Reo had to do a great deal to meet the challenge of operating in the wartime economy; according to John Tooker, who reflected on this in early 1943, the company needed to overhaul and adapt necessary machine tools and equipment on hand in the plant and procure machine tools, gauges, and equipment for war production; innovate in production techniques and in the use of critical materials; and retrain the entire organization, including new female employees, to the tasks.[34] John Tooker could not have known in 1943 exactly what the implications of this last change might be.

## The Long Wildcat Strike, 1943–1947

I think that's where everything went to hell was during the war when the women went into the factories. . . . Yeah, mother and dad both working, probably opposite shifts, and there was nobody around home and the kids were on their own and the husband would say, "We're not gonna buy this," and the wife says, "Go to hell. I've got my own money."
—Marvin Grinstern, former Reo employee[35]

The pumps were found to be in perfect condition and no reason could be found for their failure until a pair of ladies panties were taken from the suction pipe. These were undoubtedly discarded during the construction of the vessel in a moment of thoughtlessness and left lying in the tank, later finding their way into the pipeline. . . . In order that all may cooperate one hundred percent in the war effort and the total destruction of the Axis Powers, it is respectfully requested that lady workers keep their pants on during working hours for the duration.
—Senator Prentiss Brown, Democrat, member of the Army Ordnance Committee[36]

The war brought new labor relations, jobs, machines, production methods, and workers to the plant. With the departure of many of the founding fathers of the company, such as Olds, Scott, Bates, Teel, and Rath, management was freer to adapt and innovate. Henry Hund, Reo's new president and a veteran of a number of Detroit automotive companies, and his new team were free of the old paternalistic concepts of labor relations. In March 1940 the union announced the election of new officials to represent a workforce of more than 500 men. Half of the small number of foreign-born workers were from either England or Canada; their average age was 52.[37]

This was no "big factory family," but relations between labor and management were amicable during the early war years. The union and company negotiating teams met almost every week in 1941 and irregularly in 1943.[38] There was remarkably little rancor or disagreement, even over contentious issues. In March 1941, for example, "it was agreed by all those present that the number of different classifications should be kept down to the very minimum and it was suggested that three would cover everything except the welders and hammer men" (who were ranked higher). Female employees were paid 75 percent of the middle range of male rates.[39] Reo's management seemed reconciled to the closed shop and even reminded union officials when the trial period ended and workers needed to join the union.[40] The Reo benefit association was retained at the request of union leadership. The annual picnics resumed in 1941[41] and the clubhouse reopened to grateful employees in 1944.[42]

To many at Reo, the most dramatic change during the war years was undoubtedly the hiring of a large number of women. Female workers were associated with the turmoil in the factory between 1943 and 1947, but they were not its only cause. Women in the factory inspired some of their male counterparts to demand equal pay for equal work and the humane treatment of women by foremen. Many male workers recognized that women were essential to the war effort but also saw them as disruptive and disorderly, as a force that needed to be kept "in check."

There had always been a small number of female employees in the Reo plant, most of them employed as office workers and a few in the wiring and upholstery departments. During the sit-down strike of 1937, the men ushered women out of the shop and directed them to participate in the ladies auxiliary that had been organized by Lester Washburn's wife, Neva. As Reo began to gear up for war production during the early 1940s, Reo hired women in a number of different departments, but they were concentrated in the manufacturing of bomb and rocket fuses.[43] Here, workers performed operations on a variety of automatic machines (Gridleys or New Brittans) and assembled the inert fuse parts. These parts were then placed in large trays, carted away, and inspected, a precise and painstaking task subject to arbitrary review by the navy.

The presence of the new female employees presented a number of challenges. The purchasing department had to remember to stock its new Kotex dispenser;[44] supervisors had to reconsider the dress code (they decided to require that women wear pants);[45] and the legal department had to determine whether the company was required to give women longer rest periods when they were menstruating (it was not).[46] In December 1942 Reo started a training school to weed out female workers ill suited to work in the plant. Only half of the women who started were kept on. The "girls" were subjected to talks by safety engineers and were "watched very closely by the women employees of our personnel who keep a check on them and advise them regarding shop conduct."[47]

The company also hired a women's director, Bertha Tueling, who, until the end of 1945, oversaw all non-work-related matters relating to female employees.[48] Tueling revived social events and women's sports teams. One of her duties was to safeguard female employees' respectability; one of her announcements regarding a dance for male and female employees went so far as to warn the "girls" not to wear sweaters or anklets (too casual and revealing).[49] The beefed-up plant protection department not only hired female officers as the war wore on but was alert to the new pressures on the labor force brought by women employees.[50] In 1944, for example, Charles Parr, the head of plant protection, instructed the personnel department not to rehire two women who had been quarantined for venereal disease. There is no evidence that men were treated similarly.[51]

With more women around, the racial divide needed vigilant policing. The number of male and female African Americans at Reo did not increase significantly until the late 1960s, but there was a small number of black janitors and low-level factory employees. In the spring of 1943 two shop committeemen filed a complaint with Parr about "a case of a colored sweeper asking a white girl her name and address." As Parr reported it, committeeman Eugene Lewis "stated that he would like an investigation to be made at once, to find out who the colored person was, that stepped out of bounds and have him put in his place while he works here in the Reo Motors."[52] Plant protection did a full investigation of the matter but let the incident drop after discovering that the errant sweeper, Leon Maffitt, had asked the girl her name on a dare. The young woman in question, Doris White, nevertheless requested that Maffitt be moved.[53] Since Maffitt was a good worker and had a family to support, he was "put somewhere with no girls," and nothing more came of the incident.[54] Undoubtedly many Reo men experienced the presence of women in the factory as potentially explosive.[55]

Women were not the only new workers entering the plant during these years. Younger male workers and veterans contributed to the turmoil between 1943 and 1947.[56] When veterans encountered speed-ups and arbitrary supervision, they responded militantly, comparing management's actions with the arbitrary behavior of dictators and military leaders. They brought their understanding of their rights to fair treatment—not just as union members but as veterans—onto the shop floor.

Management's introduction of new production techniques mandated by the war stirred up the volatile mix of workers. The Reo plant stayed open around the clock during these years, employing three shifts, with time-and-a-half and double time for work beyond eight hours a day six days a week. Company supervisors and foremen constantly changed the way work was done to increase efficiency and to conform to capricious government regulations. Manager Al Zimmer admitted, "The continual changing of machines probably looks as if we are constantly changing our minds. In some cases this is true; mostly, though, it is the changes in design and the substitution of methods of machining due to our inability to get rapid service on tools and machine repair. There is a large waste of time involved due to the lack of planning and sufficient time between engineering changes and model changes."

Cutting labor costs was also key, and Zimmer made a lot of suggestions in this area, including retiming jobs to pick up changes in production and routing; having group piece rates reflect any reworking that needed to be done; including group leader and set-up man in time study; repairing and restocking more quickly; putting all assembly workers on group piecework; and more efficient use of workers' down time. On the last issue, Zimmer became quite passionate, suggesting that

> it should be understood that when a time study is made there is much more involved than just cutting rates. It should be understood the different departments in the Inert Division must be coordinated in time studies or the down time and loss in pieces produced will be tremendous. For instance, if a worker is making high money, he is willing to do many things that, under existing union rules, is out of his line of work, such as, moving stock, chasing tools, fixtures, oil men, etc. At least until we get our layout all completed and working, including every conveyor or chute, the time study must take all these into consideration or we will have to add more non-production help to make our present schedule.[57]

The rapid change in the work processes created pay inequities, which were exacerbated by a number of local factors. First, until 1943 women were hired in separate job classifications at lower pay. Women were also frequently "excused" from the late shift and Sunday work that paid higher wages. Second, until well into the 1950s, Reo had different pay arrangements for workers in the shop. Some were paid a straight hourly wage while others were paid by the piece (with a base rate to guard workers against slow production); still other workers were paid a group piece rate determined by dividing the output and earnings of the whole work unit by the number in the group. How a particular job or set of jobs was paid was determined by the company and was the source of ongoing tension between management and labor throughout the 1940s. Third, the wages paid for any given job were determined by a worker's seniority and by his or her productivity. Incentive pay (based on productivity) was arbitrary and was often used to tie certain workers to the company. On top of all this, time studies were applied capriciously. Workers claimed that whenever the money got too good, the company would do another time study and lower the rates. The company of course denied this, claiming that new production techniques and demands required new time studies, but delays in getting joint time studies increased worker frustration about unfair rates.

Workers were under pressure to cooperate for the war effort. Even before the actual declaration of war, the government called on organized labor to accept wage limits and a no-strike pledge for the duration of the hostilities.[58] The slogan adopted by organized labor—"equality of sacrifice for victory"—pointed to the gulf workers perceived between their own level of sacrifice and that of their corporate bosses. Workers could appeal to the National War Labor Board (NWLB) and (after the war) the

National Labor Relations Board (NLRB) when they experienced unfair or unequal treatment. The collision of these national trends and local conditions created "the long wildcat," a series of labor actions at Reo between 1943 and 1947.

Reo experienced more than fifty work stoppages, slowdowns, sit-ins and wildcat strikes between 1943 and 1946 (see Table 4 in the Appendix).[59] The appearance of larger numbers of women in the factory exacerbated inequities and precipitated many of these disturbances. By early 1943 Reo was already in trouble with Michigan's Department of Labor and Industry and the state attorney general's office because of its discriminatory pay in the navy division. Management claimed that women could legitimately be paid less than men because they did not lift the large trays of materials and were less experienced on inspections.[60] There is no evidence that Reo was penalized in any way for this inequity, but by May 1943 the company had eliminated the segregated classifications by opening to men certain jobs previously reserved for women, at a base rate of $1.05 per hour. Even so, a sexual division of labor persisted in many job classifications.[61]

One long and well-documented set of wildcats highlights many of the features of these wartime actions. As Table 4 indicates, during late March and early April 1944 the navy division, also known as the 700, particularly the automatic operators and the assemblers, were a boisterous lot. Most of Reo's female employees were located in this division, where many of the pay anomalies occurred, where the demands of war production were the most intense, and where the company therefore made many unilateral changes in production, timing, and pay rates. To make matters more volatile, the employees disagreed about whether to have rotating or fixed shifts and about when those shifts should begin,[62] exasperating even the international union's time-study man during one dispute.[63]

During the summer of 1944, management and union officials worked together and jointly filed papers with the NWLB to increase the pay of about 130 employees in the light production assembly and packers division to $1.10 an hour to eliminate inequities between these workers' pay rates and comparable classifications in the plant.[64] Pending a decision, the company sped up this work and changed the work process. Walter Foust, assistant production manager, had been experimenting with ways of getting Reo's automatics to conform to the industry standard of one worker operating two machines rather than one. Management proposed to "install the same group piece work plan in the Automatic Department that has been working with outstanding success in all other Navy Manufacturing Departments." Under group piecework, "time for reworking will be charged against the group and the O.K.'d reworked pieces credited to the group."[65] On Saturday, July 29, the company initiated the group piecework plan and the two-machine requirement. When the morning shift refused to work on Sunday, objecting as much to the method of presenting the changes as to the changes themselves, management blinked. The workers would go back to the day-rate work on only one machine, and "it was further agreed that before any plan is put into effect, it will be presented." The workers returned to work that afternoon.[66] Four days later, the NWLB denied the application for a wage increase for workers in assembly.[67] Labor and management appealed the decision[68] and on August 15 representatives of union and management appeared at the NWLB regional office in Detroit to plead their case.[69] As Reo and the union continued to supply additional information and clarification through September 1944,[70] brief slowdowns and sit-ins plagued the navy division in response to management's ongoing efforts to make this division more efficient.[71]

The 2½-hour sit-down by sixty assemblers in the 700 division on September 25 began as a protest against the NWLB's delay but soon became an opportunity for the "girls" to air a number of other grievances. Women were not allowed to go to the restroom at will, were "told they were getting old," and were called into Foust's office for individual reprimands.[72] When the NWLB approved a rate of only $1.05 per hour for the light production assembly operation and denied any increase for the packers, the navy division exploded.[73] The stewardess of the packers and assemblers, Ivah Miller, wrote an impassioned grievance claiming that the "Packers and Assemblers of the 700 Bldg. feel there has been an injustice done us, due to the fact the War Labor Board did not grant us a $1.10 increase. We feel the Union Committee and Company should be able to work out a Bonus Plan, inasmuch as we are putting forth more effort."[74] This work stoppage revealed a number of festering issues that would explode a few weeks later.

At 10:00 A.M. on October 18, the women from inert assembly met in the girls' restroom and decided to stop work to protest the ruling and Reo's inability to provide what they considered adequate compensation. The women met again in the restroom at 2:00 P.M. and refused to return to work. The next day the machine room went out in sympathy with the assemblers and packers, and work in the navy division was impaired.[75] The company was alarmed and frantically attempted to contact local union officials to get them to put their people back to work.[76] Jack Holt, the international representative, quieted the situation; he got Russell Smith to compose a third letter of appeal to the NWLB and inform the workers of the company's intention to make a quick appeal to the NWLB for the remaining five-cent-per-hour increase for the assemblers as soon as the workers returned to work.[77] He scolded the errant women and informed them that the international union was not "back of them" and that the local union was not "back of them either. They were on their own."[78] Work resumed for the first shift on October 20.

Management's response to the situation was complicated. While the company did not approve of work stoppages, it seemed somewhat tolerant of brief ones, particularly if they pursued a jointly desired end. In this case, since the union and management were tackling the NWLB jointly, management understood the workers' frustration with the maddeningly slow process. This helps to explain the press release Russell Smith issued about the events of October 18 and 19. Hund instructed Smith to be "as brief as possible. Merely factual, setting forth that it is against the W.L.B. ruling giving only half of what they asked for."[79] A *Lansing State Journal* article on October 20 referred to this episode as a strike against the NWLB, not against Reo.[80] The company seemed more interested in getting the workers their extra five cents than in blaming the workers. One might even speculate that the company recognized that the wildcat work stoppage, if kept under control, could strengthen the case for pay equity and thus increase the stability of the workforce.

A number of union stewards in the plant, however, exploited the situation and called for a larger action throughout the navy division, which naturally angered management. After the work stoppage, Reo managers began a systematic investigation, interviewing the foremen and supervisors in the divisions involved. Initially they fired a few, but after negotiating with the international they laid off only six union officials: Wayne Keeney and Bernie Bennett, both committeemen and members of the bargaining committee, Charles Kelley, Alma Wimmer, Carl Gillengerten, and Ivah Miller, all stewards; the layoffs were temporary.[81]

On November 10, 1944, Hund sent a letter to all Reo employees, explaining the company's disciplinary actions against the six union officials and blaming the sit-down on a few troublemakers. "Five of them," Hund wrote, "were disciplined because we were convinced they caused a sit-down in the machine department of the 700 building on October 19 in sympathy with a sit-down strike in the assembly department. The assembly department sit-down was in protest over a War Labor Board decision approving only a 5 cent increase in pay whereas a 10 cent increase had been jointly requested by the company and the Union."[82] That very day, in Detroit, the NWLB overturned its ruling and approved a wage increase to $1.10 for the assemblers and packers.[83]

This might have ended the unrest had Wayne Keeney not become the president of UAW Local 650. Keeney's history at Reo was brief and tumultuous. Although he was employed there during an era for which there is ample documentary evidence, the paucity of material on Keeney suggests that he shunned attention. Keeney was born on July 20, 1904, as Pete Wayne and assumed an alias some time after 1926, when he was arrested for the illegal possession of alcohol. He worked for a time as a truck driver during the 1930s and was hired in at Reo on March 24, 1941, as a tool grinder.[84] He was by all accounts a good, dependable worker. It was only late in 1942, by his own account, at the urging of his fellow workers, that Keeney became active in the local union, serving as chief steward in 1943 and as a committeeman in 1944 and becoming president of Local 650 in February 1946. Keeney was a consistent advocate for the veterans employed by Reo and caused considerable uneasiness among the company's management. Just as Washburn is held responsible for the sit-down of 1937 and the Lansing Labor Holiday, so Keeney is held responsible for the strike of 1946, the largest since the events of the late 1930s.

Keeney's election coincided with changes in personnel and production techniques prompted by demobilization after the war ended. The most immediate and serious problem was the downsizing of the workforce. During the last nine months of 1945, Reo laid off more than 3,500 workers.[85] As jobs vanished, so did the women who had done many of them, though women with some seniority could appeal for transfer to other departments.[86] Although Keeney periodically argued that women's seniority needed protection, both the company and the UAW's international representatives often agreed that the most qualified and experienced workers and returning veterans should be given priority.[87] The company attempted to retain its most senior workers, most of them male, during this period of readjustment, as it began to hire young veterans, "new to the company and factory work."

The end of the war did not mean the end of military contracts but it did change the nature of defense work from bombs and rocket fuses to trucks and other military vehicles. In addition to competing for the prized military contracts, Reo needed to compete in the private sector for a larger market share in their new products, lawnmowers (on which women were the primary workers), school buses, and a variety of civilian truck products.[88] This new product mix required greater efficiency from a diminished and relatively inexperienced workforce.

On October 16, 1945, representatives of labor and management met to chart the direction of the company in the postwar era. The company extended an olive branch to the union. Gerald Byrne, the new personnel director, called a meeting to discuss new piecework rates, "so that we may resolve these issues in advance of their being effectuated through the bargaining procedure." With Ernie Stinebower as the main spokesperson for management and Bernie Bennett, Leo Deacon, and Raymond Reed on hand for the union, the parties engaged in a frank and spirited discussion. Stinebower warned that the company "may do some things that the employees may not like, but we ask that the Committee bear in mind that these things must be done if Reo is to stay alive." Labor conceded that the new workers the war had brought into the plant were responsible for many of the troubles. Management admitted that some wartime foremen had made mistakes and expressed confidence that smoother relations would prevail in the future. Stinebower asked for patience as the company reoriented itself, and the union representatives thanked management for informing them of changes in advance.[89]

The workers themselves, however, proved less cooperative than management had hoped. In the first two months of 1946 the union filed many grievances about piecework. Some workers objected to switching from day rates to piecework; others requested a shift from day to piece rates;

while still others requested that day rates continue until new techniques were mastered and time-studied in preparation for the switch to piecework rates.[90] The grievances revealed the workers' unflagging determination to participate in decisions on issues of work and pay and to insist on "a fair, living wage."[91]

The opening of contract negotiations on March 15, 1946, provided a forum for the escalation of hostilities between union and management.[92] Since this was the first major rewriting of the contract since 1940, both sides scrutinized and debated every phrase and paragraph, dredging up old grievances and positioning themselves for future struggles.

Workers wanted some control over the pace, timing, and level of compensation of the work. As noted above, workers were far from unanimous on the issue of switching from day rates to piecework rates, although the union bargaining team demanded that the whole plant shift to day rates and a slim majority probably supported them in this. The workers did agree, however, that the company arbitrarily changed piecework rates and that the company's time studies and rate settings were fraught with problems. As union representative Charles O'Brien put it, "You are penalizing the man because of his adaptability to the job. This is the prime disagreeable feature of a piecework job—no matter how good a man is on a job you always cut him because every time he reaches a certain point you cut him and that is why people do not like piecework."[93] Bernie Bennett concurred: "As long as you have piecework here, you will never have any peace. The way it is running here, if they want to cut a job you do, and the next day you have a mess here."[94] A time-study expert from the UAW International brought into the negotiations testified that Reo had more standards under dispute than any large plant in Detroit.[95]

By mid-June management and union had worked out most of the language of the contract and turned their attention to the details of wage increases. The company's proposal of a four-cent increase per hour for piecework employees and a six-cent increase for day workers was very low.[96] In asking for an 18.5-cent increase across the board and the elimination of piecework, Reo's union officials followed the pattern set for automakers by the UAW-CIO.[97]

Management and labor based their wage proposals on different industry comparisons. The union wanted pay determined by the patterns set by the automobile industry. The union had been formed during an era when the company still made cars, not just trucks and military products, and with GM and many auto parts manufacturers in the area, Lansing was still considered an auto town. The Reo company, however, wanted to base wages on the lower industry standards for truck and lawnmower manufacturers. In addition, regional rates for smaller plants like Reo were below the 18.5-cent increase.[98] This disagreement about wages made a certain amount of sense. UAW Local 650 officials did operate in a world of autoworkers.[99] When they went to conventions, GM and Ford workers were their peers and colleagues. They also knew that they would start their bargaining from higher ground. But Reo Motors competed against other truck and lawnmower manufacturers who operated under different labor and market conditions from Ford and GM. This conflict was never entirely resolved.

By early July negotiations had stalled over whether wage rates should be determined by auto manufacturer or truck and lawnmower standards, and over day versus piecework rates.[100] Hund made two direct appeals to Reo workers. He provided data to demonstrate that wages had been rising, that piecework paid more than day work, and that most workers "prefer a system of payment on which their earnings will be dependent upon their own efforts." In an amazing piece of rhetoric, Hund simultaneously invoked Reo's legacy of low labor turnover and blamed his loyal aging workers for their frustration with piecework. "We are proud of the fact that so many of our employees have a record of years of service with the company. A recent tabulation showed the average age of all our plant employees to be 57 years, which is 17 years more than the average of the industry. However it is necessary to remember that their productive capacity is gradually decreasing and today it is not as great as it was 17 years ago."[101] The workers responded by voting to strike.[102]

During the months between the vote to strike and the actual walkout in September, the union was in turmoil, and management either created or took advantage of existing cleavages between the younger and more militant veterans and the older workers.[103] In a move that suggests that the company was in fact interfering in union affairs, Hund sent another letter to employees, and this time the gloves were off. He called the union bargaining committee "irresponsible soap orators," "rabble rousers," and "petty politicians." He resurrected the ideals of the factory family and respectable masculinity when he described the great majority of workers as "sincere and responsible" and continued, "You are aware of your obligations as good citizens and as heads of your families. You have definite goals and objectives which you pursue in your own way without interference and without regimentation. You respect orderly procedures. We feel confident that . . . you are loyal to the company."[104] Hund hoped that the remaining Reo Joes would do the right thing and vote out the troublemakers so that Reo could return to quieter times.

The membership did just that, and Keeney frantically telegrammed the international for advice, since the UAW regional director was to take over negotiations until a new committee could be formed.[105] Keeney remained on the bargaining committee but Glen Mullett and Bernie Bennett, allies of Keeney's, were voted off. Only one member of the new bargaining committee, Roland Roosa, was a Keeney ally.[106]

Even as his leadership came under fire, Keeney was very busy in export boxing and the cab department. In export boxing, where changes in production, new time studies, and rate cutting lowered pay, the workers protested "the present rate of $21.00 a truck because of no down time for stock chasing and assuming supervision duties." They requested "a guaranteed rate of $1.35 per hour until such time as wage negotiations are completed."[107] When the company insisted that the new rate stay in effect until a new time study could be done, the men sat down, and the company alleged that Keeney was behind it. The men in export boxing wanted Keeney and Mullett to argue their case before labor relations. Without any real resolution, Keeney got all but two of the men back to work on July 22.[108]

The situation in the cab department, where the issue was Floyd Schwartz's supervision, was even more critical. In the spring of 1946 Schwartz had become the foreman of the cab department, and the men found his supervision heavy-handed, cruel, and unfair.[109] On July 16, 1946, at 8:55 A.M. Keeney called a special meeting after a work stoppage on the cab line "to discuss certain protests against the company." The workers at the meeting described the situation:

> The employees in this department cannot take an interest in their work when Swartz continually pulls dirty tricks on the employees. . . . Swartz has key men working in this department who don't even know anything about spot welding. . . . He uses men so snotty that he can't hold good men in his department.

… Swartz uses the tactics of a little dictator and he does not use any diplomacy in handling men in this department. … Swartz thinks he can shove men around like a bunch of hogs. … Swartz is even standing right over the men with a stop watch driving them on to a faster production.[110]

In August, in the midst of these serious disturbances, UAW Local 650 and Reo Motors signed a labor agreement.[111] With several UAW International representatives and a state mediator present, a contract and a supplemental agreement on wages (they agreed on five cents to pieceworkers, ten cents to day workers, and money set aside for anomalies) were signed, and in September the parties began to work out the piece rates (the timing, not the pay).[112] The local and international union approved of the contract, although piecework issues were not entirely resolved. When negotiations resumed to complete the piece rate plan, it became clear that the contract had resolved nothing. George Nader of the International reiterated what Keeney had claimed earlier, that the issue was timing as well as wages.[113]

In early September the cab line added an operation that had been performed by one man on the day rate and informed the crew that the new work was to be timed for piecework; the crew got restless and threatened a work stoppage. Even after the rate department timed the job, the crews became dissatisfied as Schwartz shifted workers around to undermine their ability to control the pace of the work and affect the outcome of the time study.[114] These actions symbolized all that was wrong at Reo, and the men took action.

At 7:30 A.M. on Monday, September 16, the morning shift arrived at the cab line but grouped together rather than assume their work stations. Two workers, Al Carson and Harvey Pletcher, told Schwartz that the men would not work for him any more and wanted Schwartz to resign. Pletcher stated, "they can't run this like they run the navy."[115] The workers left the plant and convened at the union hall to decide what to do next. Keeney presided over the special department meeting at which "complaints were registered by many of the workers that his [Schwartz's] attitude was tyrannical, his demands unreasonable and that he was cheating the employees by adding operations to piece work jobs which were not rated and consequently not paid for by the company."[116] The group decided to write a grievance against Schwartz and to return for the afternoon shift at 12:30 to work through the grievance procedure. They learned upon their arrival that the two men who had spoken on their behalf, Carson and Pletcher, had been sent home. The treatment their steward and committeeman, Roland Roosa, received when he attempted to submit the grievance against Schwartz angered the workers even more. In the presence of the head of the bargaining committee, Al Salter, and the assistant production manager for the plant, Walter Foust, Schwartz refused to accept the grievance and the men once again left the plant and retired to the union hall. The strike had begun.

The workers in the cab department established picket lines around the entrances to the plant. Several "flying squadrons" (the company called them goon squads) swooped through the plant at least twice during the day to urge all employees to join the strike. According to those interviewed by the company after the strike (many of whom would not name any names), these squadrons were made up of war veterans, young, newly hired employees who had been organized by Keeney. Fred Stachel and Samuel Woolcock, foremen in machine repair, complained "there were no old Reo employees in the bunch of men who came into the motor plant" (see Table 5 for the list of participants compiled by the company). F. E. Logan, the general foreman in the lawnmower department, reported a conversation he had had with Bob Pfuhl, a participant in the "veterans' picket squad," who apparently felt that "veterans were being used as a tool to gain sympathy toward the strike movement among other employees." Floyd Whitney, the foreman in the automatics, suggested that "outsiders" were among the instigators and described a squadron leader who, "while not Jewish in appearance," "had typically Jewish mannerisms."[117]

Keeney and Roosa explained the grievances to an overflowing crowd at the union hall at noon, and the workers voted to continue the strike and to strengthen the picket lines at all gates. Throughout the day the plant remained closed and quiet; Keeney notified the press that the local union had endorsed the strike. The *Lansing State Journal* dubbed the action an "outlaw walk-out" and quoted Keeney as saying that the "spontaneous strike" resulted from "an accumulation of grievances that included the supervision dispute." Cab line workers formed a picket line on Baker Street carrying signs that read, "We Want Justice."[118]

Reo Motors and its allies in Lansing, as well as the International UAW-CIO, all sprang into action to quell the rebels. Declaring, "I won't have any drinking on the picket line!" police chief John Early closed all taverns and liquor stores in the area around the plant.[119] As the strike continued on Wednesday, September 18, Jack Holt, the international representative, publicly declared the action unauthorized. As Wayne Keeney "made a hurried trip to Detroit on an undisclosed errand," international union representatives met with management and agreed that the company would accept the grievance against Schwartz and that the union would persuade the workers to return to work.[120] During a four-and-a-half-hour meeting at the Prudden Auditorium that evening, Holt explained to union members what Walter Reuther had probably explained to Keeney in Detroit—that the strike was in violation of the contract just signed, that the company would process the grievance, and that the international union could not aid or support the unauthorized stoppage. Probably owing to pressure exerted by the international, at 8:00 P.M. Keeney telegraphed Gerald Byrne, the personnel director at Reo, that the local had voted to return to work.[121] Although the workers were ready for work and the taverns reopened on Thursday, September 19, most workers could not return to work until Monday, September 23.[122]

The *Industrial Worker*, the newspaper of the Industrial Workers of the World (IWW, known as Wobblies), began reporting on events at Reo not long after the strike began and continued reporting on work conditions in the shop and labor-management relations throughout the spring and summer of 1947. The first article, "Vets at Reo Fight for Unionism," described one part of the problem as "a long dissatisfied rank and file [motivated] largely by returned vets who resented the treatment given them under this type of unionism." The "commie, company stooges" in the union "had sold the local the rotten contract signed August 5." "During the strike," an anonymous worker wrote, "management showed a preference for dealing with the commie chairman of the Grievance Committee rather than with the non-commie President of the local." The writer understood that it was the vets who were the "good union timber at Reo."[123]

As soon as it was over, Reo launched an investigation of the strike and interviewed dozens of supervisors, foremen, and workers to determine the "facts" of the case. Company interviewers asked workers to divulge the names of coworkers who had participated. In the local CIO paper, Keeney alleged that the company was using Gestapo methods, calling workers into the office of the factory manager, often without any union representative with them, where company attorney Russell Smith grilled them about the strike.[124] Dozens of workers experienced this intimidating treatment and between fifty and seventy received disciplinary warnings for their participation in the strike. On October 5 the company released the names of those who would be discharged as a result of their role in the strike: Wayne Keeney, president of UAW Local 650, Alton Selfridge, a recreation officer who had worked at Reo on and off since 1920, and William Dowling, Reo's education officer, who had worked in truck assembly since 1944.[125]

Reo's management's and the international union's response to the September 17 action suggests that the militant rank-and-file veterans had some connections to the IWW. Weekly letters and articles about the strike and related developments appeared in the *Industrial Worker,* which someone had distributed in the plant in late October. Dowling, one of the three discharged workers, wrote to the *Industrial Worker* in June 1947. Referring to himself as one of the "so-called rebels," he explained that the journal was "the only paper one can get any truth printed in." He had recently tried to get a job at Reo under an alias but had been revealed by a stool pigeon. He reported that nothing had changed at Reo because the bargaining committee was still in league with the company and the international union.[126]

Reo's rebels, young male veterans who allied themselves with Dowling and Keeney (some of them possibly Wobblies), wanted respectful treatment and control on the shop floor. Brutal foremen and labor bureaucrats contributed to workers' problems. Writers in the *Industrial Worker* likened industrial discipline at Reo to treatment in the armed services and compared Reo's leaders to German and Italian dictators.[127] One anonymous subscriber, a worker at Reo and a member of Local 650, wanted readers to know that the members of the bargaining committee had built new homes and bought new cars. The international representative "that sold Reo their 'rotten contract,'" he wrote, "has acquired a farm, a cottage at the lake with three motor boats besides his home in Lansing and also a new car." This worker did not believe that the faction now in charge of the union worked for the "common people, struggling along trying to just keep even with the grocer and the landlord."[128]

In March 1947 Keeney was voted out of UAW Local 650 after a nasty battle that revealed the longstanding cleavages in the local union.[129] Keeney and his group, the Committee for the Revival of Unionism at Reo, engaged in red baiting and personal attacks. Keeney's handmade leaflets assailed the opposition personally (for example, they charged that Charles O'Brien fell asleep in union meetings and played golf with company officials), and proclaimed, "Down With Communistic Practices—Beware of those people who seek to RULE or RUIN—without them we'll have a better UNION."[130] The more moderate Committee for Democratic and Constructive Unionism denied allegations of communism, expressed its displeasure with the tactics of the previous year, and laid the blame squarely on "the disruptive tactics" and "dictatorship" of the "president of Local 650 and a small but noisy minority."[131] Al Salter beat Keeney in the union election by a vote of 523 to 370, a decisive victory but one based on low voter turnout.[132]

The *Industrial Worker* continued to receive reports "from the boys in the shop at Reo."[133] The strike had not changed anything. Piecework and the timing of jobs continued to cause discontent in the shop. Because of the apparent ability of "radical unscrupulous leaders" to override the majority of union members' wishes, the company reinforced its relationship to the union. Reo reasserted its prerogative to determine the content and rates of jobs, to supervise workers, and to prescribe the amount of time that union officials could engage in union business. It proposed to end the union shop, the check-off (by which the company deducted union dues from paychecks), and certain seniority provisions. This was not just punitive; Reo demanded that the union become more accountable, professional, business-like, and contractual in its dealings with the company.[134]

Negotiations on the new contract hit a number of snags, primarily on wage rates, and a strike vote loomed. Once again both workers' and management's gaze turned toward Washington, D.C., as both parties became aware of the impending implementation of new labor legislation, the Taft-Hartley bill. Although there is no definitive proof that the company was deliberately stalling, transcripts of the bargaining sessions suggest that Reo tried to postpone signing the new contract until the bill took effect. The company did not succeed, however; the contract for 1947 was signed fifteen minutes before the passage of Taft-Hartley.[135] The union lost its check-off and union shop for only one year, but the chill of Taft-Hartley put an end to the likes of Wayne Keeney.[136]

The long series of sit-down strikes had come to an end. Keeney and the IWW were the last gasp of the intense localism at Reo begun by Lester Washburn. Reo workers' contribution to the great strike wave of 1946 can only be understood as the end of a long period of resistance to the paternalistic bargain forged decades earlier. The IWW won some converts because its militant, manly stance was more appealing to returning vets than the contractual labor-management relations endorsed by the international UAW. The labor organizing of the late 1930s, the entrance of women and young male veterans into the shop, and the challenges posed by a remote union and warfare state had redefined Reo Joe's relationship to his world.

In 1948 the leadership of Reo and its union changed. Joseph Sherer, Reo's new president, joined the company during World War II. With an engineering degree from the Massachusetts Institute of Technology and many connections to the defense industry, Sherer could position Reo to take advantage of the opportunities of the Cold War era. Wayne Keeney took a job selling electrical appliances at the Lansing Consumer Cooperative and disappeared from view.[137] With the rebels quelled and a more tranquil, if challenging, future ahead, Reo's workers and managers set out to rebuild a new factory family.

## Korean Coda

Mobilization for the Korean crisis and Reo's last strike in 1951 signaled the company's adjustment to the Cold War period. The U.S. "police action" in Korea brought increased defense work, and Reo's new president knew exactly what to do.[138] Funds from the Reconstruction Finance Corporation once again provided Reo with working capital for research, development, and production to fulfill its defense contract obligations. The development of the Gold Comet Engine and the vehicle created to contain it, a 2.5-ton truck, became Reo's meal tickets.[139] When the first contract was signed in June 1949, for 5,000 vehicles at a cost of $31 million, employment and production turned around.[140] Almost 2,000 employees were added to the payroll between January 1950 and June 1951, bringing the plant to its postwar high of 3,150. Two-thirds of these employees worked on defense contracts.

Those in civilian production worked on an increasingly diverse array of products that management believed would tap into the postwar demand for consumer goods. In the immediate aftermath of World War II, Sherer, with the help of Sam Briggs, developed the lawnmower division. Reo also acquired the pal wheel goods division of Northern Indiana Steel Supply Company, which produced children's wheeled vehicles and playground equipment. In addition, Reo enhanced its sales and leasing divisions, aggressively pursuing overseas opportunities. The transition was so successful that the U.S. Departments of State and Defense identified Reo as a model for how to integrate defense and civilian production.[141]

Once again, Reo stationed representatives in Washington to pursue contracts and inside information on military spending. R. C. Orrison was stationed in Washington to head up a separate government sales division, and Colonel M. K. Barroll, a World War II veteran, was in charge of contacts, socializing, and intelligence gathering within the defense establishment. Having representatives in Washington and Detroit was essential to Reo's ability to navigate the array of Korea-related civilian industry and defense organizations and boards.[142] Whether it meant attending a troop maneuver involving Reo trucks, lunching at the Pentagon (and reporting on who was dining with whom), or throwing big holiday parties, these men "worked" the defense establishment for Reo's benefit.[143] The intelligence that technical representatives gathered from the front lines of the Cold War helped Reo produce and market a variety of products well suited for this political climate.[144]

Mobilization for Korea resurrected old problems and created some new ones. In addition to the yearly battles over wage rates, workers expressed concern over seniority irregularities, unfair discharges, key men and foremen doing line work, arbitrary or cruel supervision, sanitation and health in the workplace, and a variety of piecework issues, including compensation for down time. The down time debate involved whether a worker should be paid for the time he or she was actually present and available for work in the factory or strictly according to productivity. Since Reo used both piece and hourly rates and sometimes even elements of both, this question was not easily resolved. Workers and their representatives felt that if they were available to work, there should be some sort of compensation during slack times. Negotiations over down time revealed a struggle over the control of work assignments, since management often reassigned workers to other tasks when they were idle.[145]

New issues also arose. Starting in 1949 leaders of both the international union and Reo's local union began to press for "fringe benefits": medical insurance, cost-of-living increases, and pensions. On the national level, the leadership of the UAW and other CIO unions pushed to include welfare measures in their postwar contracts as a result of the perceived slowdown of the state in pursuing New Deal programs. Cost-of-living increases and pensions were included in pattern-setting contracts, particularly between GM and the UAW-CIO in the so-called Treaty of Detroit.[146] At Reo, benefit issues also tapped into enduring local concerns. Union officials evoked the stability and responsibility of the older, less transient workers of earlier times as the key to Reo's success, and pushed for cost-of-living and old-age security to restore this type of labor force. The union requested an across-the-board twenty-two-cent hourly increase, which, in addition to contributing to the pension plan,[147] would include money for hospitalization, medicine, disability insurance, a death benefit, and a cost-of-living adjustment.[148]

George Hill, the chairman of the Local 650's bargaining committee, and Roy Price, the international representative, laid out the argument for this unprecedented and ambitious proposal at the start of the year's negotiations. Using language from the Steel Industry Board's 1949 report to President Truman, Hill and Price suggested that just as "management has long made adequate provision as a cost of doing business, for the 'repair and retirement' of its equipment and machines," so too should management consider "the cost of worker 'repair and retirement'" as a cost of doing business. And since "private or voluntary methods do not provide the necessary funds nor the guarantee of security," they continued, "industry's social responsibility requires that it assume financial responsibility for Supplementary Security Programs established through collective bargaining when government programs are inadequate or non-existent."[149] When management balked at the inclusion of "fringes" in wage negotiations, Price argued that other auto companies already provided these benefits.[150]

As a company that prided itself on its long history of taking care of its workers, Reo found itself in a difficult position. The union called management's bluff by adding new consumer and welfare programs to their demands for wage increases. The company held firm against these proposals throughout the 1950 negotiating sessions, not on ideological grounds but out of fear about the company's economically uncertain future.[151] By summer, negotiations had reached an impasse.[152] In August, as defense contracts began to pour in and other plants in the area won contracts that included fringe benefits, Reo workers began to consider a work stoppage. The contract ratified in September 1950 did not resolve the fringe or piecework problems and created the conditions for Reo's last strike, a year later.

Nineteen-fifty-one was a troubled year at Reo. Work stoppages and discord in the shop angered the international union as much as they did management.[153] Throughout the summer, company officials made matters worse by subjecting the growing workforce to intense speedups and arbitrary foremen.[154] To present itself as a strong, united front, the union met in special session in early August to articulate its demands and vote on whether to strike, as the bargaining on the new contract entered the home stretch. The union identified its most important demands as a cost-of-living escalator clause; a pension established on a per-hour company contribution; the end of piecework in the plant and hourly day rates for all; and a long list of health and safety improvements. Ninety-five percent of the members of Local 650 voted to strike if these demands were not met.[155] By late August, as the company continued to haggle over its contribution to the pension plan, federal conciliators and even Sherer appeared at a bargaining session, while the union set up its strike committee.[156] On Friday, August 25, the union called a strike. According to the *Lansing State Journal,* as the talks on the pension plan broke down, stewards began circulating through the plant, pulling employees off their jobs. Twenty-five hundred workers left the plant, and pickets began that afternoon.[157]

As the strike extended into the third week of September, the company made a serious offer: a cost-per-hour contribution on the pension fund; guarantees on minimum levels to those workers retiring in the next five years; safeguards on pensions in the future; increases in the general wage levels; an escalator clause; and a pool for wage inequities. Piecework and the labor process were still contentious issues, but eventually the union settled for fringe benefits and accepted the offer.[158] On September 20, 1951, the union rank and file ratified the five-year contract, abandoned the pickets, and returned to work after a work stoppage of nearly a month. The overall package added 17.5 cents per hour to wages, including an escalator clause, contributions to an inequity pool, a ten-cent hourly wage increase, and company contributions to a pension plan, with minimum payments guaranteed.[159]

With a five-year contract in place, ongoing meetings between labor and management were no longer necessary. After the 1951 strike, the union and management handled disturbances in the shop through the grievance procedure. Seniority, pay-rate irregularities, and work reassignments continued to create discord, but handled as individual grievances these issues no longer formed the basis of collective action. For the rest of its history (with the exception of the union's amalgamation of an office workers' union, the technical, office and professional workers, in 1968),[160] UAW Local 650 was characterized by an apathetic membership held hostage by Reo's financial uncertainty, overshadowed by the international and the larger, more important GM locals in Lansing, and distracted by other concerns and activities. In 1954 there were just over 1,000 workers in the plant, and by the time the contract was renegotiated in 1956, just a few hundred. The 1956 supplemental agreement between workers and Reo Motors contained a provision lowering "rates to be paid for direct and indirect labor to be performed on this contract for military vehicles . . . 10% from present levels."[161]

The security union members thought they had won in 1951 proved fleeting. In the summer of 1953, Dollie Beadle, the recording secretary of Local 650, reported in her "Reo News" column in the *Lansing Labor News* that uncertain times were ahead because of the reduction in defense contracts. In this time of trouble she drew on the collective nostalgia so powerful at Reo. Reo workers "want to come to work each and every day with the thought that we want to give a good day's work to the company and we in turn want and need a good day's pay. So if we all buckle in as the old timers did to keep Reo on the map, we may realize other fields of production other than defense contracts."[162] Religion provided solace to some workers. In 1955 A. H. Gibbons wrote in the Reo column, "if you have done everything that you can and cannot obtain happiness, try praising God. In thanksgiving and praise is peace." H. W. Forsemen described the leaders he hoped might revitalize the union in the early 1960s. They "should be leaders of men and set an example of wholesome living not only in the shop but also be so recognized in their everyday living, on their street, their community and be affiliated with a church of their choice. Church and labor have a lot in common. People who violate or have no respect for the 'ten commandments' have no right to hold office or represent the people who do respect it and live accordingly."[163] These sentiments owed as much to Reo's past as to the company's successful efforts to revive the factory family during the 1950s.

# 5

# A Cold War Factory Family

In September 1953 Reo employees turned out in large numbers, not for a strike but for the Reo family fall fair. The fair had not been held for years, but the company revived it as a way to celebrate the approaching fiftieth anniversary of Reo. Old and new members of the Reo family competed for prizes for produce and livestock, fine arts and photography, handicrafts and collectibles, fancy work, baked and canned goods, displays of curios and antiques, Indian relics and war trophies, and even a baby clinic. Floyd Schwartz, the strong-arm foreman who provoked the 1946 strike, cochaired the produce and livestock competition. Described as an "old-fashioned country fair," the fair was in part a fund-raising event, organized by the Reo girls' club, for the Marian Ilic Cancer and Benefit Fund, established in memory of a Reo employee who had died of cancer and devoted to the aid of Reo families similarly stricken. Pictures in the new company publication, *Reo Items*, attested to the success of the event, which drew local and state dignitaries, including Governor G. Mennen Williams.[1]

The 1953 family fall fair revealed a powerful nostalgia for the "factory family" of the 1920s. Perhaps this nostalgia signaled an awareness that the company, community, and nation had entered a new era. Ransom E. Olds had died in 1950. Gerald Byrne, the

Portions of this chapter are reprinted from "Rights of Men, Rites of Passage: Hunting and Masculinity at Reo Motors of Lansing, Michigan, 1945–1975," *Journal of Social History* 33 (summer 2000): 805–23.

director of personnel and a veteran of many labor-management committee battles, reflected:

> The Family Fall Fair revealed to us how little our people know of Reo's history. If that is true at home, then it is time that the whole story of Reo be revealed to the public. It has been said that "history is something that never happened, written by someone who wasn't there." Not so with Reo's history. It did happen and it can be written by people who were there. It should be void of any appearance of a publicity job. It would be well printed, illustrated and bound, with the finished volume reflecting the progressive attitude of its present management.[2]

In the wake of two strikes, the company and even some union members sought to re-create some (though not necessarily the same) features of the prewar company in changed circumstances. During the late 1940s and particularly the 1950s, however, workers and management forged a new shared company culture. This new factory family assumed and accommodated the existence of the union and state intrusions into plant operations, and it provides a good example of how welfare capitalism persisted into the late twentieth century.[3]

The welfare capitalism of the teens and twenties had tied white working-class men to their managers through shared bonds of whiteness, localism, and masculinity. Company programs and labor arrangements provided workers with what managers had: a home, a family wage, some job security, and at least a minimum level of consumption and leisure (the last often in the form of organized activities at Reo itself).

An editorial in *Reo Items* (an updated version of *Reo Spirit*) entitled "Spring Has Come Again to America" revealed many features of the new Cold War factory family. As the writer reflected on the state of his hometown, he was struck by the "general well being—the look of the well fed, comfortably clothed, adequately cared for citizenry. Automobiles of all types roll by, driven by the ordinary American man. He may be on his way to work, to play golf, to his home, for a drive." Despite the scars of conflict, "there is good food on his table, fire in the furnace, warm clothing for his family, medical care, educational opportunities and time for play and relaxation." This bounty was the fruit not only of America's triumph in World War II but also of the American way of life, which gave "a man . . . [the] right to compete as an individual to satisfy any equitable desire he may have."[4] The American way of life, the very antithesis of collectivism, allowed a new and improved standard of living. The fruit was there for the picking, for worker and employer alike.

The economy of Lansing developed in familiar ways, based on cars and related automotive products, state government, and the expanding Michigan State University to the east.[5] Despite the migration of a small number of African Americans and Mexican Americans, Lansing remained a white city throughout the 1950s. In the introduction to Birt Darling's history of Lansing, written in 1950, Paul D. Bagwell, two-time gubernatorial candidate, past president of the U.S. Junior Chamber of Commerce, and Michigan State University professor, described the history of Lansing as the "story of Free America . . . a city with an estimated population of over 100,000; a city where thirty major industries employ approximately 25,000 workers; a city with a debt-free public school system with modern and up-to-date physical facilities. A city with no bonded indebtedness, no red light districts, and no vice of any consequence." In the 1950s, Lansing Community College began operating downtown, and the Lansing area's first shopping mall, Frandor, opened in an expanse of land on a former golf course between Lansing and East Lansing.[6] The people, the industries, and the borders of Lansing all grew during the 1950s, but for the most part in familiar ways.

## The Domesticated, Sexualized Firm

On the face of it, Reo revived the ethos of the factory family along familiar lines: the fall fair, the new company journal, sports teams, and paternalistic rhetoric. *Reo Items* published poignant photos of real Reo families employed in the plant; one of the most moving of these appeared on the cover of the Thanksgiving 1948 issue (see Illustration 11). It featured the entire Aves family seated around a table full of holiday fare. Both Layton and Otto (Ted), whom I interviewed forty years later, and their wives, father, siblings, and children were featured, linking the generations' commitment to the company. The caption read, "Of four generations of Aves pictured on the cover, 3 generations are employed here at Reo." Frank Aves, the patriarch, worked in the heat treat department. His son Lloyd worked in the experimental garage. Lloyd's wife (the mother of Layton

ILLUSTRATION 11. Aves family Thanksgiving. Cover of *Reo Items*, November 1948, Reo Papers, box 52, folder 52, Michigan State University Archives and Historical Collections. Photo courtesy of Michigan State University Archives and Historical Collections.

and Otto) worked in the lawnmower division. Layton was a key man checker in the receiving room and Otto on the Reo coach line. The photo's message was clear: Reo still supported the family and allowed white male workers to live the American dream, while also providing appropriate employment for women.[7]

Women not only worked in a number of Reo plant divisions (most notably in the lawnmower division) but also made up an increasingly visible presence in the growing clerical and office force. The additional administrative responsibilities involved in pursuing both defense and commercial production activities required more record keeping. In addition, during the late 1940s and 1950s, Reo pursued a vigorous sales program, enlisting a growing number of branches throughout the country in a variety of advertising campaigns. The men and women employed in this "nonproductive" work contributed to changing the culture of the company.

The organization of the company and the programs devised to tie employees to it in the postwar era divided workers by sex and class in ways consistent with the dominant gender ideology of the 1950s. Blue-collar factory workers and union members, the children of the factory "family," required paternalistic guidance; the newly enlarged and energized corps of salesmen and advertisers, who coalesced around a sales department newsletter, were cast in the role of young, randy bachelors, not only tolerated but also indulged by their elders; supervisors and administrators organized through the steering gear club retired to their clubroom on the third floor of the clubhouse to drink, smoke, and fulfill their role as the fathers of the firm; and the members of the Reo girls' club, who occupied space in the basement of the clubhouse (where the cafeteria was located) were the mothers of the company. What Elaine Tyler May has called "domestic containment," the hegemony of the middle-class family informed and reinforced this arrangement with the promise of prosperity, consumer goods, and leisure.[8]

## Mothers and Fathers

As the mothers of the company, the Reo girls' club actually took on many of the functions that had once been the business of male company officials like Cy Rath. Officially open to all female employees and wives of employees, the Reo girls' club was primarily run by female office workers and other non-blue-collar staff. In fact, many of the club's most active members were secretaries to the personnel officers of the company.[9] Reorganized in 1949, the girls' club came into its own during the 1950s with more than 200 members.[10] The club's purpose was "to unite in an organization, the women employed by Reo Motors to encourage and promote friendship, better cooperation, to sponsor projects of worthy cause and to encourage the cultural and professional welfare of its members." The club emblem, which appeared on the cover of a brochure for an event in March 1953, featured the silhouettes of three women: an office worker, a nurse, and a factory worker.[11]

The girls' club organized fund-raising drives and social events for worthy causes and seasonal events. In addition to the fall fair, the club sponsored a style show for the muscular dystrophy association, held harvest and Christmas evening celebrations, decorated the clubhouse for the holidays, and organized a mother-and-daughter banquet for Mother's Day. The cards, flowers, and sick calls committee sent cards to committee members on their birthdays, if they fell ill, or if they experienced a death in the family; they put roses on the desks of new brides, and they arranged for visits to sick members in the hospital or at home. On April 13, 1953, the club sponsored its first "Boss Night" in the ballroom of the Reo clubhouse. Office workers invited and paid for their bosses to accompany them to a dinner where they heard Mr. C. W. Otto, the manager of the Lansing Chamber of Commerce, on promoting "better human relations."[12]

Former members of the Reo girls' club have extremely fond memories of the activities and the bonds these activities created within the plant and the community. Doris Dow, who worked in both factory and office during her years at Reo, remembered it as "a real good girls' club" with a big membership. "We used to put on ... showers. We put on style shows. We had Christmas parties. We put on several charity ... different things." These activities extended into the community and had the full support of management. Years later Doris still found it hard to drive past the location of the old clubhouse, because of her poignant memories of the place.[13]

By using what was universally acknowledged as women's club work, the Reo girl's club provided the opportunity for cathartic and positive cross-class activities, which helped to create that "family feeling."[14] When Mabel

McQueen, an office worker at Reo, was asked what the girls did when they met, she responded, "Talked and ate!"[15] Marjorie Koehler, Mabel's good friend (they now live in the same trailer park in Dimondale, Michigan), started working at Reo in 1947, first for Gerald Byrne and then for Carl Ogden. She described the many features of the fair she participated in but became particularly animated when describing the mock jail. When asked who ended up in the jail, Koehler responded, "Oh, a lot of the bosses." It was primarily the workers who put them there, she explained, "and they loved every minute of it."[16]

If the girls' club resembled a women's club, the steering gear club was a combination of a men's private club, a civic club, and a fraternal order. Supervisors, administrators, and some of the important foremen belonged, and membership was a sign of belonging to the inner circle in the company. Opened in 1952, the clubroom was located on the third floor of the clubhouse[17] and was dominated by a large steering gear hung from the center of the room as a chandelier. The room contained tables, chairs, a large, well-stocked open bar, a TV, and, at one time, even a slot machine.[18]

The club activities provided cohesion among the salaried employees for their work both within and outside of the plant. Camaraderie among management was an important outcome. Al Zimmer, production manager, plucked Lewis Garcia off the punch press line two years before his apprenticeship training was completed to become, as Lewis himself described it, a "straw boss." Garcia was proud of his membership in the club and even served as its president. This status allowed him access to the president and vice president, an honor he clearly treasured. He claimed that "it kept the unity" among groups of supervisors who might get into "a hell of an argument 'cause you slow my production and you thought you was gaining your production, so you go over there and drink a few drinks and forget about it."[19] Vivern Haight, who ran the clubhouse during these years and tended bar in the steering gear room, remembered Garcia as a man who "liked his drinks." "You knew every foreman," Haight recalled, "when I'd come in they'd say, ... we want a triple shot, a triple to calm 'em down 'cause you know, all keyed up during the day and they'd have double shots and we'd have parties up there. They'd play cards ... till one or two o'clock in the morning, but you never saw anybody get boisterous, want to get up and fight. They were all buddies. That's all there was to it. They were friends. We all were."[20] In addition to monthly dinners for the members and their wives and baseball excursions to Tigers games, the club organized a variety of charity and seasonal events that supplemented or supported the activities of the girls' club or Local 650.[21] The Tuesday before Thanksgiving, 1952, for example, management and the union cosponsored a Thanksgiving feather party to raise money for the less fortunate.[22] The steering gear club also participated in the activities of the industrial executive club and foremen's organizations organized by the YMCA of Lansing, which linked their activities to others in the city and throughout the nation.[23]

The men who worked in the sales and advertising divisions were also part of this fraternity. Through their memos, bulletins, and publicity material, these managers drew upon sexualized and often misogynist images of the relationship between the sexes as a way to enhance their business prospects, tapping into the growing national awareness that "sex sells." In 1953, for example, J. M. Struble of the advertising department reported on the recent American Trucking Association convention in Los Angeles, where Reo had a publicity booth. In addition to information about the product (which was less than prominent), the suite offered playing cards for guests under a sign that read, "Let's Have a Showdown—Play Us a 'Cold Hand.'" If this was not enticement enough, the suite also featured Miss Gold and Miss Comet, two beautiful young models wearing tight sweaters with their names emblazoned across the front. Two thousand truckers participated in the drinking, games, and whatever else took place in the suite. Reo's culture had come a long way from the "dry days" of the 1920s and early 1930s.[24]

The bulletin of the sales and advertising department, *Reo Gold Comet Record Buster*, provided the counterpoint to *Reo Items*. If the latter represented respectable family values, the former offered an outlet for a more raucous, sexualized masculine culture reputed to be a part of the life of the salesman. One issue of *Record Buster* featured a chain letter designed to "bring relief and happiness to the tired businessman." The reader was instructed to send a copy to five businessmen and send his wife's name to the man at the top of the list, then add his own name to the bottom of the list. "When your name comes to the top of the list," the letter read, "you'll get 16,478 women, and some of them will be dandies." It continued, "have faith ... do not break the chain. One man broke the chain and got his old lady back.... As of this date of writing a friend of mine received 183 women. They buried him yesterday and everyone said he had a smile on his face for the first time in his life." The bulletin featured jokes and ditties along the same lines. One began,

> "How did you spend the weekend?"
> "Fishing through the ice."
> "Fishing through the ice? For what?"
> "Olives."[25]

The postwar factory family contained this newly emerging masculine culture, available primarily to more elite elements in the firm.[26]

As in the early years of welfare capitalism, the company encouraged men and some women to join a variety of sports and leisure activities. Gerald Byrne, Reo's personnel manager, believed that "people who play together as a team, team well together at work" and "that many a dispute can be the more readily settled across the desk or conference table if the parties concerned can match skills or laughs outside of working hours."[27] In the 1950s fewer workers participated, and those who did engaged in just a few sports, segregated by class and sex. Reo still had a baseball team, but now only one all-star team competed in the city league. Rifle teams still attracted members, but golf and bowling teams were most popular among men and some women in the company.

Building on the decades-long association between golf and exclusive country clubs, Reo's management dominated golfing activities.[28] Some union officials (like Charles O'Brien, who was denounced for golfing with management during the disturbances of the late 1940s) participated in the golf league, but few regular workers found the time to play. Golf tournaments probably brought together lower-level management and higher-level male workers and union officials.

Bowling was a more popular game among the working-class constituencies in the plant and brought some workers and managers together. Bowling fees were reasonable, and those who played out the season were treated to a free annual banquet at the clubhouse. Reo bowling league teams had five men, usually from the same section of the plant. The best bowlers in various departments formed themselves into the motors, puddlers, lawnmower, service, engineering, experimental, maintenance, tool room, and punch press teams. There were also the Tigers, Pirates, Stragglers, Lucky Bums, and Wild Cats, whose members did not necessarily come from the same workspaces. Over the years the composition of these teams was fairly fluid, so a certain amount of competition for good players must have gone on. It is hard to know exactly how much "playing out" of union-management tensions occurred. One of the most active participants in the bowling league was Gerald Byrne. There is also evidence that Alton Selfridge, one of rebels of the 1946 strike, was on a bowling team during the late 1940s. One wonders whether these combatants "bowled the strike," or whether, and how, the actions on the lanes and at the negotiating table affected each other.[29]

## Worker Sons at Work

The management at Reo once again came up with a combination of programs, policies, and policing to control its labor force and labor relations. In an era when the relationship between the "big three" auto makers and the UAW-CIO was characterized by long-term contractual relationships, Reo's management began to pay increasing attention to the dynamics on the shop floor and in particular to the role of the foreman. It is not surprising that Gerald Byrne and other Reo managers believed that fine-tuning the role of the foreman might provide the solution to the problems of labor turnover, absenteeism, and grievances. To address the labor turnover problem, management instituted an elaborate employee rating system, overseen by foremen who would "make an immediate appraisal of all employees and discuss their merits or shortcomings with them as soon as practical." Since management believed that workers did not leave simply because of wages, it was the foreman's job to help the worker "feel that he belongs."

Byrne changed the way foremen handled absenteeism and disciplinary discharges resulting from infractions of the rules. Foremen had had enormous power and discretion in following up on excessive absenteeism, even making visits to errant workers' homes to verify their stories. Reo's management changed this policy because of the potential abuses, the demands on the foreman's time, and its failure to act as a deterrent. For any violation of rules, foremen issued an exit pass to the employee. While the worker was at home, the foreman made a written report that became part of the material management considered. According to company documents, "decisions established by two or more qualified persons, basing their actions on facts and equity, usually command respect. Penalties that stick have great influence on employee discipline and labor turnover."

To aid the foreman in his new role, management devised a new foreman's handbook and also instituted an "indoctrination program" for new employees.[30] The company devised its own "general rules and rules for personal conduct," which identified dozens of specific behaviors and the penalties for them. Insubordination, absences, lateness, "horseplay, scuffling or throwing things," smoking or possessing a weapon, gambling, abusive language, or fighting could result in punishment that ranged from a warning to discharge. Distributing literature of any description on company premises without permission could be punished by anything from a warning to a two-week layoff. Deliberately restricting output might result in a one-week layoff, or the offender could be fired, and immoral conduct or indecency could likewise result in layoff or discharge.[31]

Management included the union in appropriate ways in its welfare capitalist activities and featured news of the union and union members in *Reo Items*. A 1952 article entitled "When Opinions Differ. . . ." spoke volumes about how management understood the union's role in this new factory family. The article described Reo as a village of 3,000 people. Each employee had his or her particular personality, individual rights and responsibilities, and personal attitude toward them. "Could so many souls anywhere work or play together without problems of some kind cropping up—misunderstandings, disputes, even an occasional challenging of the rules? It would hardly be human," the article reasoned. The labor-management contract, operating procedures, schedules, rules, and general policies maintained order and fairness. Reo's labor-relations men, "the vital body through whom most of these problems are eventually funneled and resolved," offered the wise and impartial counsel that kept the system working properly. The article featured a photo of the labor-relations team—four representatives from management dressed in suits and ties, seated, and seven workers in their dungarees and work shirts standing behind them.[32] The composition of the picture made clear who management felt was better equipped to offer that wise and learned counsel and who created the problems requiring, as they put it, "human engineering": the workers.

Male workers used their union and grievance procedure to address workplace problems, but on the shop floor errant sons challenged "human engineering" by engaging in horseplay. Although this kind of behavior was hardly new, it certainly seems to have increased with the infusion of new workers during World War II and Korea. Perhaps those engaging in horseplay during the first decades of the twentieth century did not last long at Reo. This youthful, exuberant, and potentially threatening behavior may have been a response to the changed company culture during the Cold War. Raymond Fuller, who worked in the truck repair department at Reo between 1943 and 1975, recalled that it was young people who participated in this kind of playfulness. "Well, back then when I first hired in there, them old birds they didn't do none of that stuff."

Horseplay itself did not necessarily represent working-class resistance (or acquiescence), but it does provide a window into an underground work culture with its own "hidden transcripts."[33] Horseplay on the shop floor revealed a working-class masculinity no longer premised on the somber dignity of putting in a full day's work; this was an antiwork masculinity rooted in leisure, fun, and play. Unauthorized collective playfulness may have allowed workers to perform acts of control over their workspaces.

The context of and response to any episode imparted a particular meaning to the event. For example, Raymond Fuller recounted four episodes of horseplay, none of which was apparently punished. First, he described how one worker used to "break in" new men by feeding them what he said was candy but instead was that "black stuff they put on fenders to close up the cracks" with sugar on it. Another worker, angry that during his break the two chocolate-covered donuts he brought everyday had mysteriously vanished, "went home one night and . . . got a couple of plain donuts and . . . melted some Ex-Lax and dropped them in there and let them harden." He discovered who the thief was as "he sat over in the can all afternoon." The third episode involved Fuller replacing a hard-boiled egg with a raw one in the lunch pail of a coworker who had bragged that he could tell the difference between a raw and a cooked egg without breaking it open. After the predicable mess was made, the coworker screamed, "damn you, Fuller!" Finally, Fuller recalled that when they were working with grease in the truck pits, workers used to paint the toes of anyone who happened to walk by. Even supervisors, "if they came along, they'd get it too, it didn't make any difference."[34]

Fuller's descriptions suggest that this horseplay relieved tension and provided welcome relief and cohesion to the factory floor, involving workers of all ranks in the joke. It connected workers in a bond of transgression. Horseplay that went too far and involved potentially dangerous activities did attract the attention of management, and some workers got in trouble. One of the better-documented cases involved two employees, Joe Brzak and Arthur Trescott, lift drivers. On December 9, 1953, Brzak allegedly goosed Trescott, who made chase to return the favor, causing disruption and some danger in a crowded workspace. Neither Brzak nor Trescott had brought any of this to the attention of management or the union; it was two supervisors, M. D. Murray and Garth Barrett, who witnessed the episode and dismissed Brzak for horseplay. Brzak believed that the harsh penalty was retaliation for a grievance he had filed against the company years before, and he filed another grievance. The impartial chairman ruled that, "while both the alleged gooser and alleged goosee deny alleged goosing," obviously something potentially dangerous occurred, and the men admitted they were "fooling around." On the basis of penalties in other horseplay cases, the impartial chairman ruled that the discharge was too harsh, and Reo reinstated Brzak with full seniority and compensation for lost time minus a one-week penalty.

If management's effort to curb horseplay, or episodes of "rough masculinity," as Stephen Meyer describes it, was a way to restore order or promote a more respectable and sober masculinity at work, the effort was not entirely successful.[35] The domesticated firm had created spaces for groups defined by class and gender to perform their roles. When workers on the shop floor engaged in horseplay, they were forging an antiwork masculine culture. Understood within the context of the era, horseplay at Reo Motors provides one example of how class and gender divisions hardened during the 1950s, as workers at Reo absorbed the lessons of the prevailing domestic ideals. Company managers did not permit horseplay, but they probably expected it; after all, boys will be boys.

## Workers at Play

Cheek that is tanned to the wind of the north,
Body that jests at the bite of the cold,
Limbs that are eager and strong to go forth
Into the wilds and the ways of the bold;
Red blood that pulses and throbs in the veins,
Ears that love silences better than noise;
Strength of the forest and health of the plains:
These the rewards that the hunter enjoys.

Forests were ever the cradles of men;
Manhood is born of a kinship with trees.
Whence shall come brave hearts and stout muscles, when
Woods have made way for our cities of ease?
Oh, do you wonder that stalwarts return
Yearly to hark to the whispering oak?
'Tis for the brave days of old that they yearn:
These are the splendors the hunter invokes.[36]
—"The Hunter" by Edgar A. Guest (1916)

Horseplay was not management's only problem. Management was also only moderately successful in curbing absenteeism, a growing problem in the postwar era. During negotiations over piecework rates on October 12, 1948, a remarkable exchange took place between management and labor.[37] Ernest Miller, a union representative, asked if the plant would be open on Friday, since management did "not seem clear on the agreement that we arrived at as far as deer hunters are concerned." Barnes, for the union, continued, "People that waived a portion of their vacation in the summer time, it was agreed when we set up the vacation period, they would take it during deer season." Management responded that if the supervisor had approved, then the worker could go hunting. Barnes then added, "From what I hear and the people have told their supervisors, about 50% will not be here Friday." When management pointed out that the deer season did not begin until noon, Barnes responded, "By the time they get oiled up and their guns ready it would be noon." Raymond Reed, president of the union, added, "Last year they did shut down for the day if I recall." To which Gerald Byrne replied, "We were forced to shut down. We attempted to start the line."

RUSSELL SMITH [assistant secretary to the president of Reo]:
   The year before last, wasn't that?

BARNES: It was the year before and we sent them home at 10.

SMITH: Last year, we found in advance we were going to have the
   same situation so they did not run at all, as I recall.

FOUST [management]: There is just as good hunting on Saturday
   as on Friday.

REED: It is only normal they want to go out the first day.

BYRNE: You are telling us now that we can expect about 50% absenteeism on Friday.

BARNES: I would not say it would be full 50% but there will be a
   lot of them off.

REED: This is every year.[38]

This exchange about hunting occurred in the middle of a negotiating session devoted to resolving piecework issues, but both sides had to accept
that letting men off for the opening of hunting season was not negotiable.
Union officials, like management, were sometimes inconvenienced when
meetings were scheduled in October and November because deer hunting
came first (see Illustration 12).[39]

From the mid-1940s through the 1950s, the company and the union
sought to codify the relationship between vacation time and hunting leave.
The company policy was that "time off during fishing or hunting season
should be discouraged excepting to employees eligible for regular vacations," and Reo's management objected to the practice of supervisors who
granted so-called deer-hunting leaves to employees who lacked seniority or
had already used up their vacation time.[40] When a foreman dispensed hunting leave he could be accused of favoritism and unequal treatment. Grievances and sometimes discharges resulted when certain employees were held
to the letter of the law while their peers experienced privileged treatment.[41]
The dispensation of hunting leave may have been one of the last prerog-
atives of the foreman in the period after World War II. Reo's management
had its hands full with workers eager to make for the forests and foremen
determined to follow the language of the contract.[42] None of this seemed
to make any difference. In 1957 the plant experienced an epidemic of
Asian flu on Monday, October 21, the first day of pheasant-hunting season.[43]

ILLUSTRATION 12. "You can do it with a Reo." General Photo Collection, State Archives of Michigan. Photo courtesy of State Archives of Michigan.

The Reo Company and the UAW Local 650 papers, and the Lansing and Michigan labor journals, all reported extensively on the opening and closing of various hunting seasons, printed information about places, gear, and weather conditions, and welcomed accounts of humorous or dangerous hunting trips, controversies over unauthorized vacations at hunting time, and reports about activities related to hunting (drinking, card playing, and so on). Ted and Layton Aves talked about their annual excursions to their hunting camp up north with male coworkers and relatives. They both insisted that farming was better than working in the factory and that hunting was better than farming. Their eyes sparkled and they came to life when they talked about hunting pheasant or deer.[44]

Masculinity studies, auto labor history, and work culture-leisure studies are virtually devoid of any discussion on the relationship between the automotive working class and hunting. In the new area of "men's studies," working-class men are relatively understudied; but when hunting is considered, it is presented as a throwback, a carry-over of a primitive male behavior. Peter Stearns, in *Be A Man! Males in Modern Society* (1979), suggests that the expressions of masculinity in the modern era are largely an attempt to re-create the challenges, skills, bonding, and values associated with hunting and war in much earlier times. Ancient "hunting societies provided models for personal identification that long survived their economic basis and remain valid simply because models are needed," according to Stearns. Because most of us today live in a "post-hunting" culture, war, sports teams, secret societies, and the like have replaced hunting as a means of enacting and transmitting masculine characteristics and values. Perhaps because Stearns focuses primarily on European working-class men, the actual activity of hunting itself is not explored as an enduring source of masculine identity.[45] Recent works on manhood in U.S. history are similarly silent on hunting as a social phenomenon in the twentieth century.[46]

Although there is a growing body of excellent historical, anthropological, and sociological work that considers working-class leisure and culture, virtually nothing has been written in these fields about hunting.[47] Pathbreaking works of the 1980s by Roy Rosenzweig and Kathy Peiss proposed that an exploration of leisure and nonworking activities of the working class can reveal spaces in which alternative (but not necessarily oppositional) working-class culture can be forged and worked out.[48] Historians like Ronald Edsforth, Lizabeth Cohen, and George Lipsitz, interested in the rise of mass consumer culture throughout the twentieth century and its effect on the working class, have explored consumption patterns, radio, television, the roller derby, car customizing, country music, rock and roll, and film. Often these forms of leisure are understood as safety valves, sources of alternative (or diversionary) class consciousness, sites of resistance or opposition that remain safe and manageable, or means by which workers participated in (or were co-opted by) a national consumer culture.[49]

Hunting in the twentieth century does not lend itself to this kind of analysis. Even though it is certainly an ancient activity bound up with notions of masculinity, it changed and evolved throughout the twentieth century. Scholars in many fields have revealed that it was and continues to be a sort of craft passed down from father to son, often in ritualized fashion.[50] Although hunting involves the consumption of gear and, ultimately, game, it is a different kind of consumption from the consumption of soap or soap operas. It is a sport, but it is not organized or attended like a baseball game. And even though there are local variations, all hunting came under state regulation during the twentieth century.[51] Members of the working class came to understand their own access to the land and its game as both a right of American citizenship and an emblem of a particular type of working-class masculinity.[52]

The turn of the century saw the first meaningful efforts by the state to regulate the taking of game. In response to the depletion of deer by market hunters supplying out-of-state suppliers and loggers with venison and fur, Michigan in 1895 passed its first law limiting seasons, regions, and amount of deer taken. Hunters have reminisced at least since the 1920s about "the good old days," when hundreds of deer roamed the countryside in plain sight, but this golden age went out of existence after 1850.

Three constituencies were interested in preserving game animals and their habitat: professional conservationists, sportsmen, who tended to be from more elite classes, and workers. Sportsmen, "in high boots and whipcords, armed with fine gunnery, who kill for sheer joy of the hunt and seeing things die," formed their own private clubs to ensure their access to land, given the poor enforcement of the early regulations.[53] The desire of the growing urban labor force, and particularly of autoworkers, for outdoor recreation placed a greater strain on an already stressed resource. WPA researchers identified the growth of the auto industry, the availability of cheap cars, and the improvement of roads as the key factors that brought more people to the woods of Michigan to hunt. Urban workers invaded farming regions contiguous to cities during hunting season. In the words of one researcher, "The city amateurs respected the rights of neither the farmer nor the sportsman, but raided the farm and reserve alike, sometimes killing pets and livestock. This stirred hot rural resentment and eventually brought the farmer into the sportsmen's camp."[54] The result was the creation in 1921 of the Department of Conservation, which began to innovate to accommodate these various constituencies.

In his 1931 report on game management in the north central states, one of the United States' most important conservationists, Aldo Leopold, applauded Michigan, with its "able leadership in the conservation department, and an extraordinary pressure of hunters by reason of the heavy industrial populations of the automobile manufacturing towns," for its efforts to provide public lands for hunting and for establishing creative ways to ease conflicts between hunters and farmers.[55] As the Department of Conservation became mired in bureaucracy, hunters from many constituencies became concerned that appointments and policies would reflect political patronage rather than hunters' admittedly diverse interests. In 1937 sportsmen formed the Michigan United Conservation Clubs, an amalgamation of the scores of sportsmen's clubs throughout the state. Functioning as both clearinghouse and lobbying group, Michigan United Conservation Clubs (MUCC, now one of the largest sportsmen's clubs in the nation) disseminated information about hunting throughout the state and monitored the actions of the Department of Conservation.[56]

## Rites of Masculinity

Throughout the twentieth century, hunting tapped into a number of enduring sources of masculine identity, including many factory workers' rural roots.[57] Ties to the land, like hunting, was a quiet yet constant refrain from the beginning of Reo's existence. In August 1919, for example, the company gave 111 employees the "privilege of volunteering to assist the farmers of Ingham and surrounding counties" and held these employees' jobs for them until they returned. An analysis of the names of the employees and those of the farmers they were helping shows that at least forty-one of them had the same last name, and therefore may have been related.[58] Reo's annual labor reports revealed that between 1918 and 1938 the number of workers leaving to "go to farms" was consistent overall but peaked during years of economic crisis (see Table 3 in the Appendix).

And many worked on farms and in the factory even after World War II. Glen Green, who worked for Reo between 1937 and 1975, recalls that the company "started in working winters because they could hire farmers that couldn't work on the fields ... and then in the spring when it came time for planting they'd shut down and maybe build up a supply of parts to work the next winters." Green's dad, Howard, had a farm north of Potterville in the 1920s and 1930s. "He would come home from work, jump on the tractor and go out after work and run until dark, come back up and milk cows, go back out and run until close to midnight, get up at 3:00 in the morning to dawn—he had twenty-six cows to milk by hand—and milk those cows, go down to Reo, work all day and come back out."[59] The popular annual fall fair, which started during the teens and was revived one last time in 1953, resembled in many ways rural country fairs. At least one-third of the people interviewed for the Reo Oral History Project came from farming backgrounds; two of our interviews were actually conducted in the farm homes of former Reo workers, and these were farms on which they had lived since the 1940s or 1950s.[60] Through the 1950s, farmer-workers at Reo were still being identified in the *Lansing Labor News* as a distinctive group.[61]

Even more important as a source of masculine identity, however, was the association of hunting with war. Throughout the century, but particularly during the periods of the World Wars, the links between hunting and military preparedness were often asserted. As Theodore Roosevelt put it in 1905, "the qualities that made a good soldier are ... the qualities that made a good hunter."[62] The *Michigan Sportsman* later echoed this sentiment, arguing that "free shooting and fishing must not be allowed to disappear, for directly thereon rest not only the health and happiness of thousands of our citizens, but in a large measure our national security." The editors called upon the federal government, the states, private associations, and philanthropic individuals to "set aside at once as many public hunting preserves as possible to ensure that our nation is composed of strong, healthy men, not only ... prepared for future military service, but ... better able to withstand the duties of a successful civil life."[63]

Reo workers were informed about the association between hunting and military preparedness in the *Reo Spirit*. In 1918 an editorial humorously reported that "hunting is a disease that attacks human beings, but comes in the most virulent form during the fall and winter months ... making men do strange things," then turned serious, claiming that "just now there seems to be much good in it, for several gentlemen so infected are in Europe, hunting the Kaiser. That gentlemen thinks Huntergetis a bad disease, wishes that all who have it had been quarantined."[64] This language undoubtedly resonated with the scores of employees who joined the Reo national rifle club.[65]

During World War II, hunting was even more popular among autoworkers who took to the woods to supplement the diets of their families. On November 14, 1944, the *Lansing State Journal* reported that "excessive absenteeism due to deer hunting season" had brought on an unprecedented number of cases of "grip, severe headache, rheumatism, and other ailments," which affected production at Reo, Motor Wheel, and Fisher Body, with whole shifts canceled at Oldsmobile. It was reported that Carl Swanson, regional director of the UAW-CIO (Flint and Lansing region) had suggested to local civil defense committees that "we in the state of Michigan should get to-gether all the DeerHunters and put them in squadrons to help with the home defense . . . they have high powered rifles and if put together they could help in case of invasion as a temporary relief." Swanson, himself a deer hunter, estimated that "there were over 100,000 deer hunters in the state of Michigan."[66]

One of the largest single increases in hunting occurred directly after World War II, when veterans returning to the factories sought an outlet for their new skills, cash, and leisure. In the late 1940s and 1950s hunting was endorsed as an antidote to what were widely perceived as two hallmarks of the era: domesticity and the new factory system. As veterans came home from abroad and their wives and girlfriends journeyed homeward, hunting became a form of family leisure, though usually one restricted to fathers and sons. A poem in the Grand Rapids *Sportsmen's Voice* (1948) began, "If you have a son mister, give him a gun, plus a dog and a reel and a rod, / For the lad who knows both water and wood has a keener knowledge of God."[67] Hunting was also described as an antidote to the stresses of modern life, an adventurous way to refresh and renew oneself. After reporting on those who had returned victorious from the "battle of the North," the writer of one *Reo Items* column in the *Lansing Labor News* described the condition of those who returned empty-handed: "long and lean from the need of a well-cooked meal; bleary eyed from lack of sleep, and glassy eyed, not always from driving straight through; perhaps disappointed but not dismayed; full of stories and an experience never to be forgotten. They'll invade the woods again en mass next season. Even if only a brief respite, you're not thinking of all your everyday problems while peering in the quiet woods for the sign of a spike" (see Illustration 13).[68]

Hunting was not just a masculine rite, an activity associated with the land and war and manly characteristics and values, it was also a right that had to be negotiated. By the post–World War II period, Michigan autoworkers had developed a collective consciousness about their rights to the land. In 1957, when the Republican legislature was preparing to get Governor Williams to sign a bill allowing for the creation of private game

ILLUSTRATION 13. Rites of passage. General Photo Collection, State Archives of Michigan. Photo courtesy of State Archives of Michigan.

preserves with longer hunting seasons and virtually no restrictions, the Michigan CIO Council asked Williams to veto the bill. The president of the Michigan CIO Council, August Scholle, wrote, "This is the worst kind of class legislation. It permits wealthy people who are able to spend large sums of money to hunt on these preserves to buy themselves a license to hunt 120 days of the year, while the rest of the population of Michigan would be restricted to the very limited season for bird hunting." Many of these preserves would be created, "gobbling up every potential bird hunting area in the state. It would ultimately evolve into the same situation as prevailed in most European countries where hunting was reserved for the aristocracy, and the only sport in which a working man could indulge would be bush-beating for the aristocrats."[69]

By the postwar era, a great deal of land had already been set aside for recreational uses, including hunting. Because of the state's retrieval of marginal and abandoned farmland, particularly around urban areas, there was a well-established network of nature areas.[70] Workers applauded any increase in land for hunting or better accessibility to that land, and they protested any restrictions. Workers and their unions understood the issue of land accessibility as a class issue. In 1958, for example, there was universal praise for the building of the Mackinac Bridge, which connected the lower and upper peninsulas in Michigan and radically diminished the travel time between the two, which previously involved taking a ferry.[71] Sunday hunting bans persisted through the 1950s, although they were determined by individual localities, which created a patchwork of regulations throughout the state. Farmers in areas that allowed Sunday hunting, particularly around large cities, felt invaded during open seasons. Workers pushed for uniform laws that would allow them to hunt on their day of rest.[72]

During the 1960s and early 1970s, the history of hunting in Michigan and the history of Reo intersected in several ways. In the late 1960s, at the height of protests against militarism and the unpopular Vietnam War, the number of workers who hunted game increased, and they became more assertive about their right to bear arms. The "Reo Local Sportsman," column in the *Lansing Labor News* reported in 1969 that "the anti-gun forces have been quietly awaiting an opportunity to force their 'hangups' on you the sportsman. . . . Don't let Clubwomen and sentimental popgun crusaders disarm you and arm the criminal."[73] The 1960s also saw an increase in less "respectable" masculine behavior associated with hunting. Hunting was an opportunity for men to escape from their wives, abandon daily rituals of hygiene, play cards, and drink a lot. As one joke went, "Six men on a deer hunting trip ran out of provisions and sent one of their men to a nearby town to shop. He returned with six bottles of wine, a case of beer, a bottle of whiskey, and loaf of bread. One of the group was heard to exclaim, 'Good boy! You've even brought something for the birds.'"[74] The values associated with hunting ranged from the sacred to the profane, all masculine and having enormous appeal for all men.

As hunting reached new heights of popularity during the 1960s and early 1970s, Reo was in decline. In the increasingly depressing Reo columns in the *Lansing Labor News*, the juxtaposition of articles on the company's decline and joyful accounts of hunting trips was striking. In October 1963, along with news that the company that had taken over Reo had engaged in yet another merger, the men formed a buck club and every year thereafter had buck contests.[75] In 1968, the year the Reo local formed its own sportsman's club and signed 150 members in its first month, the company changed its production manager, personnel director, supervisory staff, and foremen.[76] The following year, amid continuing concerns over the viability of the company in Lansing and the threat that the plant might relocate, the men of the Reo sportsman's club affiliated with the MUCC and began publishing their own column in the *Lansing Labor News*, the only Lansing local to do so.[77] Packed full of information, the first column alone announced classified ads relating to hunting and the opening of a club library at the 650 union hall, wholesale buying at a sportsman store for union members, a fishing contest, information about shooting carp, news about the smelt run and a special turkey-hunting season in May, state congressional hearings about financing of state recreational facilities, meetings of the MUCC, and information about a local shooting range. These sorts of activities continued until the Lansing plant's demise.

It wasn't that hunting diverted the energies and attention of workers from useful protests against their alienating work, their place in an increasingly global capitalist system, the increasing bureaucratization (or ineffectiveness) of their union, or the threat to their jobs and pensions. Perhaps some of the workers at Reo responded to these developments by retreating to the woods as often as they could; others may have been motivated enough to engage in political protest (whether from the left or from the right). A number of factors were undoubtedly at work: the deskilling of the workplace, the bureaucratization of the unions, the co-option of the workers by good wages and fringe benefits, the politically repressive atmosphere of the Cold War, the challenges to traditional masculinity made by the civil rights and women's movements. All of these forces probably contributed to the growing popularity of hunting as a form of leisure for Michigan autoworkers. Hunting may be understood as a particular response of the working class to their "blue-collar blues" during the 1960s and 1970s, a response similar to the middle-class men's flight from job and family that Barbara Ehrenreich described in *The Hearts of Men*.[78] The increasing popularity of hunting among the automotive working class may be evidence of the "remasculization" that Susan Jeffords described in *The Remasculinization of America: Gender and the Vietnam War*.[79] Hunting might also be seen as a midwestern automotive version of the hypermasculine "hard hat" phenomenon of the late 1960s and early 1970s so well documented by Joshua Freeman.[80]

But the reasons for the increasing popularity of hunting among auto-workers in the late twentieth century, and its importance as a source of white, working-class masculine identity, needs to understood as proactive rather than merely reactive. There is no question that many men who took to hunting did so because it was considered one of the few remaining authentically masculine activities. The act of hunting, the yearly ritual of taking to the woods with workmates, friends, and male kin cannot be reduced to an act of resistance, the reaction of men under assault. Because of hunting's long history in Michigan (and elsewhere), its regulation by the state, and the consistent and varied ways working men sought to ensure and extend their rights to land and game, it needs to be understood as a right earned and won. As surely as Reo workers came to expect to earn a living wage, to rely on the state to ensure minimum wages, hours, working conditions, and fringe benefits, to be treated equally and fairly in their workplace and communities, they also expected to have the time and space to hunt. For Reo workers, the right to hunt was all they were left with after 1975, when their plant closed down.

Just as they had probably been doing for the forty years since the building of the Reo clubhouse, a group of men were sitting around the lunch table in the cafeteria. It's September 1957, and "fishing is nearly done at the lunch table and the boys have started killing deer. Biggest deer killed Tuesday at lunch was by Gene Lewis, weight 566 pounds with 42 points. Longest deer carried was by Eddie Phile, who said he chased the deer eight miles thru a swamp then carried him eleven miles back; deer weighed 220 pounds. Ed said he didn't mind the weight of the deer much, but the horns kept probing his back."[81] After World War II, for many white male workers in automotive industries, and certainly for the men who worked at Reo, hunting and other outdoor activities became an important part of their lives as working-class men. With rebellions quelled and the rebels expelled, with the company's future tenuous and the union emasculated, many Reo Joes took to the woods. For Eddie, Gene, and many of the men at Reo, it was the activity of hunting that tied them to their fellow workers, and filled their days and minds with excitement and joy.[82]

# The "Fall" of Reo, 1955-1975

On October 16, 1965, approximately 150 students from Michigan State University, in one of the earliest demonstrations against the Vietnam War in the Lansing area, marched in front of the Lansing Division of White Motors. Fred Parks, writing for UAW Local 650 in the *Lansing Labor News,* reported that "this un-American committee picketed the Lansing Division because we build military trucks," many of them destined for Vietnam. "The government should have set up an induction center on Baker Street and drafted each one as they strolled by," he wrote angrily.[1] The last two decades of Reo's existence brought demoralizing changes to its stalwart employees. The company was taken over three times, challenging union members and management alike to make their peace with working for remote corporate owners. Military production was increasingly the lifeblood of the Lansing factory. The persistence of residential and occupational segregation, as African American and Hispanics populations increased, created some unrest, forcing city leaders to devise solutions.[2] One of these solutions, urban renewal, altered the very look of the city. Remote corporate ownership,

This chapter is reprinted from "The 'Fall' of Reo in Lansing, Michigan, 1955–1975," in Jefferson Cowie and Joseph Heathcott (editors), *Beyond the Ruins: The Meanings of Deindustrialization* (Ithaca: Cornell University Press, 2003). Copyright © 2003 Cornell University. Reprinted by permission of the publisher.

defense contracts dependent on federal policy, and urban renewal ended forever Reo's cherished tradition of local control. The international union and larger GM local unions overshadowed UAW Local 650. The Reo family persisted through this difficult time nonetheless, providing those in the plant with a way to understand and respond to a changing and sometimes troubling world.

The organizational and rhetorical expressions of the Reo family were the lifeboat in which Reo's workers navigated the turbulent seas of the 1960s. Reo's company culture provided comfort when the plant closed its doors in 1975. A few weeks before the closing, when everything was auctioned off for $11 million, Reo employee Lee Magielski wrote in the *Lansing Labor News*, "When Diamond Reo seems to be going down like a sinking ship ... we remember we once were and still are a people of class, manufacturing one of the greatest trucks on the road. Whatever happens from here on in, it is important that the few of us that are left at work go about our tasks with the dignity and class that made us great. Let's keep that dignity and class to the very end like a captain going down with the ship."[3]

The closing of the Reo plant is part of a larger story of de-industrialization that brought about what is often referred to as the postindustrial economy.[4] Many scholars have represented the late twentieth-century phenomenon of de-industrialization as a macro political and economic event with micro personal and economic consequences.[5] Writers at opposite ends of the political spectrum, who disagree about the role government should play in this economic transition, agree that large multinational corporations have been allowed to put their balance sheets above the lives of their workers, and that this era of mobile capital and high technology allows them to do this more often and more thoroughly than ever before.[6] The large body of literature that describes plant closings provides poignant, ground-level accounts of the demise of individuals, families, and communities. Michael Moore's film *Roger and Me*, a controversial postmortem on Flint, Michigan, is a good example.[7]

The plant closings of the late twentieth century involve the intersection of global, national, regional, and local causes and consequences, and any given closing may therefore be unique by reason of its time and place, and not simply in terms of degree.[8] The closing of a plant always involves many stories, and each closing, in its details, is unique. The closing of Reo's plant brought Reo's story to an end, but automotive production in Lansing and the surrounding area continued. Why, then, did Reo fall?[9]

Reo's decline began in 1955, when the plant was absorbed by a larger, distant corporation and began producing trucks for the military. Remote ownership and over-reliance on one product seemed a logical step in the early years of the Cold War, but it ultimately spelled disaster for the company. The story of Reo's demise is bound up with efforts by both city and federal officials to rid municipalities like Lansing of "urban blight," which included aging factories like Reo. By the early 1970s, Reo's corporate owners had failed in their attempts to secure federal urban-renewal dollars to move the plant to newer, up-to-date facilities outside the city. Instead, they sold the factory to a private entrepreneur—not a large multinational but a very old-fashioned capitalist—who squeezed everything of value left in the people and the facilities for his own gain.

It is probably a coincidence that the Vietnam War and Reo Motors ended in the same year, but it is a meaningful one. Reo failed primarily because it could not make the transition to civilian production and became dependent upon military truck contracts for its survival. Not that it didn't try. By 1952, as the Korean conflict wound down, Reo's president, Joseph Sherer, began to plan for the Cold War era. His diversification plan reoriented Reo's production to consumer goods. In addition to the already healthy lawnmower division, Reo launched a new industrial and marine engine division, a children's wheeled goods division, new truck sales branches, and a new truck leasing division.[10] The company already produced urban and school buses and the civil defense vehicle "Calamity Jane."[11]

In the meantime, Reo's dependence on military contracts continued even after the Korean conflict ended; in 1953 70 percent of Reo's business volume was related to defense.[12] In September of that year, just a few months before Sherer left, Reo announced that it had scored a major truck contract, becoming one of only two producers of the 2.5-ton truck and upsetting the new "single producer policy" through its successful public relations program at the Pentagon.[13] Some evidence suggests that a decision was made (or perhaps forced) to pursue this line of defense work at the expense of other high-tech defense work.[14] It is not entirely clear whether Sherer left Reo because he felt he had accomplished his mission of getting Reo back on its feet in the Cold War world, or whether he decided that he had reached the limits of what he could do.

During Sherer's last year, 1954, things began to go downhill: workers experienced layoffs, shutdowns, and short weeks; when they showed up for work they found little red tags tied to the die settings throughout the plant.[15] Ed Wright wrote, "it means their job is done. 'Final' is the word written across the card. It means that particular die has made its last run on the part it was built for. It means the contract for Uncle Sam that has kept our shop so noisy and so busy for so long will soon come to a close."[16] Henney Motors Company of Freeport, Illinois, began the process of purchasing the company. Henney, recognizing that the plant's chief product was trucks, sold the lawnmower division to Motor Wheel (another long-time local manufacturer) and did away with the children's toy division. When it received another government truck order, Henney pledged to shoot for the number-one spot among truck independents.[17] The company remained in limbo as the acquisition deal stalled. By the end of 1954 it became clear that the president of Henney had decided not to purchase Reo after all. He transferred the entire arrangement to Bohn Aluminum and Brass of Detroit in a complicated financial deal that benefited only his stockholders and board of directors.[18] John Tooker, who had worked at Reo since the mid-1920s and was second in command under Sherer, took the reins. For many years he had been Reo's representative in Washington and was known in ordnance and defense circles throughout the city.[19]

Defense contracts trickled in, the union obliged the company with grudging concessions, and things limped along.[20] When White Motors of Cleveland stepped in to buy the company in 1957, even union members hailed the development.[21] White was one of a number of small, struggling, independent truck producers in a market dominated by Mack Trucks. In the 1960s White engaged in an aggressive merging spree that made it one of the largest truck producers—and one of the top 100 primary defense contractors—in the country.[22] In this national corporate environment, Reo was purchased to play a specialized role: to manufacture trucks, a large percentage of them for military purposes, and to lease, sell, and service those trucks, wherever they might be found. Reo was part of an organization that held one-quarter of the growing truck market and was the second-largest truck producer in the United States.[23]

Between 1960 and 1969, Diamond Reo (as it came to be called after the merger of Reo and Diamond T trucks of Chicago) produced trucks and filled millions of dollars of orders for 2.5-ton trucks for military ordnance. It can be tentatively surmised that military contracts amounted to an average of $13.5 million each year (see Table 6 in the Appendix). Zenon C. R. Hansen, a forty-year veteran of the truck industry, remembers his years as president of Diamond Reo in Lansing and executive vice president of the White Motor Corporation until 1965 as "extremely successful."[24] This prosperous era was not to continue.

The corporate tactics that absorbed Reo into White Motor Company and brought initial success and prominence eventually began to weaken White Motors. By the late 1960s, as a result of many mergers and much diversification, particularly into farm equipment, White began to show losses.[25] White's managers put their energies into aggressive marketing and "let manufacturing take a back seat."[26] To accomplish the necessary corporate housekeeping, the company's CEOs turned to familiar tactics: they proposed a merger with White Consolidated, another Cleveland-based company that produced consumer goods. In the summer of 1970 the merger seemed a possibility, scuttling some preliminary negotiations that were underway with Francis Cappaert regarding the purchase of the Reo Plant.[27] Early in 1971, the antitrust division of the U.S. Justice Department found that the merger violated the Clayton Anti-Trust Act and ordered an injunction to block it. Rather than go to court, White abandoned the merger and sold Reo to Cappaert.[28]

Why managers at White decided to sell Reo and not one of its many other holdings is not clear, especially in light of the actions of W. L. Peterson, the president of the White Motors truck division. When Peterson tried to delay the merger because, he claimed, the truck division was financially healthy, he was fired.[29] News releases after the sale often claimed that the trucks made at Reo were in direct competition with other White products, but waning demand due to cutbacks in military contracts explains why this competition had become a problem in the late 1960s.[30]

Students of the industrial economy in the Cold War era have concluded that the Midwest did not benefit to the same extent as other regions of the American "gunbelt," and that the region lost the prominence it had had during World War II and Korea as military dollars shifted to high-technology industries. The authors of *The Rise of the Gunbelt: The Military Remapping of Industrial America* assert that "the industrial heartland never captured a sufficient share of the cold war aerospace defense contracts" and conclude that "midwestern habits of making and selling were better suited to the car dealer and the housewife than to the Pentagon colonel."[31] Because it had specialized in ordnance trucks, the Diamond Reo plant was decidedly low-tech and not competitive with more sophisticated technologies. If Diamond Reo no longer pulled its weight by bringing in government contracts, White's management reasoned, it was expendable. In fact, a *Forbes* magazine article on White's new CEO, "Bunkie" Knudsen, explained that "when Diamond Reo Truck division, which had been losing money for five years, lost a key US government order, Knudsen sold it off."[32] The combination of remote ownership and overspecialization was Diamond Reo's undoing.

Its over-reliance on competitive military contracts was not Diamond Reo's only problem. The aging inner-city plant was starting to become a corporate liability, requiring "significant investment in new equipment to bring its facilities up to optimum productivity."[33] By the end of the decade, both the Reo Plant and Lansing were in dire need of an infusion of capital and energy to restore their infrastructure. White's inability to secure federal and municipal funds to modernize and relocate Diamond Reo sealed the plant's fate. Lacking both sufficient military contracts and corporate welfare, White decided to abandon Reo.

Lansing's municipal history helps provide the context (though not necessarily the exact causes) of this unfortunate outcome. Although it lagged behind larger industrial cities in this respect, by the early 1960s Lansing had begun vigorously and successfully to pursue federal funds for highway construction and the "Great Society" programs designed to create model U.S. cities.[34] But what began as an effort to modernize and to eradicate "urban blight" ended up, tragically, destroying downtown businesses and residential districts where poor, predominantly African American families lived. After World War II, Lansing became a more diverse city. Its nonwhite population doubled every decade between 1950 and 1970, growing from 3,046 in 1950 to 6,794 in 1960 and 12,232 in 1970. Lansing was not as diverse as Flint, Grand Rapids, or Kalamazoo, but its African American neighborhood, established at the beginning of the century, was expanding rapidly (see Table 7 in the Appendix). One scholar of residential patterns in Lansing claimed that "residential segregation or spatial concentration of the blacks represents the most obvious and extreme expression of racial prejudice in Lansing."[35] It was in this traditionally African American neighborhood that the removals began.

The first assault was the building of an interstate highway right through the heart of the city. Interstate 496 replaced Main Street, which ran east to west just south of the capitol building and the main business district on Washington Avenue, which ran north to south. The new interstate separated the downtown from one of the large Oldsmobile plants and from Diamond Reo, both located south of the highway. Interstate 496 cut through much of the African American community, destroying 890 dwellings and displacing many more families.[36] Although the destruction of the neighborhood and the removal of families against their will was the most serious consequence of this highway, there was another outcome: the destruction of the Ransom E. Olds mansion on the corner of Main Street and South Washington Avenue. Once a testament to the heterogeneous mixing of classes (though certainly not races) in the downtown neighborhoods, Olds's house was within walking distance of his plant, the downtown business district, the homes of other Reo managers, and the more modest workers' homes and boarding houses. By the early 1960s these once sumptuous mansions had begun to be broken up into apartments and to become run down. Despite some effort to preserve and to move it to another site, the Olds house eventually came down, another victim of urban renewal and the desire for better traffic flow.[37]

By the mid-1960s the city of Lansing had also identified three urban renewal projects designed to clean up and modernize the most blighted and depressed areas of the city's business and residential areas.[38] Urban Renewal Project #1 comprised a business district near the capitol building, with late nineteenth-century two- and three-story buildings that housed locally owned small businesses and about 130 families, primarily African American. These were bought up and razed, and tall glass-and-steel boxes were erected in their place. Urban Renewal Project #2 included a variety of residential and business areas west and east of the capitol building. Altogether, 372 dwellings, again largely occupied by black families, gave way to a large, impersonal, boxy glass-and-steel capitol complex,

a series of office buildings for use by the federal, state, and local government, and Lansing Community College.[39] The removal of these businesses and homes coincided with the building of scattered-site housing
projects designed to provide an alternative to low-income housing in the
city, but they were certainly inadequate in both quality and quantity.[40]
Local plants such Olds and Motor Wheel exacerbated the situation in two
ways. First, they fueled in-migrations of workers who needed low-cost
housing, and, second, the expansion of their facilities meant the razing of
still more houses and apartments, which put additional pressure on existing housing stock.[41]

Understandably, by the mid-1960s Lansing had developed a housing
problem, and many understood this housing problem as a race problem,
since the two episodes of racial unrest that Lansing experienced in these
years occurred on the west side. The first, in June 1964, involved a mob
of 700 throwing rocks, which the *Lansing State Journal* characterized simply as disorderly conduct.[42] The disturbance began when a resident called
the police to report a fight. When the police arrived, there was swearing,
a scuffle, and an arrest. A nearby house party emptied into the street soon
afterward, and the crowd became angry about the heavy-handed police
action. Several hours of rock throwing and disorderly conduct prompted
the arrival of 130 policemen in riot gear. The more serious events, which
took place in August 1966, revealed the source of the problem. For two
nights youths roamed the downtown, engaging in violence and defacing
property. The police shot four of these youths during the disturbances.
Two of Lansing's religious leaders, who headed youth organizations,
claimed that the two days of rioting were the fruit of grievances that had
been festering since 1964. Reverend Kenneth Favier, the pastor of the
Cristo Rey Catholic Church, which served the Mexican American population of the city, and Bishop S. C. Cole of the Church of God in Christ,
a member of the Inter-faith Council, cited the lack of recreational facilities and employment opportunities for youth, poor minority representation in municipal government, job discrimination, and the scarcity and
poor quality of housing as the causes of the violence. A youth group
formed in the wake of the violence proposed that the city open and staff
new recreational facilities on the west side to serve both white and African
American youth.[43]

Local groups struggled to address these problems, but change came slowly. Leaders of the African American community worked with police to curb violence and proposed new youth centers for the schools, but racism persisted.[44] During the first night of violence in August 1966, "bands of white youths yelling 'shoot them, kill them' fanned the flames."[45] When a 1968 survey by the Ministerial Council (an ecumenical group representing twenty-one churches) revealed that downtown stores were not hiring blacks, the group threatened a "Black and Brown Easter," a boycott of downtown stores for Easter. A meeting between representatives of the Downtown Businesses' Association, the Ministerial Council, the NAACP, and Lansing's Human Relations Commission produced a plan to address the problems and averted the boycott.[46] As late as 1970 the prospect of a Negro History Week celebration at a west side high school provoked the threat of a white student boycott and caused scuffles and fights.[47]

As citizens of Lansing struggled to respond to these challenges to the status quo and end discriminatory practices in education, housing, and work, Urban Renewal Project #3 began. The affected areas included a corridor extending southward from the capitol building, traversing the newly built highway, Interstate 496, to the businesses and neighborhoods beyond. Diamond Reo and the neighborhoods and commercial districts surrounding it were designated as "blighted" and slated for drastic change. J. N. Bauman, the president of White Motors, proposed a novel way to fund corporate welfare and community development simultaneously.[48] His plan provided for moderate- and low-income housing on the deteriorating south side without a single removal, while at the same time giving the old Diamond Reo plant land and capital for the retooling it needed by moving the plant out of the inner city. Bauman proposed that the city appeal to the U.S. Department of Housing and Urban Development (HUD) for funds to buy the existing Diamond Reo factory and site from the parent company, White Motors. With that money and a generous land and tax deal from the city of Lansing, Diamond Reo would relocate to a site in the northern part of the city, with a new and improved facility and additional space to grow. The old site would then be razed and become available for the private development of moderate- and low-income housing.

White Motors, still enjoying some success at its Lansing plant, announced its plans to build a new manufacturing plant at the city limits.[49] It appeared willing to work with the city council and with the citizens' district council for district area 3, created to provide community input into the urban renewal process.[50] After some delays, funding was obtained for a feasibility appraisal, the first step in the process of HUD approval of the final funding.[51] By the start of the new decade, Local UAW 650, the citizens' district council, the *Lansing State Journal,* and the township and county of Diamond Reo's new home had all approved the arrangement.[52] The success of the project hinged on HUD's appraisal of the worth of the factory and site. Independent appraisers had calculated that it was worth between $4 and $5 million, an amount that would have been acceptable to White Motors and put the whole plan into action. HUD, however, offered only $1.8 million for the project, and neither White Motor executives nor the local congressman could get HUD to budge. White Motors rejected the deal.[53]

The summer of 1970 was a turning point for White Motors and Diamond Reo. The poor offer from HUD and the Justice Department injunction against the merger with White Consolidated dealt two serious blows to the Lansing division. Urban Renewal Project #3 was never funded, probably a casualty of changing policies of HUD at the national level.[54] The mechanisms designed to realize a new Lansing rendered local city planners dependent on money from the federal government. Like the dwindling of military contracts, the lack of cooperation from HUD dealt Reo a serious blow. The plant remained in an area designated as "urban blight."

There was nothing left for White Motors to do but sell the Diamond Reo plant. In 1971 White sold Reo to a man who had been a shadowy figure in the injunction against the merger between White Motors and White Consolidated: Francis Cappaert. When he bought the plant, Cappaert pledged to restore Reo to its former glory as an independent truck producer, and there was some reason to believe that he would. Cappaert, like Ransom Olds, was a native son, born, raised, and schooled in the Alma/ Mt. Pleasant area, just an hour north of Lansing. When Cappaert bought Diamond Reo, he was fifty years old, living in Mississippi, the father of the mobile home business and owner of numerous holding companies in electronics and oil drilling and of land holdings in Las Vegas and throughout the southern United States (he also owned a herd of 25,000 Black Angus cattle). A free-wheeling, intensively private independent entrepreneur, Cappaert was considered one of the richest men in America, with a reputation for either making a big profit, fast, or dumping the whole project. Cappaert affected the "good ol' boy" image. He drank Schlitz instead of cocktails aboard his BAC-11 jet, his sumptuous flying home, a $3.5 million British-made plane that held seventy to eighty passengers.[55]

Throughout the years of remote ownership, employees of all ranks worked very hard to keep Reo's company culture alive. The groups of the early 1950s—the Reo girls' club, the steering gear club, golfing, bowling, and hunting clubs—all persisted throughout the 1960s in the face of changing ownership and periodic cutbacks and layoffs. UAW Local 650 continued to negotiate contracts every three years throughout the 1960s and managed to keep cost-of-living increases, pensions, and wages (which all became day-rate during this period) consistent within the pattern bargaining that prevailed in the automobile industry and the local market.[56] In 1967 the office employees voted 183 to 107 to create the technical, office, and professional department (TOP), and in 1968 they created an amalgamated Local 650.[57]

Although Local 650 processed its share of grievances, and although strikes were frequently threatened as contract deadlines approached, Reo workers never struck again after 1951. The union remained an important recourse for shop floor problems and an outlet for political and civic service for some, but larger GM unions overshadowed the smaller Reo local.[58] Many union members became apathetic. G. Sanders, writing in the *Lansing Labor News,* chastised union members for a lackluster strike vote in 1962, when a speedup on the main assembly line had prompted some of the men to walk off for a few hours. He chastised those who were too young to remember 1937.

> You've never had to fight for anything; you've never had to defend anything, not even your indescribable pride. Your latest demonstration in exercising your right to vote fully illustrates one point. You don't care about the vital things that make this nation a great one. You want someone else to do your job, unless the reward is monetary.... Most of you were quite verbal in speaking out that you didn't want a strike, as Christmas is near.... Your pride in being a man among men is showing, but in the opposite direction. Your family will be proud of you, if you can return to them after a good day's work, reasonably tired, but happy, confident and exuding pride in yourself and your union.[59]

Despite the appeal to working-class manhood, the strike vote failed. For those who had joined the new TOP union, identification with the girls' club remained strong. The *Lansing Labor News* "Off the TOP" column reported on the activities of its sister organization. In 1970, for example, the "Off the TOP" column reported that the Diamond Reo girls' club had assisted those displaced by urban renewal by collecting and distributing necessary household items.[60] Working at "the Reo" provided the important source of identification for those who persevered in the factory.

Those who worked at Reo during these years identified a number of values that made Reo a unique place to work, values summed up in the phrase "family feeling." As Lewis Garcia recalled, "the family never lost its culture. The Reo family, whenever it started—and that's before my time, but whenever it started—that culture carried down." Garcia spoke of how Reo contributed to community charities and the feeling of fellowship among the workers. Many spoke of the difference between working for Reo and working for the larger Oldsmobile plant in town. Glen Green didn't look for a job at Olds because there he would "just be a number." At Reo, "everybody [had] a place in the operation of this big machine and I didn't want to give that up to become nobody at Olds." Doris Dow, who worked as an office worker between 1950 and 1975 and was active in the TOP, described Reo as a "family-oriented place. The people that worked for Reo really liked and enjoyed their jobs, I think most of 'em. They all complained, we all complained, but I really think the people that worked there enjoyed their job or enjoyed . . . the other people that worked there . . . and so they wanted their sons there." Doris Faustman, who worked on and off as a white-collar worker throughout the post–World War II period recalled, "It was kind of a family place, a lot of them, they still kind of cling to each other."[61]

Threats to this imagined community, the Reo family, came from both within and without. Federal affirmative action programs required that more minorities be hired. A number of Reo's employees felt that these minorities, and other new workers, lacked the proper work ethnic and commitment to product and reputation. One worker at Reo recalled:

> We didn't have enough colored people in the Reo, so NPC [NAACP] made 'em hire some. Well, I don't know why, but they bused fifty colored people out of Jackson on a bus come in here every morning, fifty black ones come in every Monday, every day from Jackson. Within a six weeks' time, I don't think there was only two of them left. Every one of them that come in there worked a day

or two and he hurt his back. Every one of them went out on workman's compensation. And after that, if you had the slightest back trouble you didn't get into Reo. Well, my boy has got a bad back and he couldn't get into Reo.[62]

Another supervisor remembered, "there were the days when the government said you have to hire so many minority workers.... I'm not against the minority people or anything like that, but so many of them would come here to go to work and it would take two of them to do what one older worker used to do."[63] Finally, one worker who started in the shop and ended in supervision remembered that in the 1960s more "crazy-time people" entered the shop. The Vietnam era brought veterans, those just out of college, and "the ones that couldn't go to the army for some reason or other and they had a different attitude . . . and they was smokin' marijuana and they start gettin' into LSD. . . . Then you got the little butterfly people, you know, you don't know whether women or men."[64] The African Americans, hippies, and homosexuals who entered Reo during the late 1960s posed a threat to the Reo family.

There were other problems in the plant. Despite OSHA and other programs designed to improve workplace heath and safety, the Reo plant became a dangerous place to work, with an aging plant and equipment making matters worse over time. In 1973 the union identified a long list of problems: hazardous working conditions, substandard first aid, cockroaches that crawled from every corner and wallboard, unsanitary restrooms, ceilings and lights that shook and jiggled overhead, rodent droppings in the vending machines, unsafe noise levels in certain areas, diesel exhaust fumes that drifted into many work areas.[65] Many workers also identified a creeping corruption that coincided with Cappaert's ownership of the company. Some mentioned that certain managers and foremen stole from the company and that even Cappaert was guilty of theft.[66]

Cappaert also began to tamper with the pension fund, and this provoked a brief episode of union militancy. Although the union rejected the company's efforts to renegotiate the pension agreement in 1972, by 1973 the fund was depleted.[67] UAW Local 650 president Roger D. Foster reported the unsuccessful talks to the rank and file but was still conciliatory. "Our union has never been labeled radical or strike-happy and we still would only use a strike as a last resort."[68] The local student groups, so eager to picket Reo when it was making trucks destined for Vietnam, now offered their assistance. They suggested in their alternative paper that "if the plant goes out, [students should] drop by the pickets at the plant and express your solidarity."[69] With no assurance on worker pensions, the union settled in March 1973. The company announced the appointment of a new director of industry and community relations, Tom Shelley, who explained to the bargaining committee that he was going to start a weekly company newspaper, company sports teams, and a suggestion program.[70]

The pension situation was a symptom of a much more serious problem. One spring day in 1975, Diamond Reo workers arrived at work to find their plant padlocked. Even though this outcome had been twenty years in the making, the several hundred workers still left in the plant were shocked. Former employees offered vivid and painful recollections of the plant closing. Seventeen years later, it was still quite real for Doris Dow.

> I'm walking down the street, there down Washington Avenue, and I'm, why is there this crowd of people there in front? Why aren't they going in? Well, it was, it was April, it was the spring of the year so you're thinking, well, it's nice out, it was quite common to see people standing out in front with a cup of coffee or something like that in the spring of the air, if it was a nice day, you know, and it was nice that day. But that was too many people and then, as you get there closer, you see the chains on the door. You know something has happened and, of course, you're looking at the chains on the door and you say, why. . . ?[71]

Dow and many others told of suicides and other problems after the shutdown. Calvin Chamberlain, an engine worker and time-and-motion specialist between 1950 and 1975 who "helped turn out the lights," turned to drink.[72] Raymond Fuller, who worked on truck repair between 1943 and 1975, took the closing very hard, even though he had expected it.

> Oh yes, I know it was coming. I was on repair for it. I stayed until all the trucks was gone. Sure I know exactly when I was going to leave. You know, I was fifty-eight years old when that thing closed. Now, where do you go to look for a job when you are fifty-eight years old? I sat around here. I guess we went to Florida, I remember, that winter, and then I come back and went ice fishing. Come along the first of March I told my wife I got to find something to do, this is driving me crazy.[73]

Former Reo workers identified Cappaert as the reason for their factory's closing.[74] The overwhelming number of informants who offered an opinion on why Reo closed stated quite baldly that Francis Cappaert ruined the company and deprived them of their pensions in the process.

Of course, these informants were drawn from the various Reo retiree groups that still exist in Lansing, which were formed after efforts to pursue the pension money failed. These individuals had collectively discussed and formulated their own version of the narrative of the plant's demise. The consistency of their story suggests that this group continues to reinforce this narrative at retiree luncheons that still occur each month.[75] Arthur Frahm, who worked in accounts payable and purchasing between 1947 and 1972, claimed that Cappaert's "prime interest was to just liquidate the place." Herbert Heinz, who worked as an electrician and in truck repair between 1951 and 1974, said, "the old Cappaert, he is the one that bankrupt the company. . . . When Cappaert took off, when he went bankrupt in that place, he took six million dollars of our pension fund." Wayne Nunheimer, a mechanic and spot welder between 1945 and 1975, asserted passionately, "Reo could have been operating today if it hadn't been for Cappaert." Only one worker, Lewis Garcia, felt no hostility toward Cappaert, but even he claimed that Cappaert had confided in him over drinks that he was going to close the place down.[76]

Some informants acknowledged that the many buyouts had weakened Reo before Cappaert arrived, but none saw this as the cause of Reo's demise. Cappaert was guilty; he probably had no intention of making a go of Reo and certainly not of restoring the company to its former glory. He used brutal tactics that this labor force was unused to; and he deprived these workers, many of whom had worked at Reo for more than twenty-five years, of any decent retirement. Nevertheless, Cappaert was not the sole villain of the piece, however understandable the feelings of these workers may be. Cappaert's mismanagement was the straw that broke Reo's back, but the company had been progressively weakened for years before he arrived on the scene, and his reign coincided with many other disruptive and disturbing changes in the factory and the community.

The many buyouts the company had suffered and the remoteness of its corporate owners had crippled the ability of local business, municipal, and union officials to exert any meaningful control over the workings of the plant. Reo's over-reliance on federal dollars for a single military product probably kept the company afloat longer than other truck independents, but ultimately, when the Cold War began to wind down, White Motors was forced to make a decision about Reo's future. Had the HUD funds to retool and relocate the plant been forthcoming, Reo might have survived. For reasons that are still somewhat obscure, however, these funds did not materialize. The Diamond Reo plant, abandoned by federal and local governments and its various owners, but remembered by its workers to this day, shut down forever.

## Post Script—Destruction and Resurrection

The abandonment of Urban Renewal Project #3 and the closing of the Diamond Reo factory created an eyesore of more than forty acres in South Lansing. The mayor and those living near the plant believed that this firetrap needed to be cleared as quickly as possible, but that would cost money. In 1978, after the city made a commitment to redevelop the site, the Lansing city council learned that the National Register of Historic Places had declared the site a historic monument. Ralph J. Christian, a resident of Nashville, Michigan, apparently visited the site in 1976 and "just thought the nomination was a good thing to do." Jerry Rogers, chief of the Interior Department's architectural and historical preservation unit, defended the decision to preserve the Reo buildings as part of the nation's heritage. Mayor Gerald Graves declared, "We are talking industry and jobs for Lansing and they are talking junk. We're pretty upset with it but if it holds up we can't tear the buildings down."[77]

The city council and the people of the neighborhoods surrounding the site had some legitimate concerns: the plant was a fire hazard, a point that Mayor Graves hammered home in his many attempts to demolish the complex.[78] Finally, a memorandum of agreement was drafted that allowed for the demolition of the site if the city would, in good faith, explore the possibility of incorporating any of the existing structures in future development. The U.S. Commerce Department contributed $1 million to making the site into an industrial park.

On July 23, 1979, the demolition began anyway. The *Lansing State Journal* featured a picture of a jubilant Mayor Graves operating the machinery.[79] Less than a month later, when it was disclosed that the city had not lived up to its commitment as outlined in the memorandum, the wrecking ball was stilled. On October 30, 1979, the remaining structures

ILLUSTRATION 14. Clubhouse ballroom before demolition. Photo courtesy of Library of Congress, Prints and Photographs Division, Historic American Engineering Record, Reproduction Number HAER, MICH, 33-LAN, 1-3.

burned to the ground in what many interviewed believed was a suspicious fire. By the start of 1980 there was nothing left on the site that had manufactured hundreds of thousands of cars and trucks, employed hundreds of thousands of people, and been one of Lansing's premier industries for more than seventy years. After the fire, the site was declared environmentally unsound. A few businesses occupy part of the space today, but most of it remains open and unoccupied, a testament to a city that cared little for those who worked there and less for its own history (see Illustrations 14 and 15).

In an industrial park surrounded by forest and farms near the village of Charlotte, about twenty minutes southwest of Lansing, one may visit the reincarnation of Reo, Spartan Motors. It was founded in 1975 by George Sztykiel, a former engineer at Reo, in conjunction with several other refugees from Diamond Reo. The company produces mobile home chassis, school buses, and fire engines. With additional facilities in Mexico, the company did very well in the 1990s.

ILLUSTRATION 15.  Reo before the fall. Photo courtesy of Library of Congress, Prints and Photographs Division, Historic American Engineering Record, Reproduction Number HAER, MICH, 33-LAN, 1-14.

Spartan Motors is in many ways a worthy successor to Reo. In addition to the populist philosophy of its founder, the workforce and personnel policies are eerily like those of the company that spawned Spartan Motors. Spartan prides itself on its "homegrown" workforce, blue collar and white collar alike. In 1992, "of 380 employees at Spartan, only eight have college or advanced degrees. The preponderance come from inside the county, off the farm and out of the local high school." Spartan's chief financial officer and personnel manager calls the Spartan workforce "'vocationally literate' and 'not afraid to work.' Many grew up on farms, tending—from an early age—not only livestock but to broken tractors as well. Many still rebuild car engines in their spare time. Many come from families in which generations have worked at GM's big Oldsmobile plant in Lansing."[80]

Labor relations at Spartan resemble those at Reo in the 1920s. This nonunionized plant prides itself on its hands-on relationship with the workers. A reporter for *Inc.* magazine described how Sztykiel made a point of talking to the men each quarter; at the talk overheard by the reporter, Sztykiel invoked the concept of the factory family. "Sztykiel took his windbreaker off and laid it on top of the cardboard box in the corner of the room. He climbed a small stepladder, sat on the top step, and ... began, 'Welcome, We think this is a good corporation. It's run on the same principles that a family is, because we think that's the most effective way human beings have managed to get along.'" Spartan Motors "distributes 10% of pretax profit quarterly among its workers" and in the 1990s committed itself not to lay off its workforce. Sztykiel explained, "You wouldn't do that in your family. If you have 10 children and times get tough, you wouldn't send the three youngest ones out the door. It's not only immoral, it's stupid. Why? Those who have been let go are soon forgotten—screw them—and the ones who stay haven't learned anything from the experience." "We don't recognize the terms labor and management here. I am not the boss. I am the number one servant of this corporation."[81]

On March 25, 1992, I toured Spartan Motors. The tour guide described the supervisors, including Sztykiel, as willing to get their hands dirty. "It is not uncommon to find him working out in the shop." There was no assembly line, although progressive work stations with computer terminals were evident. The representative took a great deal of pride in the custom work the company performed. "If a customer wants ten pounds of coffee in a one pound can, we'll figure out a way to do it," he said. As far as I could tell, all of the 360 to 370 workers at Spartan were white men. Loud country and western music played throughout the plant, and the various work stations displayed pictures of babies and babes: the workers' children as well as their favorite female forms. One work station featured a confederate flag. In the offices, a male employee's cubby sported a sign stating, "sexual harassment in this department will not be reported—However, it will be graded." The spirit of Reo lives on in Spartan Motors in an updated form. Spartan seems successfully to have re-created the industrial community Ransom E. Olds fashioned at his first Reo Motor Car Company in Lansing in 1904: a small workplace in a small community with a homogeneous, white, native-born labor force drawn from the surrounding farming countryside, where everyone is said to belong to a big factory family.

The resurrection of Reo as Spartan Motors and the return of GM to Lansing resulted from favorable tax abatements, corporate perceptions of the "well-qualified labor force," and "very good labor relations" in the region. If Spartan Motors, a small, independent, rural, nonunion automotive producer is the wave of the future, then we need to recognize the ways in which it is also powerfully rooted in its past. The padlocking of Reo was not the end of the story for the workers or for manufacturing activities in the region, but the closing of one complicated chapter.

# Epilogue

*Reo of the Mind*

**I loved it. . . . I still dream about the Reo.**
—Vivern Haight, former Reo worker

The doors of the Diamond Reo plant might have closed in 1975, but Reo lives on today in the hearts and minds of many of its former workers and in the city itself. It is this ongoing relationship with a company long since gone that has made the history of this place, this company, and these workers so distinctive and compelling.

Since the plant closed, former Reo workers have been meeting in a variety of retiree organizations. These organizations were initially a response to the efforts to pursue the pensions squandered by Reo's last owner, Frank Cappaert, as he divested the company of its worth for his own private gain.[1] As wronged former employees came together to appeal for their pensions, they coalesced into three retiree groups, each continuing the Reo organizations started in the post–World War II period. One group, composed primarily but not exclusively of former union members, meets at one of the local UAW union halls each month, primarily for socializing and bingo. The second group, former members of the steering gear club, meets monthly at a south side Lansing restaurant. The third group, former members of the girls' club, also meets each month for lunch. The former steering gear group and the former girls' club group

169

maintain their sex and class exclusivity, but the group at the union hall includes all ranks and sexes. Every August, all former Reo workers meet for a huge luncheon. Until the late 1990s there was a similar annual event in Florida as well. Just as they had done while working at Reo, the members of the girls' club group took the lead in organizing the annual events and informing former employees of the various activities.

Shirley Bradley, a local historian who works at the R. E. Olds Transportation Museum and who is a member of a Reo family herself, and I interviewed thirty former Reo workers and attended the gatherings of all of these retiree groups. As the word got out about our project, we also received letters from former Reo workers who lived too far away to be interviewed, but wanted to tell us their stories. While each of the organized groups had its own distinctive characteristics, it was through the repeated meeting and contact with other former employees that Reo workers forged collective memories, revived relationships, and re-created the world of their former lives.

I first made contact with Shirley in the fall of 1991 at a reception for former Reo workers sponsored by the R. E. Olds Transportation Museum in downtown Lansing. We attended our first meeting of former union members on December 18, 1991. The group made announcements about friends, socialized, shared refreshments, and played bingo in the main meeting hall of UAW Local 724. It was at this gathering that we learned about the monthly luncheon of the steering gear group.

On January 9, 1992, Shirley and I had lunch at the Casa Nova with that group. Our contact was Lewis Garcia, the Mexican-born informant Al Zimmer had plucked off the punch press line to become a "straw boss." He was also the worker who had the most positive relationship with Cappaert. Casa Nova, which has since gone out of business, was an Italian restaurant on Lansing's south side, right across the street from the now defunct Lindell Drop Forge. It was a large restaurant with vinyl booths and an atmosphere and prices right out of the 1950s. The dozen men were seated in a dark corner of the restaurant. When Shirley and I arrived, the men immediately referred to us as "those dancing girls 'Louie' said would be coming." The camaraderie and joviality was palpable and the conversation was directed almost entirely at us.

Almost immediately the men began discussing "that family feeling and where it came from." They claimed the company took care of its employees and allowed them to plan for the future. They told us the story of how Garcia was promoted. They acknowledged that there had been plenty of disagreements, conflicts, incompetent workers, and unfair bosses, but they insisted that if you met a fellow Reoite outside the plant, he was kin—you were family. It was their unanimous collective opinion that Reo was the best place to work and that Reo workers were the best people. Reo treated its workers right, not like Olds and other plants, where workers were just numbers. The men had fond memories of the clubhouse. They delighted in listing for us its many activities and features and in describing how big and well equipped it was. Their fondest memories were of their times in the steering gear club, where the monthly meeting fostered fellow feeling among the men. "Then," they continued, "we drank. Sometimes women, too." There was alcohol at this luncheon, too, and toward the end the men began to do some of their regular business. They read letters from retirees living elsewhere, exchanged news, and told jokes. The men passed around a cartoon of a woman with wet hair in her eyes standing in front of a sink, her hand extended to receive a hairdryer. Her husband, however, was handing her a revolver. On our way out, Shirley and I were invited to the August luncheon, "to meet the women. We're proud of them," the men proclaimed.

On February 26, 1992, we attended the former girls' club luncheon at a diner-like restaurant on the south side. This was a much larger event, attended by twenty to thirty women. It was more difficult to get a general sense of the group under these circumstances. Nevertheless, certain standard rituals occurred: a prayer, news of retirees not present, and of recent deaths, and socializing. This group was more formal and business-like than the steering club group. Shirley and I mingled and made as many contacts as we could, but it was harder to establish connections. The leaders of this group proved the most resistant to interviews. One got the sense that they were still honoring the confidences of bosses they had worked for years before.

Throughout the 1990s, former girls' club members organized the annual luncheons, which were usually attended by about 180 people.[2] At the affair in 1993, the meal was preceded by a prayer of thanks that they could all get together to remember and celebrate their good times at Reo. After lunch, various individuals from the dais and the tables approached the podium and made announcements, told stories and jokes, and oversaw a raffle. In addition to news of births, deaths, anniversaries, and sickness, people shared stories about the past. This was an oral supplement to a table covered with memorabilia and historical materials. The luncheons we attended in 1995, marking the tenth anniversary of the Reo retiree association, and again in 1999 all followed the same script.

One of the speeches at the 1995 luncheon was particularly memorable for the "work" that all of these gatherings accomplished in the collective memories of these individuals. Karen Douglas was something of a local celebrity, a regular columnist for the *Lansing State Journal* who also happened to be the daughter and wife of Reo workers. She described her father, a skilled tradesman who had worked at Reo between 1929 and 1963, as a "dedicated employee and a real team player." After remembering the people, the clubhouse, and the products at Reo, "which drew skilled tradesmen from throughout the Midwest," she declared that the highest honor was to be a part of the Reo family. "Whatever name, the company was more than a plot on South Washington Avenue. . . . Reo people . . . Reo workers . . . they were a Reo family." A number of people cried through this speech. It spoke directly to their sadness about a world they had lost.

Even though the Reo factory family's history dates back to the 1910s, the version of the family that Shirley and I witnessed was no simple continuation of the 1950s incarnation. The factory family that these retirees shared was only a memory of a time and place that no longer existed. Their narratives of the family factory bound together a particular generation of Reo workers. They had shared good times and bad, and the act of re-creating the factory family provided them with social and emotional support. Their memories of the Reo family emphasized the positive aspects of the company's paternalism—the parties, charity work, and community events—and completely left out the more insidious and even repressive aspects of supervision, control, and conflict.[3]

Karen Douglas's comments at the 1995 luncheon provide an additional insight into this feature of the retirees' collective memory. Douglas's father was a Local 650 member and a union steward who had participated in the sit-down of 1937 as well as the wartime and postwar conflicts. But Douglas did not dwell on this part of Reo's history. She merely mentioned briefly that her father had been a steward and union member and that therefore he had participated in incidents of labor-management conflict. "Those things happened," she said, and then moved on to more positive things.

It was not that those who had been union members had forgotten. Many acknowledged, when asked, that the union had brought welcome changes. Their apparent amnesia pertained only to the episodes of conflict and strife. No one volunteered any information about his or her own participation in or impressions of any of the strikes at Reo.

The most powerful illustration of this collective amnesia was the text on the historical marker recently established to commemorate Reo. In 1995 a blue ribbon committee formed from the retiree association and composed primarily of former steering gear and girls' club members met many times to draft the wording for the marker.[4] Both Shirley Bradley and I were invited to attend the July 19, 1995, meeting to offer suggestions on the evolving language. By this time I understood that these former Reo workers had been collectively constructing and reconstructing their memories of the past ever since the plant closed. Reo still played a key role in their social life and sense of self, and they believed that they owned this history.

Once I had seen the proposed text for the marker, I offered a number of minor changes and suggested one major addition. The draft that I saw made no reference to any union activity, to the 1937 strike, the Lansing Labor Holiday, or any subsequent labor activities. I suggested that, along with the Flint sit-down, the Reo sit-down had been an important local event and was worthy of mention, since it brought the UAW-CIO to the plant for the remainder of its history. The two-sided historical marker, which was dedicated almost a year later, made no mention of the union (see Illustration 16). One side highlighted the technological, manufacturing, and managerial history of the company; the other side described the Reo clubhouse, "one of those policies implemented by Reo to cultivate the loyalty of its workers. Years after the Diamond Reo plant closed in 1975, "former employees recalled the sense of family fostered by the company."

A viewer of this marker might be tempted to conclude that the elites of the company simply whitewashed Reo's past in this omission, but the archival and oral evidence does not support that conclusion. Those who

ILLUSTRATION 16.  Reo historical marker, side one and side two. Photos courtesy of Laura Rose Ashlee.

wrote the text for the historic marker offered a vision of a homogeneous, harmonious, and humane workplace with employers and employees all able to live out a version of the American Dream.

It has not always been easy to reconcile the historian's responsibility to tell a story grounded in the record with one's personal desire to honor the ownership of one's informants' lives and stories; indeed, at times it has been wrenching. When the interview process was winding down, I received funding to have the tapes transcribed. It was a cold, wintry day when I toted the boxes filled with thousands of pages of testimony. That night my dreams began. Over the next two weeks I had the same nightmare three times. It was always the same: in my dream, I have gotten the transcripts from the typist one at a time. As I hold the single transcript in my hand, I am gripped with terror as I remember how I have murdered the individual whose words I am holding. Slowly I recall how I have completed the interview, killed my informant (although just how is never clear), and buried him under the floorboards. In my nightmare, I have blocked the memory of the murder, but now that the transcript is finished and is about to be made public, my misdeed will certainly come to light (literally: in my dream I picture the authorities axing the floorboards to reveal the body). I am doomed. During the course of the dream, this scenario plays out several times, as I remember my shameful act with the arrival of each transcript. So vivid was this dream that, after waking, I had to repeat to myself over and over that, no, I had not committed murder, no, I had not repressed some horrible past event. It was a powerful feeling that took a long time to fade.

The burden, the responsibility I felt then to tell the right stories, my fear that I might mangle and mutilate that which was so precious to my informants, is no less intense today, when at least a third of my informants have passed away. My feeling of obligation to render their lives and stories properly and with respect is more important than ever. The lives they lived, the world they knew, the past they celebrated and worked so hard to preserve and share with others, is a worthy story. It is the story of Reo Joe, the white Protestant working-class man and his family, and of how they all navigated with honor and dignity in a midwestern auto town throughout the twentieth century. I hope I have done justice to all of the Reo Joes and their families, and the lesson of their lives.

> Maybe the Master Builder will have a fine mansion for Joe's kind in that other world. Maybe that's the vision—the hope—that keeps him going. Gee, I hope so. If it's just for Joe.[5]

# Appendix

*Tables*

TABLE 1. Reo Oral History Project Participants

| Name | Date of interview | Position[a] | Tenure | Place of interview (if not Lansing) |
|------|------|------|------|------|
| Russell Alberts | Apr 16, 1992 | assembly | 1928–39 | |
| Mildred Alspaugh | Feb 25, 1992 | Reo family | | |
| Layton Aves | Aug 8, 1995 | chip handler, plating, lawnmower, export | 1941–75 | |
| Otto Aves | Jan 4, 1993 | sweeping, repair floor, final assembly | 1945–72 | |
| John Bowles | June 9, 1992 | spray painter, inspection | 1946–55 | |
| Sue Ellen Brown | Mar 2, 1993 | Reo family, witnessed fire | | |
| Calvin Chamberlain | June 11, 1992 | engine worker, time-and-motion specialist | 1950–75 | |
| Marilyn Uptegraft Chamberlain | June 11, 1992 | Reo family | | |
| Vern Cook | Feb 5, 1992 | sweeper, stock | 1944–47 | |
| Doris Dow | Feb 19, 1992 | office worker | 1950–75 | |
| Jack Down | Feb 18, 1992 | assistant sales engineer | 1947–48 | |

*(continued)*

177

**TABLE 1** *(cont.)*

| Name | Date of interview | Position[a] | Tenure | Place of interview (if not Lansing) |
|---|---|---|---|---|
| Doris Faustman | June 23, 1992 | office worker | 1945–47, 1949–51, 1967–75 | Williamston |
| Arthur Frahm | Feb 10, 1992 | accounts payable, purchasing | 1947–72 | |
| Raymond Fuller | Mar 19, 1992 | truck repair | 1943–75 | Mulliken |
| Lewis Garcia | Jan 28, 1992 | press room, superintendent | 1946–75 | |
| Glen Green | Jan 22, 1992 | receiving dept., machine repair, foreman | 1937–75 | |
| Norma Grimwood | Mar 26, 1992 | Reo family | | |
| Marvin Grinstern | Dec 3, 1992 | janitor | 1965–75 | |
| Vivern Haight | Feb 4, 1993 | managed clubhouse | 1945–75 | Webberville |
| Herbert Heinz | Mar 16, 1993 | electrician, truck repair | 1951–74 | Dansville |
| Harold Janetzke | Feb 26, 1992 | mail boy, time keeping, engineering | 1936–75 | |
| Eileen Janetzke | Feb 26, 1992 | office worker | 1940–43 | |
| Marjorie Koehler | June 16, 1992 | office worker | 1947–75 | Dimondale |
| Mabel Shreve McQueen | June 16, 1992 | office worker | 1953–75 | Dimondale |
| Eileen Nortman | Jan 28, 1993 | spline grinding | 1943–45 | East Lansing |
| Wayne Nunheimer | June 18, 1992 | mechanic, spot welder | 1945–75 | |
| Edward Rankin | Jan 30, 1992 | inventory, pricing, export | 1947–73 | |
| Hilda Smith | Feb 12, 1992 | ran employment office | 1923–64 | |
| Lester Washburn | May 30, 1986, May 27, 1988 | carpenter, export shipping, Reo Union | 1927–39 | Milwaukee, Wisconsin |

All interviews conducted by Lisa M. Fine and Shirley Bradley, except for Russell Alberts, by Shirley Bradley, and Lester Washburn, by Ken Germanson of Allied Industrial Workers of America.

[a] "Reo family" means that family members, but not the informant, worked for Reo.

TABLE 2. Number of Employees at the Reo Motor Car Company, Lansing, Michigan, 1905–1939

| Year | Number | Year | Number |
|------|--------|------|--------|
| 1905 | 437    | 1922 | 4,074  |
| 1906 | 559    | 1923 | 4,462  |
| 1907 | 705    | 1924 | 4,335  |
| 1908 | 603    | 1925 | 4,463  |
| 1909 | 832    | 1926 | 4,660  |
| 1910 | 1,024  | 1927 | 5,621  |
| 1911 | 538    | 1928 | 5,308  |
| 1912 | 1,835  | 1929 | 4,532  |
| 1913 | 1,865  | 1930 | 3,453  |
| 1914 | 2,534  | 1931 | 3,067  |
| 1915 | 3,819  | 1932 | 2,556  |
| 1916 | 4,123  | 1933 | 2,390  |
| 1917 | 5,399  | 1934 | 2,841  |
| 1918 | 4,378  | 1935 | 2,554  |
| 1919 | 3,855  | 1936 | 1,994  |
| 1920 | 4,711  | 1937 | 2,233  |
| 1921 | 3,928  | 1938 | 1,534  |

Figures for 1905–1908 from *Annual Reports of the Bureau of Labor and Industrial Statistics I* (Lansing: Wynkoop, Hallenbeck, Crawford Co., State Printers, 1906–1909). These are figures for all employees at the company.

Figures for 1909–1919 from *Annual Reports of the Department of Labor of the State of Michigan* (Lansing: Wynkoop, Hallenbeck, Crawford Co., State Printers, 1910–1920). These are figures for all employees at the company.

Figures for 1920–1939 from *Memorandum on Personnel Data* from Cy Rath, dated Jan. 10, 1939 (1939 figures added by hand). Reo Papers, box 73, folder 53. These are figures for employees on the factory payroll only.

TABLE 3. "Going to Farms"

| Year | Number of voluntary quits[a] | Number "going to farm" | Percentage "going to farm"[b] |
|---|---|---|---|
| 1918 | 4,045 | 272 | 6.7 |
| 1919 | 5,059 | 259 | 5.1 |
| 1920 | 5,435 | 527 | 9.7 |
| 1921 | 984 | 129 | 13.1 |
| 1922 | 1,212 | 67 | 5.5 |
| 1923 | 1,996 | 94 | 4.7 |
| 1924 | 885 | 68 | 7.7 |
| 1925 | 994 | 51 | 5.1 |
| 1926 | 947 | 61 | 6.4 |
| 1927 | 1,343 | 63 | 4.7 |
| 1928 | 2,276 | 75 | 3.3 |
| 1929 | 1,959 | 87 | 4.4 |
| 1930 | 871 | 66 | 7.6 |
| 1931 | 432 | 26 | 6.0 |
| 1932 | 106 | 12 | 11.3 |
| 1933 | 147 | 6 | 4.1 |
| 1934 | 363 | 14 | 3.9 |
| 1935 | 606 | 10 | 1.7 |
| 1936 | 467 | 14 | 3.0 |
| 1937 | 513 | 9 | 1.8 |
| 1938 | 105 | 3 | 2.9 |
| 1939 | 90 | 0 | 0 |

All information from "Annual Reports of Labor Department," 1918–1938, Reo Papers, box 66, folders 2–54.

[a]Voluntary quits include these categories: "better job in city," "better job out of city," "leaving the city," "dissatisfied with wages," "dissatisfied in other ways," "sickness and poor health," "can't make good on job," and "other." Some early labor reports provided even more categories. Voluntary quits do not include "no work, out of stock."

[b]Rounded to the nearest tenth.

TABLE 4. The Long Wildcat at Reo, 1942–1946

| Date | Where / reason | Duration | Number of workers | Com-mittee-man |
|---|---|---|---|---|
| Nov 1942 | 700 div. / piece rate | 2 hours | 10 | Williams, Bennett |
| Jan 7, 1943 | 700 div. / foreman discharge | 4 hours | 40 | Williams, Bennett |
| Jan 1943 | 700 div. / shift change | 8 weeks, off and on | 1,100 | Bennett |
| Mar 1943 | time clerks / rate increase | 4 hours | 20 | Bennett |
| Nov 1943 | motor plant / food machines, piece rates | 1 full shift | 16 | Lewis |
| Nov 1943 | 700 div. / discharge of employee due to too much scrap | 2 hours | 22 | Bennett, Reed |
| Feb 10, 1944 | motor plant / food machines, piece rates | 1 week, off and on | 75 | Lewis |
| Feb 28, 1944 | motor plant / tube line rates | 4 hours | 14 | Lewis |
| last week of Mar 1944[a] | 700 div. / automatics, rate adjustment | slowdown | 78 | |
| Mar 31, 1944[a] | 700 div. / automatics, rate adjustments | 3 hours | 26 | |
| Apr 1, 2, 3, 1944[a] | 700 div. / automatics, rate adjustments | sit-downs, several hours in each shift | | |
| May 1944 | 700 div. / shutter line rates | 2 hours | 14 | Bennett |
| May 1944 | 700 div. / Gisholt group time study | ½ hour | either 14 or 30 | Bennett |
| second week of June 1944[a] | 700 div. / automatics, rate adjustments | sit-down, 2 shifts at 2 hours each | 10 | |
| June 12, 1944[b] | lower gear carrier support group / results of time study | 2 hours | | Bennett |
| June 29, 1944 | 700 div. / head line, working conditions | 4 hours | 12 | Bennett |
| July 10, 1944 | 700 div. / automatics, two-machine operation | 8 hours | 16 | Bennett |
| July 23, 1944 | 700 div. / automatics and motor plants, piecework | 8 hours | 75 | Lewis |

(continued)

**TABLE 4** *(cont.)*

| Date | Where / reason | Duration | Number of workers | Com-mittee-man |
|------|----------------|----------|-------------------|----------------|
| July 31, 1944 | 700 div. / automatics, two-machine operation | 8 hours | 15 | Bennett |
| July 31, 1944*c* | 600 div. (navy) / no reason given | | 24 | |
| Aug 15, 1944 | Timken floor / change gate entrance | ½ hour | 150 | Lewis |
| Third week of Aug 1944*a* | 700 div. / automatics, piecework | 7 hours | 25 | |
| Second week of Sept 1944*a* | 700 div. / assembly, NWLB delay | 2½ hours | 60 | |
| Oct 7, 1944 | dept. 85 / gov't. inspection, working conditions | 2 hours | 150 | Deacon |
| Oct 18, 1944 | 700 div. / inspection, working conditions | 8 hours | 40 | Deacon |
| Oct 19, 1944 | 700 div. / sympathy with inspection | 8 hours | 300 | Bennett, Deacon |
| Oct 20, 1944 | dept. 85 / gov't. inspection, working conditions | 3 hours | 150 | Deacon |
| Nov 9, 1944 | 700 div. / assembly pay (5-cent increase from NWLB) | 1 hour | 75 | Bennett |
| Nov 10, 1944 | 700 div. / assembly pay (5-cent increase from NWLB) | 1 hour | 75 | Bennett |
| Dec 7, 1944 | dept. 20 / sheet metal superintendent appointment | 8 hours | 50 | Reed |
| Dec 10, 1944 | export dept. / wage increase | 2 weeks, off and on | 75 | Lewis |
| Jan 12, 1945 | truck line / overtime rate | 4 hours | 7 | Bennett |
| Jan 15, 1945*d* | axle machine dept. of Timken div. / waiting for conciliatory service to do time study | | | |
| Jan 22, 1945*d* | same as above | | | |
| Jan 24, 1945*d* | same as above | | | |

*(continued)*

TABLE 4  *(cont.)*

| Date | Where / reason | Duration | Number of workers | Com-mittee-man |
|------|---------------|----------|-------------------|----------------|
| Jan 20, 1945 | transmission / working conditions | 8 hours | 3 | Lewis |
| Feb 19, 1945 | truck line / working conditions | 2 hours | 4 | Bennett |
| July 16, 1945 | 700 div. / automatics, rates | 1 hour | 14 | O'Brien |
| July 25, 1945 | paint line / foreman appointment | 8 hours | 600 | Bennett |
| July 25, 1945 | 700 div. / automatics, methods of pay | 3 hours | 41 | O'Brien |
| Aug 3, 1945 | motor plant / dept. 35 rate adjustment | 1 hour | 60 | Lewis |
| Mar 20, 1946 | cab line, dept. 15 / rates | 2 hours | 50 | Bennett |
| Apr 22, 1946[e] | lawnmower dept. / rate cutting | A.M. | | |
| Apr 23, 1946[e] | same as above | A.M. | | |
| July 19, 1946 | export dept. 22 / rates | 8½ hours | 18 | Lewis, Keeney |
| Sept 16, 1946 | cab line, dept. 15 / selection of supervision | 8 hours | 70 | Roosa, Keeney |
| Sept 16, 1946 | entire plant / unauthorized strike | 8 hours | 2,334 | full com-mittee |

NWLB, National War Labor Board.

Except as noted otherwise, information from "Report on Strikes and Work Stoppages from 1941–1946, Exhibit 1-A" (exhibit prepared by Reo for an NLRB hearing of 1949), Reo Papers, box 54, folder 6, MSU Archives and Historical Collections.

[a]From one of two sheets that go together regarding work stoppages in 1944. See "Work Stoppages in 1944," Jan. 4, 1945, and the list following this sheet, Reo Papers, box 69 folder 41.

[b]From office memorandum, Walter E. Foust to Mr. Hund, June 12, 1944, Reo Papers, box 67, folder 40.

[c]From Reo Papers, box 67, folder 61.

[d]From Reo Papers, box 69, folder 55.

[e]From Union-Management Committee Meeting, April 23, 1946, Reo Papers, box 67, folder 70, and UAW Local 650 Papers, box 7, Reuther Library.

TABLE 5. Participants in the 1946 Wildcat Issued Disciplinary Warnings

| Name | Hired | Age | Veteran |
|------|-------|-----|---------|
| Wm. Bickard | July 22, 1943 | 23 | yes |
| Gerald Ohmer | July 10, 1946 | 20 | yes |
| Leon Spencer | Apr 12, 1942 | 29 | no |
| Eugene Alward | July 10, 1946 | 22 | yes |
| Richard Edding | Jan 12, 1942 | 43 | no |
| Jerry Rabbage | Nov 13, 1941 | 23 | yes |
| Carl Sitts | May 27, 1942 | 38 | yes |
| Neal Dasbon (or Darbin) | Apr 27, 1942 | 26 | yes |
| F. Neal | July 9, 1946 | 22 | yes |
| R. Harris | June 7, 1944 | 24 | no |
| G. Nicholas [Nicholos] | Jan 27, 1942 | 24 | yes |
| H. Loudenslager | July 22, 1942 | 27 | yes |
| G. Hopp | Apr 25, 1942 | 25 | yes |
| K. Gilbert | Apr 21, 1942 | 25 | yes |
| H. Joy | May 23, 1942 | 23 | yes |
| R. Seidlitz | Aug 6, 1943 | 21 | yes |
| L. Heilman | Aug 14, 1946 | 25 | yes |
| John Frye | Nov 22, 1943 | 43 | no |
| R. Reed | June 27, 1946 | 27 | yes |
| C. Richard | July 2, 1946 | 23 | yes |
| G. Heilman | Aug 14, 1946 | 25 | yes |
| R. Pfuhl | July 1, 1942 | 22 | yes |
| J. Watson | no information | | |
| D. LaPratt | July 28, 1941 | 25 | no |

Attachment to letter from Reo Motors Management (probably from Gerald Byrne or Henry Hund) to J. A. Salter, chairman of Local 650 Bargaining Committee Reo Papers, box 68, folder 20, MSU Archives and Historical Collections. The letter stated, "We are attaching hereto list of the Reo employees to whom disciplinary warnings are being issued who participated but only those who were positively identified. It seems that the larger part of members who took part in this type of activity were comparatively new employees. As a matter of fact, the average length of employment with Reo of over 80% of them is less than five months and we believe that this accounts for the fact that they allowed themselves to be used by unscrupulous leaders."

TABLE 6.  Military Contracts Awarded to Lansing Division of White Motors
Announced in Newspapers

| Year | Amount (in millions of dollars, rounded to nearest tenth) |
|---|---|
| 1960 | 13.5[a] |
| 1961 | 22.0 |
|  | 1.4[b] |
|  | 8.3[c] |
| 1962 | 7.0[d] |
| 1963 | 12.3[e] |
| 1964 | — |
| 1965 | 1.2[f] |
| 1966 | 10.0[g] |
| 1967 | 10.4[h] |
|  | 9.8[i] |
|  | 18.3[j] |
| 1968 | 5.8[k] |
| 1969 | 3.5[l] |

[a] "Reo Awarded Large Army Truck Contract," *Lansing Labor News*, July 7, 1960, 1.

[b] "White Motor Unit Contract," *Wall Street Journal*, July 5, 1961, 3.

[c] "Pentagon Awards Over $120 Million in Defense Orders," *Wall Street Journal*, Nov. 9, 1961, 7.

[d] "Pentagon Awarded More Than $236.2 Million in Defense Contracts," *Wall Street Journal*, Jan. 2, 1962.

[e] "Army Gives White Motor $12,278,464 Truck Order," *Wall Street Journal*, May 6, 1963, 8.

[f] "Defense Contract," *Wall Street Journal*, March 4, 1965, 7.

[g] *Wall Street Journal*, May 10, 1966, 17.

[h] "Army Gives White Motors a $10,433,090 Truck Job," *Wall Street Journal*, March 15, 1967, 5.

[i] "White Motor Gets $9,844,869 Army Contract for Trucks," *Wall Street Journal*, June 9, 1967, 9.

[j] "Pentagon Awards $575 Million Jobs as Fiscal '67 Year Ends," *Wall Street Journal*, July 3, 1967, 2.

[k] "Borg Warner Division Gets $6 Million Navy Bomb Order," *Wall Street Journal*, May 23, 1968, 3.

[l] "Air Forces Gives TRW Satellite Work Valued at Up to $37.7 Million," *Wall Street Journal*, March 4, 1969, 16.

TABLE 7. Percentage of Nonwhite[a] Population in Michigan and Selected Cities in Michigan, 1950, 1960, and 1970

| Place | 1950[b] | 1960[c] | 1970[d] |
|---|---|---|---|
| Michigan | 7.1 | 9.4 | 11.7 |
| Detroit | 16.4 | 29.2 | 44.5 |
| Flint | 8.6 | 17.7 | 28.6 |
| Pontiac | 9.5 | 17.0 | 27.5 |
| Saginaw | 9.3 | 17.0 | 25.0 |
| Grand Rapids | 3.9 | 8.3 | 12.0 |
| Kalamazoo | 4.4 | 6.7 | 10.6 |
| Lansing | 3.3 | 6.5 | 10.1 |

[a]Nonwhite in all three censuses included Negroes, Indians, Japanese, Chinese, and other Asian nationalities. It did not include Mexican-born inhabitants or people of Mexican descent or other Hispanics.

[b]U.S. Bureau of the Census, *Census of the Population: 1950; A Report of the Seventeenth Decennial Census of the United States*, vol. 2, *Characteristics of the Population* (Part 22: Michigan) (Washington, D.C.: U.S. Government Printing Office, 1952).

[c]U.S. Bureau of the Census, *Population: 1960*, vol. 1, *Characteristics of the Population* (Part 22: Michigan) (Washington, D.C.: U.S. Government Printing Office, 1963).

[d]U.S. Bureau of the Census, *Nineteenth Census, 1970*, vol. 1, *Characteristics of the Population* (Part 24: Michigan) (Washington, D.C.: U.S. Government Printing Office, 1973).

# Notes

## Introduction

1. J. R. Connor, "They Call Him 'Reo Joe,'" *Lansing Industrial News*, Oct. 20, 1939, 1.

2. Ibid.

3. Ibid.

4. Ibid.

5. Ely Chinoy, *Automobile Workers and the American Dream*, 2d ed., ed. Ruth Milkman (Urbana: University of Illinois Press, 1992), 1, 24, 25.

6. Joan Wallach Scott, "Gender: A Useful Category of Historical Analysis," in Joan Wallach Scott, *Gender and the Politics of History* (New York: Columbia University Press, 1988). On how to apply this to U.S. labor history, see Ava Baron, "Gender and Labor History: Learning from the Past, Looking to the Future" in *Work Engendered: Toward a New History of American Labor,* ed. Ava Baron (Ithaca: Cornell University Press, 1991).

7. Richard Oestreicher, "Separate Tribes? Working-Class and Women's History," *Reviews in American History* 19 (June 1991): 228.

8. Nick Salvatore's *Eugene V. Debs: Citizen and Socialist* (Urbana: University of Illinois Press, 1982), and David Montgomery's *The Fall of the House of Labor: The Workplace, the State, and American Labor Activism, 1865–1925* (New York: Cambridge University Press, 1987) were among the first works to analyze ideas of masculinity in working-class culture.

9. Malcolm X, with Alex Haley, *The Autobiography of Malcolm X* (New York: Grove Press, 1964), 5.

10. Peter Goldman, *The Death and Life of Malcolm X* (New York: Harper and Row, 1973), 26–28.

11. See Thomas Sugrue, *The Origins of the Urban Crisis: Race and Inequality in Postwar Detroit* (Princeton: Princeton University Press, 1996).

12. Michelle Brattain, *The Politics of Whiteness: Race, Workers, and Culture in the Modern South* (Princeton: Princeton University Press, 2001), 4. See "Scholarly Controversy: Whiteness and the Historians' Imagination," *International Labor and Working-Class History* 60 (fall 2001), with contributions by Eric Arnesen, James R. Barrett, David Brody, Barbara J. Fields, Eric Foner, Victoria C. Hattam, and Adoph Reed Jr. I first began thinking about the concept of whiteness after reading David Roediger's *The Wages of*

*Whiteness: Race and the Making of the American Working Class* (London: Verso, 1991). I have also found very helpful Kevin Boyle, "The Kiss: Racial and Gender Conflict in a 1950s Automobile Factory," *Journal of American History* 84 (Sept. 1997): 496–523.

13. This is a reference to Lizabeth Cohen's *Making a New Deal: Industrial Workers in Chicago, 1919–1939* (New York: Cambridge University Press, 1990), 324.

14. See Alan Brinkley, *Voices of Protest: Huey Long, Father Coughlin, and the Great Depression* (New York: Random House, 1983), and Michael Kazin, *The Populist Persuasion: An American History* (New York: Basic Books, 1995) on the importance of local orientation and assertions of local control in the face of national, bureaucratic, and cosmopolitan influences in twentieth-century life.

15. See Howard Kimeldorf, *Battling for American Labor: Wobblies, Craft Workers, and the Making of the Union Movement* (Berkeley and Los Angeles: University of California Press, 1999.) I would like to thank Rick Halpern for this reference and for all of his help on this issue.

16. "The Family Spirit Never Leaves," *Lansing State Journal*, Aug. 14, 1991, 2C.

17. Scott, *Gender and the Politics of History*, 44.

18. See, for example, Eugene D. Genovese, *Roll, Jordan, Roll: The World the Slaves Made* (New York: Vintage Books, 1976,), and Mary Beth Norton, *Founding Mothers and Fathers: Gendered Power and the Forming of American Society* (New York: Knopf, 1996) for two very different works that employ this type of analysis.

19. Jacquelyn Dowd Hall et al., *Like a Family: The Making of a Southern Cotton Mill World* (Chapel Hill: University of North Carolina Press, 1987), xvii.

20. Ronald Edsforth, *Class Conflict and Cultural Consensus: The Making of a Mass Consumer Society in Flint, Michigan* (New Brunswick: Rutgers University Press, 1987), 216. See also Cohen, *Making a New Deal*; Gary Gerstle, *Working-Class Americanism: The Politics of Labor in a Textile City, 1914–1960* (New York: Cambridge University Press, 1989); Elizabeth Faue, *Community of Suffering and Struggle: Women, Men, and the Labor Movement in Minneapolis, 1915–1945* (Chapel Hill: University of North Carolina Press, 1991); Steve Fraser and Gary Gerstle, eds., *The Rise and Fall of the New Deal Order, 1930–1980* (Princeton: Princeton University Press, 1989).

21. The three counties in which Reo employees lived, Clinton, Eaton, and Ingham (Lansing's county), voted overwhelmingly Republican in presidential elections except in 1932 and 1936 (FDR), 1960 (Kennedy by a slim margin), and 1964 (Johnson). Ingham County went for Clinton in 1992 and 1996 and for Gore in 2000. See John P. White, *Michigan Votes: Election Statistics, 1928–1956*, (Papers in Public Administration No. 24, Bureau of Government, Institute of Public Administration, University of Michigan, 1958), and *Official Canvass of Votes*, comp. Michigan Secretary of State (Lansing, 1952, 1956, 1960, 1964, 1968, 1972, 1976).

22. See, for example, Nancy MacLean, *Behind the Mask of Chivalry: The Making of the Second Ku Klux Klan* (New York: Oxford University Press, 1994). Recent works have established the impact of national labor organizations on the liberal politics of the postwar period. Although this is a worthwhile endeavor, it is no substitute for an exploration of local working-class constituencies. See Kevin Boyle, ed., *Organized Labor and American Politics, 1894–1994, The Labor-Liberal Alliance* (Albany: SUNY Press, 1998).

23. Nelson Lichtenstein, *State of the Union: A Century of American Labor* (Princeton: Princeton University Press, 2002), 192.

24. Kathleen Lavey, "GM a 'Family Operation,'" *Lansing State Journal*, Jan. 8, 2002, 1.

25. Norma Grimwood, interview by author and Shirley Bradley, Lansing, March 26, 1992. There is also information on the Leyrer family in the 1920 Lansing Census and in an obituary that appeared in *Reo Items*, July 1948, 8, Reo Papers, box 52, folder 56, Michigan State University Archives and Historical Collections (hereafter MSUAHC).

26. Grimwood, interview.

27. Layton Aves, interview by author and Shirley Bradley, Lansing, Aug. 8, 1995.

28. Otto (Ted) Aves, interview by author and Shirley Bradley, Lansing, Jan. 4, 1993.

29. Glen Green, interview by author and Shirley Bradley, Lansing, Jan. 22, 1992.

30. Green, interview.

31. Ibid.

32. Adolph and Caroline Janetzke appeared in the 1910 Lansing Census. At this point their household included five-year-old Matilda, four-year-old Henry, two-year-old Ernest, and Adolph's eighteen-year-old-brother, Jacob, who had recently immigrated from the same community in Poland and who was also working at Reo. Shirley Bradley and I interviewed a Janetzke son born after 1910, Harold Janetzke, and his wife Eileen, who also worked at Reo. Eileen and Harold Janetzke, interview by author and Shirley Bradley, Lansing, Feb. 26, 1992. See also Harold Janetzke's obituary, *Lansing State Journal*, Dec. 6, 2000, 7D.

33. Janetzkes, interview.

34. Ibid.

35. Ibid.; "Edgar A. Guest: Guest of Reo," *Reo Items*, April 1948, 3, Reo Papers, box 52, folder 52, MSUAHC.

36. Biographical information on Edgar A. Guest from Royce Howes, *Edgar A. Guest: A Biography* (Chicago: Reilly and Lee Co., 1953); "Edgar A. Guest," in *Current Biography, 1941* (New York: H. W. Wilson Co., 1941), 354–55; "Edgar A. Guest, Poet Dead at 77," *New York Times*, Aug. 6, 1959, 27; Edgar A. Guest, *My Job as a Father and What My Father Did for Me* (Chicago: Reilly and Lee Co., 1923).

37. "Edgar A. Guest," *New York Times*, Aug. 6, 1959; "Edgar A. Guest," *Current Biography, 1941*, 354.

38. Edgar A. Guest, *Mother* (Chicago: Reilly and Lee Co., 1925). This collection contains poems such as "Unchangeable Mother" and "Ma and the Auto." See also Edgar Guest, *Faith* (Chicago: Reilly and Lee Co., 1932). Edgar Guest is also described as Middletown's favorite poet in Robert S. Lynd and Helen Merrell Lynd, *Middletown: A Study in American Culture* (New York: Harcourt, Brace and World, 1929), 238.

## Chapter One

1. Charles M. Killam to Charles Davis, Dec. 3, 1924, Papers of the Lansing Chamber of Commerce (hereafter LCC Papers), box 11, folder 1, State Archives of Michigan (hereafter SAM).

2. Since the groundbreaking work of E. P. Thompson, U.S. labor historians have taken as axiomatic that the Industrial Revolution involved the transition from rural/organic conceptions of time and work to routinized industrial discipline. See, for example, Gunther Paul Barth, *City People: The Rise of Modern City Culture in Nineteenth-Century*

*America* (New York: Oxford University Press, 1980); Daniel Nelson, *Farm and Factory: Workers in the Midwest, 1880–1990* (Bloomington: Indiana University Press, 1995); Jon Teaford, *Cities of the Heartland: The Rise and Fall of the Industrial Midwest* (Bloomington: Indiana University Press, 1993); Peter Laslett, *The World We Have Lost: England before the Industrial Age* (New York: Scribners, 1971); E. P. Thompson, *The Making of the English Working Class* (New York: Vintage Books, 1963); E. P. Thompson, "Time, Work-Discipline, and Industrial Capitalism," *Past and Present* 38 (1967): 56–97; Gerd Korman, *Industrialization, Immigrants, and Americanization: The View from Milwaukee* (Madison: University of Wisconsin Press, 1967); Alan Dawley, *Class and Community: The Industrial Revolution in Lynn* (Cambridge: Harvard University Press, 1976); Herbert G. Gutman, *Work, Culture, and Society in Industrializing America* (New York: Vintage Books, 1977); Daniel T. Rodgers, *The Work Ethic In Industrial America, 1850–1920* (Chicago: University of Chicago Press, 1978). Recently many U.S. labor historians have revised how we understand the transition from rural, pre-industrial, organic notions of time to industrial, rationalized time discipline in a way that captures the fluidity and the blurring of boundaries between city and country, farm and factory, industrial and rural so characteristic of Lansing at this moment. One of the best examples is Jacquelyn Dowd Hall et al., *Like A Family: The Making of a Southern Cotton Mill World* (Chapel Hill: University of North Carolina Press, 1987).

3. See Olivier Zunz, *The Changing Face of Inequality: Urbanization, Industrial Development and Immigrants in Detroit, 1880–1920* (Chicago: University of Chicago Press, 1982), and Donald Finlay Davis, *Conspicuous Production: Automobiles and Elites in Detroit, 1899–1933* (Philadelphia: Temple University Press, 1988).

4. See Birt Darling, *City in the Forest: The Story of Lansing* (New York: Stratford House, 1950): "Economically, there was no reason whatever for a city to be planned and built on the site of Lansing. It did not have such natural advantages as the waterway at Grand Rapids; the magnificent black loam farmland of Kalamazoo, or the obvious transportation cross-roads location of Jackson and Marshall," 11–12.

5. There is comparatively little scholarly work on Lansing's history. The best work is Justin L. Kestenbaum, *Out of a Wilderness: An Illustrated History of Greater Lansing* (Woodland Hills, Calif.: Windsor Publications, 1981). Other, less reliable works are Sallie M. Manassah, David A. Thomas, and James F. Wallington, *Lansing: Capital, Campus, and Cars* (East Lansing: Contemporary Image, 1986), a work sponsored by the Lansing Chamber of Commerce, and Darling, *City in the Forest*.

6. See Kestenbaum, *Out of a Wilderness*, 63, and Manassah et al., *Lansing*, 19.

7. Kestenbaum, *Out of a Wilderness*, 24.

8. Ibid., 22.

9. See, for example, *Lansing Illustrated* (New York: International Publishers Co., 1888); *Lansing Illustrated* (Coldwater, Mich.: J. S. Conover, 1889).

10. Local historians often note the similarity of place names in Ingham county and upstate New York and New England.

11. See Nelson, *Farm and Factory*, chap. 1; Lew Allen Chase, *Rural Michigan* (New York: Macmillan, 1922); Jeremy Atack and Fred Bateman, "Yankee Farming and Settlement in the Old Northwest: A Comparative Analysis," 77–102, and William N. Parker, "Native Origins of Modern Industry: Heavy Industrialization in the Old

Northwest before 1900," 243–74, both in *Essays on The Economy of the Old Northwest*, ed. David C. Klingaman and Richard K. Vedder (Athens: Ohio University Press, 1987); William N. Parker, "From Northwest to Mid-West: Social Bases of a Regional History," in *Essays in Nineteenth Century Economic History: The Old Northwest*, ed. David C. Klingaman and Richard K. Vedder, 3–35 (Athens: Ohio University Press, 1975); C. Warren Vander Hill, *Settling the Great Lakes Frontier: Immigration to Michigan, 1837–1924* (Lansing: Michigan Historical Commission, 1970); Jeremy W. Kilar, *Germans in Michigan* (East Lansing: MSU Press, 2002); Marcus Lee Hansen, *The Mingling of the Canadian and American Peoples*, vol. 1 (New Haven: Yale University Press, 1940), 215; Sidney Glazer, "Labor and Agrarian Movements in Michigan, 1876–1896," Ph.D. diss., University of Michigan, 1932; Sidney Glazer, "The Rural Community in the Urban Age: Changes in Michigan since 1900," *Agricultural History* 23 (April 1949): 130–34; Sidney Glazer, "Patrons of Industry in Michigan," *Mississippi Valley Historical Review* 24 (Sept. 1937): 185–94; Fred Trump, *The Grange in Michigan: An Agricultural History of Michigan over the Past 90 Years* (Grand Rapids: Dean Hicks, Co., 1963).

12. The best work on Olds is George S. May, *R. E. Olds: Auto Industry Pioneer* (Grand Rapids: Eerdmanns Publishing Co., 1977). See also Glenn A. Niemeyer, *The Automotive Career of Ransom E. Olds* (East Lansing: Bureau of Business and Economic Research, Graduate School of Business Administration, Michigan State University, 1963), and Duane Yarnell, *Auto Pioneering: A Remarkable Story of Ransom E. Olds, Father of Oldsmobile and Reo* (Lansing: Franklin DeKleine, 1949). Yarnell's biography was commissioned by Olds himself, and he owned the copyright.

13. May, *R. E. Olds*, 68, 80–81.

14. Charles Franklin Kettering and Allen Orth, *American Battle for Abundance: A Story of Mass Production* (Detroit: GM, 1948), 50–54.

15. Yarnell, *Ransom E. Olds*, 83–84.

16. Ibid., 84–85.

17. Ibid., 89.

18. May, *R. E. Olds*, 152–58.

19. See David Gartman, *Auto Slavery: The Labor Process in the American Automobile Industry, 1897–1950* (New Brunswick: Rutgers University Press, 1986), chap. 2, esp. 21–22.

20. See "The Art of Cutting Metal," in David Montgomery, *The Fall of the House of Labor: The Workplace, the State, and American Labor Activism, 1865–1925* (New York: Cambridge University Press, 1987), 171–213.

21. "Thirty Men Quit," *Lansing Journal*, April 1, 1898, 1.

22. Ibid.

23. Yarnell, who got his facts from Ransom, put a different spin on this story and attributed Ransom's decision to leave Lansing in part to these labor/family troubles. He also claimed that Ransom felt he was not fully appreciated by the city. *Ransom E. Olds*, 65–75. See also Niemeyer, *Ransom E. Olds*, 21.

24. According to a report in the *Lansing Journal* (Feb. 19, 1898, 1), Ransom had already been receiving offers from other cities for the relocation of his factory before the April strike.

25. Montgomery, *Fall of the House of Labor*, 259–69.

26. The running account of these events appeared in the *Detroit Free Press* on May 18, 19, 20, 21, 23, 24, 25, 26, June 1, 5, 7, 14, 15, 26, 1901.

27. May, *R. E. Olds*, 200–203.

28. May describes this incident in great detail. The letters between Olds and Smith are in the R. E. Olds Collection, MSUAHC.

29. May, *R. E. Olds*, 261–85.

30. Yarnell, May, and Niemeyer all describe these events similarly and in detail.

31. "The Chamber of Commerce and its Relation to the City," (1912), LCC Papers, box 1, folder 11, SAM.

32. Lansing Chamber of Commerce, *Lansing, Michigan: A Progressive American City* (Lansing: Dick Short and Co., 1926), 5; Lee Papers, box 19, folder 26, SAM.

33. "Diary of the Secretary," Feb. 18–25, 1921, and May 10, 1924, LCC Papers, box 7, SAM.

34. *Report of the 26th Annual Convention of the Michigan Federation of Labor,* Sept. 21–25, 1915, Traverse City, Michigan, 45.

35. Manufacturers' and Jobbers' Club, June 4, 1912, LCC Papers, box 4, folder 5, SAM. "The demand made by the strikers when sifted down to bare facts consisted mostly of the recognition of the shop committee and the unionizing of the foundry."

36. "Molders Sued by Seagers," *Lansing State Journal,* July 6, 1912, 10; "Five Molders Are Arrested," ibid., July 10, 1912, 7.

37. "Chamber of Commerce Now Has 900 Members," *Lansing State Journal,* June 5, 1912, 1; "Molders' Strike to Be Investigated," ibid., June 5, 1912, 1; "Striking Molders Parade Street," ibid., July 11, 1912, 10.

38. "Striking Molder Is Sentenced," ibid., July 24, 1912, 7.

39. "Manufacturers Take Firm Stand," ibid., June 26, 1912, 10.

40. "Manufacturers' and Jobbers' Club, July 29, 1912, LCC Papers, box 4, folder 12, SAM.

41. C. A. Henry, general superintendent, Seager Engine Works (formerly Olds Gas Power Co.) to F. H. Stambaugh, Lansing Commercial Club, n.d. [1912], Manufacturers' and Jobbers' Club (1911–1912), LCC Papers, box 4, folder 12, SAM.

42. Manufacturers' and Jobbers' Club, Jan. 9, 1913, and Chamber of Commerce, "Information Sheet," May 10, 1919, LCC Papers, box 5, folder 11, SAM.

43. President Carl Young of the Michigan Federation of Labor stated, "A meeting was advertised at which I was to speak by invitation or solicitation and one of the men, who was a Trade Unionist working in a certain plant in the city, during the noon hour on the streets handed out some little hand bills announcing the meeting. We had a real good meeting that night, but the next that Brother didn't have a job. He was out. I know and I feel that *there is a system in vogue that means a black list,* in my opinion, of unequal proportions to any city in the State of Michigan that exists here" (emphasis added). *Proceedings of the 30th Annual Convention of the Michigan Federation of Labor,* Lansing, Sept. 16–19, 1919, 6.

44. Cy Rath, director of personnel to Mr. Lauzun, factory superintendent, Oct. 24, 1918, Re: #1577 Harry J. Marion by Foreman Gardner, Reo Papers, box 67, folder 54, MSUAHC.

45. "Lansing Report: Report of Organizer Dickerson," *Auto Worker,* Sept. 1919, 13.

46. Report from Charles E. Dickerson, general organizer, *Convention Proceedings of the 6th Biennial Convention*, held by the United Automobile, Aircraft, and Vehicle Workers of America, Cleveland, Sept. 13–19, 1920, 12.

47. "Resolution," Nov. 2, 1915, LCC Papers, box 1, folder 11, SAM.

48. Letter from the Ingham County Local Option Committee, Feb. 26, 1912, LCC Papers, box 1, folder 16, SAM.

49. *The New Republic* (special Lansing edition): Westerville, Ohio, March 24, 1916, LCC Papers, box 20, folder 13, SAM.

50. Kestenbaum, *Out of a Wilderness*, 84, 86.

51. *Proceedings of the 28th Annual Convention of the Michigan Federation of Labor*, Grand Haven, Michigan, Sept. 18–22, 1917, 19.

52. "Diary of the Secretary," July 7, 1923 and June 7, 1924, LCC Papers, box 7, SAM.

53. "Resolution No. 16," *Proceedings of the 18th Annual Convention of the Michigan Federation of Labor*, Detroit, Sept. 17–20, 1907, 13.

54. See Mark C. Carnes and Clyde Griffen, eds., *Meanings for Manhood: Constructions of Masculinity in Victorian America* (Chicago: Chicago University Press, 1990); Mark C. Carnes, *Secret Ritual and Manhood in Victorian America* (New Haven: Yale University Press, 1989); Mary Ann Clawson, *Constructing Brotherhood: Class, Gender, and Fraternalism* (Princeton: Princeton University Press, 1989).

55. "Greater Lansing 1859–1906," Lansing Journal, 1906, 10. See also the *Chilson and McKinley's Lansing City Directory*, 1911 (Lansing: Wynkoop Hallenbeck Crawford Co., 1911), 9–12, which lists more than forty-one local fraternal orders, ten of them women's auxiliaries and one a "colored" Masonic Lodge.

56. *Lansing Masonic Directory, 1909*, Lansing Local History Collection, Lansing Public Library (hereafter LLHC).

57. *Lansing City Directory*, 1912.

58. *Lansing Lodge #196, B.P.O.E. Elks, Dedication and Diamond Jubilee, 1891–1966*, Jan. 25–28, 1967, souvenir program, LLHC.

59. The Lynds, in their examination of Muncie, Indiana, noted that the lodges had become more inclusive of members of the working class during the early twentieth century. See Lynd and Lynd, *Middletown*, 306.

60. *Report of the Proceedings of the 15th Annual Convention of the Michigan Federation of Labor*, Jackson, Michigan, Sept. 20–23, 1904, 49.

61. *Proceedings of the 25th Annual Convention of the Michigan Federation of Labor*, Lansing, Sept. 15–18, 1914, 3.

62. Ezra B. Breithaupt, *The History of the Young Men's Christian Association of Lansing, Michigan: 1877–1977* (Lansing: YMCA, n.d.), 3–7; "Foreman's Club Has a Unique Place," *Lansing State Journal*, Jan. 2, 1928, 14.

63. "Industrial Department of the YMCA Unique," *Lansing State Journal*, Jan. 1, 1925, 6.

64. The nationalities specifically mentioned were Syrians, Phoenicians, and Scottish. See "The Young Womens' Christian Association of Lansing, MI," Sept. 1927, and "YWCA—50th Anniversary," Feb. 6, 1939, Pamphlets—Organizations—YWCA, LLHC.

65. "History of Central United Methodist Church, 1850–1976," 8–9, and "Weekly Calendar" (Sunday, April 18, 1915), Pamphlets—Religion—Central United Methodists, LLHC.

66. Frederick C. Aldinger, "History of the Lansing Public Schools, 1847–1944," 12, LLHC.

67. The 1910 Manuscript Census names came from the 1910 Lansing City Directory.

68. Of the 176 Reo workers identified who were not male heads of household, 88 were boarders (unrelated to the head of household), and 48 (the next-largest number) were sons. There were 11 daughters.

69. See David Jacobson, "Lansing's Jewish Community," manuscript, n.d. but probably 1970s, 9, Pamphlets—Religion—Jews, LLHC.

70. Mildred Alspaugh, interview by author and Shirley Bradley, Lansing, Feb. 25, 1992.

71. The 1920 Lansing City Directory, in addition to providing street addresses, also indicated whether a person worked at Reo.

72. In 1921 R. E. Olds lived at 720 South Washington, R. H. Scott lived at 109 W. Main, Donald Bates lived at 720 Seymour Street, H. Thomas lived at 114 S. Walnut, Cy Rath lived at 140 Garden Street, and Harry Teel lived at 210 E. Mount Hope Road.

73. *Proceedings of the 30th Annual Convention of the Michigan Federation of Labor*, Lansing, Sept. 16–19, 1919, 4–7.

## Chapter Two

*Epigraph:* Edgar A. Guest, "The Workman's Dream," in Edgar A. Guest, *All That Matters* (Chicago: Reilly and Lee Co., 1922), 74–75.

1. Antonio Gramsci, *Selections from the Prison Notebooks of Antonio Gramsci*, ed. and trans. Quintin Hoare and Geoffrey Nowell Smith (New York: International Publishers, 1971), 285.

2. Gramsci quoted in David Harvey, *The Condition of Postmodernity* (Cambridge: Blackwell, 1989), 126.

3. Kenneth Park, "Here and There with the Editor," *Reo Spirit,* June 1920, Reo Papers, box 53, folder 2, MSUAHC.

4. Duane Yarnell, *Auto Pioneering: A Remarkable Story of Ransom E. Olds, Father of Oldsmobile and Reo* (Lansing: Franklin DeKleine, 1949), 200–201.

5. Ransom E. Olds to Charles Warren of the Union Trust, Oct. 14, 1912, Detroit, R. E. Olds Papers, box 1, folder 11, MSUAHC.

6. Ransom E. Olds to Mayor J. G. Reutter, Nov. 18, 1912, R. E. Olds Papers, box 1, folder 12, MSUAHC.

7. Alfred E. Brose, "Trend of Industrial and Municipal Recreation in the Lansing Community," master's thesis, Michigan State University, 1934, not only claimed that Reo "has carried on a more extensive recreation program than any of the other industries," but also that these programs were key to the creation and success of municipal recreation in the city, 33, 107–16.

8. Laurence Veiller to Smith Young, May 10, 1916, Lansing, R. E. Olds Papers, box 9, folder 9, MSUAHC. Conservative Progressive Laurence Veiller is described by

Daniel T. Rodgers in *Atlantic Crossings: Social Politics in a Progressive Age* (Cambridge: Harvard University Press, 1998), 194.

9. "Sagamore Hill Land Company," Dec. 24, 1924, Reo Papers, box 53, folder 7, MSUAHC.

10. Ransom E. Olds to James G. Cannon, president of Men and Religion Forward Movement, May 6, 1912, New York, R. E. Olds Papers, box 1, folder 9, MSUAHC.

11. Ibid., box 9, folders 7–20.

12. Ibid., box 9, folders 15 and 19.

13. *"Oldsmar: For Health, Wealth, Happiness,"* Publicity Brochure, n.d., R. E. Olds Papers, box 9, folder 22, MSUAHC.

14. Glenn A. Niemeyer, *The Automotive Career of Ransom E. Olds* (East Lansing: Bureau of Business and Economic Research, Graduate School of Business Administration, Michigan State University, 1963), 118. The edifying effects of the environment and the arrangement of the community would benefit the working class as well as the developers. Fred Cook of Detroit, who as president of the Reo Farms Company worked closely with Olds on the development of the property, apparently consulted with Reverend J. Sparks of the American Baptist Publication Society in 1916 on Olds's suggestion. See Walter J. Sparks, reverend and special representative of the American Baptist Publication Society, to Ransom E. Olds, Oct. 18, 1916, R. E. Olds Papers, box 9, folder 10, MSUAHC.

15. See Lisa M. Fine, "'Our Big Factory Family': Masculinity and Paternalism at the Reo Motor Car Company of Lansing, Michigan," *Labor History* 34 (spring–summer 1993): 274–91.

16. Irving Bernstein, *The Lean Years: A History of the American Worker, 1920–1933* (Boston: Houghton Mifflin, 1960), and *The Turbulent Years: A History of the American Worker, 1933–1941* (Boston: Houghton Mifflin, 1970).

17. Gerald Zahavi, *Workers, Managers, and Welfare Capitalism: The Shoeworkers and Tanners of Endicott Johnson, 1890–1950* (Urbana: University of Illinois Press, 1988); Gerald Zahavi, "Negotiated Loyalty: Welfare Capitalism and the Shoeworkers of Endicott Johnson, 1920–1940," *Journal of American History* 70 (1983): 602; Lizabeth Cohen, *Making a New Deal: Industrial Workers in Chicago, 1919–1939* (New York: Cambridge University Press, 1990), chap. 4. On the welfare capitalism program at Reo, see Peter Iversen Berg, "Welfare Capitalism at the Reo Motor Car Company," *Michigan History* 69 (Nov.–Dec. 1985): 37. On welfare capitalism generally, see David Brody's chapter on "The Rise and Decline of Welfare Capitalism," in *Workers in Industrial America: Essays on the 20th-Century Struggle* (New York: Oxford University Press, 1980); Stuart D. Brandes, *American Welfare Capitalism: 1880–1940* (Chicago: University of Chicago, 1976); Daniel M. G. Raff, "Ford Welfare Capitalism and Its Economic Context," in *Masters to Managers: Historical and Comparative Perspectives on American Employers*, ed. Sanford Jacoby (New York: Columbia University Press, 1991). Most helpful are Andrea Tone, *The Business of Benevolence: Industrial Paternalism in Progressive America* (Ithaca: Cornell University Press, 1997), and Sanford Jacoby, *Modern Manors: Welfare Capitalism since the New Deal* (Princeton: Princeton University Press, 1997).

18. Cohen, *Making a New Deal*; Ronald Edsforth, *Class Conflict and Cultural Consensus: The Making of a Mass Consumer Society in Flint, Michigan* (New Brunswick: Rutgers University Press, 1987).

19. See, for example, Jacquelyn Dowd Hall, et al., *Like a Family: The Making of a Southern Cotton Mill World* (Chapel Hill: University of North Carolina Press, 1987). For a different perspective, see Nikki Mandell, *The Corporation as Family: The Gendering of Corporate Welfare* (Chapel Hill: University of North Carolina Press, 2002).

20. "WREO Logbook," 1924–1925, Reo Papers, vol. 39, MSUAHC.

21. On the "square deal," see Zahavi, *Workers, Managers, and Welfare Capitalism.*

22. See Joyce Shaw Peterson, *American Automobile Workers, 1900–1930* (Albany: SUNY Press, 1987); David Gartman, *Auto Slavery: The Labor Process in the American Automobile Industry, 1897–1950* (New Brunswick: Rutgers University Press, 1986); Nelson Lichtenstein and Stephen Meyer, eds., *On the Line: Essays in the History of Auto Work* (Urbana: University of Illinois Press, 1989); Charles Reitell, "Machinery and Its Effect upon the Workers in the Automotive Industry," *American Academy of Political and Social Sciences: The Annals* 116 (1924): 37–43.

23. A series of articles that appeared in 1928 in *Automotive Industries* also supports these assertions. See K. W. Stillman, "Reo Crankshaft Machining Methods," *Automotive Industries* (Sept. 15, 1928), 374: "In the plant of the Reo Motor Car Company at Lansing, Michigan, practically all the parts used in Reo cars and trucks are produced. Here, as in other plants, the production methods employed are generally those in common use."

24. David Montgomery, *The Fall of the House of Labor: The Workplace, the State, and American Labor Activism, 1865–1925* (New York: Cambridge University Press, 1987), 32, 204–5; Mary Ann Clawson, *Constructing Brotherhood: Class, Gender, and Fraternalism* (Princeton: Princeton University Press, 1989); Mark C. Carnes and Clyde Griffen, eds., *Meanings for Manhood: Constructions of Masculinity in Victorian America* (Chicago: Chicago University Press, 1990).

25. "Time Books, 1905–1906," Aug. 5, 1905, Reo Papers, vols. 36–37. Of the 306 employees listed at this early date, 99 worked in the assembly room and 95 were listed as in the manufacturing department; 10 were listed as common labor.

26. Cy Rath, "Pertinent Facts Regarding Day Workers at the Reo Motor Car Company, April 1, 1922," Reo Papers, box 73, folder 38, MSUAHC.

27. Throughout much of this period, Cy Rath painstakingly kept monthly turnover rates, determining the reasons with exit reports. These rates were continually reported and compared with earlier times and other plants. The goal was clearly to keep the rates as low as possible.

28. Cy Rath to Leon B. Royce, superintendent of the Reo factory, Jan. 2, 1925, Reo Papers, box 67, folder 48, MSUAHC.

29. *Reasons for Reo*, 1923, 16, LLHC. See also internal memos in Reo Papers, Personnel, box 67, folder 47, which contain hiring preferences for men over twenty-five and married men (except in the case of returning servicemen) and for replacing workers from inside the factory.

30. Reo Motor Car Company, welfare department, *Facts and Figures: A Ready Reference of Valuable Information* (Lansing, 1915), 2, R. E. Olds Transportation Museum, Lansing.

31. "The Labor Department," *Reo Spirit*, June 1918, 4, Reo Papers, box 52, folder 57, MSUAHC.

32. "The Real Reo Spirit," *Reo Spirit,* April 1916, 3, Reo Papers, box 52, folder 56, MSUAHC.

33. See *Reo Spirit,* "Our First Aid to the Stuck," Jan. 1916, 4–6, box 52, folder 56; "Reminiscences: Old Time Shops As They Were," Aug. 1917, 8, box 52, folder 57; "Old Timers' Section," Sept. 1920, 6–7, box 53, folder 2; "Old Timers' Section," Nov. 1920, 8–9, box 53, folder 2; "Old Timers' Number," Jan. 1921, box 53, folder 2; "Old Timers' Number," Jan. 1923, box 53, folder 3, MSUAHC.

34. H. C. Teel, "Old Timers, Masters of Their Art," *Reo Spirit,* Jan. 1920, 2, Reo Papers, box 53, folder 2, MSUAHC.

35. "Old Timers Get Together," *Reo Spirit,* Dec. 1922, 5, 16, 17, Reo Papers, box 53, folder 3, MSUAHC.

36. "Old Timers' Section," *Reo Spirit,* Dec. 1920, Reo Papers, box 53, folder 2, MSUAHC.

37. Lester Washburn described the apprenticeship program positively. See also Tone, *The Business of Benevolence,* and Gartman, *Auto Slavery,* 245.

38. "Labor Turnover—Reo Motor Car Company—Lansing, Michigan," April 20, 1925, Reo Papers, box 66, folder 18, MSUAHC.

39. Reo Papers, box 52, folder 29, MSUAHC (on apprenticeship course).

40. "The Men Who Make Reo," *Reo Magazine,* Factory Number, 1914, 2, LLHC.

41. "Annual Report of the Reo Motor Car Company," 1921, Reo Papers, box 11, folder 1, MSUAHC.

42. *Reasons for Reo,* 1923, 20, LLHC.

43. C. J. Shower, "Reo's Clubhouse for Workers," *Automotive Industries* (June 13, 1918), 1136–38; "Reo Clubhouse Marks New Era in Lansing's Industrial Life," *Lansing State Journal,* Jan. 1, 1917, 10; "Reo Club House Anniversary," *Reo Spirit,* May 1920, 17; "Editorial," *Reo Spirit,* Oct. 1919, 4; "Noon Hour Gossip," *Reo Spirit,* April 1920, 23; "Club House Activities—Year, 1927," clubhouse materials, Reo Papers, box 52, folder 13, MSUAHC; Mrs. Willis Hartley, "Reo Memories Happy Ones," *Lansing State Journal,* Sept. 8, 1975.

44. "Editorial," *Reo Spirit,* Oct. 1919, 3, Reo Papers, box 53, folder 1, MSUAHC.

45. "Sticking to the Job," ibid., April 1924, box 53, folder 4, MSUAHC.

46. Ibid., Aug. 1928, 7–11, box 53, folder 5, for reports.

47. In fact, Peter Berg suggests that the excessive enthusiasm may have prompted company officials to harness this energy into organized athletics. Berg, "Welfare Capitalism," 44.

48. "Constitution and By Laws of the Reo Bowling League," 1925–1926 [?], Reo Papers, box 52, folder 10, MSUAHC.

49. "Teamwork," *Reo Spirit,* July 1920, 18, Reo Papers, box 53, folder 2, MSUAHC.

50. "Reo Bowling League," 1926–1927, Reo Papers, box 52, folder 10, MSUAHC.

51. "Membership List—Reo Bowling League," n.d., but probably 1921–1922 season, Reo Papers, box 52, folder 9, MSUAHC.

52. Joe Blanco, "That Ball Game," *Reo Spirit,* Sept. 1924, 15, Reo Papers, box 53, folder 4, MSUAHC.

53. "Sixth Annual Reo Bowling League Banquet," March 29, 1923, Reo Papers, box 52, folder 9, MSUAHC.

54. Nativity of Auto Workers—in United States and at Reo (%):

|       | Year | Native born, white and black | Foreign born |
|-------|------|------------------------------|--------------|
| U.S.  | 1920 | 64.1                         | 35.9         |
|       | 1930 | 68.7                         | 30.3         |
| Reo   | 1925 | 88.1                         | 11.9         |
|       | 1927 | 89.6                         | 10.4         |
|       | 1935 | 89.9                         | 10.2         |

U.S. figures from Peterson, *American Automobile Workers*, 15. The whole number for 1920 is 204,505 and the whole number for 1930 is 285,674. I altered Peterson's percentages to make them more accurate. Reo figures from "Nationality Statistics," Feb. 16, 1925; "Statistical Data on Group Ages and Average Age, Length of Service, Home Owning and Buying, Nationality," Aug. 2, 1927 and Dec. 1, 1935, Reo Papers, box 67, folder 35, MSUAHC.

55. "Educational Course Planned," *Reo Spirit*, Aug. 1919, 4; "Americanization Class Starts," ibid., Dec. 1919, 3, Reo Papers, box 53, folder 1; Letter from Cy Rath, Oct. 16, 1920, Reo Papers, box 52, folder 48, MSUAHC.

56. Letter from Cy Rath, Nov. 25, 1919, Reo Papers, box 52, folder 48, MSUAHC.

57. "Foreigners Must Change Their Ways," *Reo Spirit*, June, 1916, 6, Reo Papers, box 52, folder 56, MSUAHC.

58. "Practical Bolshevism," ibid., June 1920, 20, Reo Papers, box 53, folder 2; ibid., July 1918, 3, Reo Papers, box 52, folder 57, "We All Suffer," ibid., June 1919, 4, Reo Papers, box 53, folder 1, MSUAHC. "We All Suffer" equated spring fever and its attendant absenteeism with Bolshevism!

59. "Election Information," *Reo Spirit*, Oct. 1916, 1, Reo Papers, box 52, folder 56, MSUAHC; Justin L. Kestenbaum, *Out of a Wilderness: An Illustrated History of Greater Lansing* (Woodland Hills, Calif.: Windsor Publications, 1981), 84.

60. "Prohibition and Immigration," *Reo Spirit*, Aug. 1919, 4, Reo Papers, box 53, folder 1, MSUAHC.

61. "Are We Bums?" ibid., March 1919, 5, Reo Papers, box 53, folder 1, MSUAHC.

62. "How Wives Can Prevent Accidents," ibid., June 1916, 4, Reo Papers, box 52, folder 56, MSUAHC.

63. "Delicate Hands for Delicate Work: National Coil Assembly Room," ibid., June 1917, 7, Reo Papers, box 52, folder 57, MSUAHC.

64. Ibid.

65. "Working Schedule: For Ladies in Reo Factory Effective Monday June 4, 1928," Reo Papers, box 67, folder 52, MSUAHC.

66. "Reo Girls Sponsor Dance," *Reo Spirit*, Jan. 1928, 17, Reo Papers, box 53, folder 5, MSUAHC.

67. "Join City Clubs," ibid., June 1920, 3, Reo Papers, box 53, folder 2. On clerical workers rituals, see Lisa M. Fine, "Between Two Worlds: Business Women in a Chicago Boarding House," *Journal of Social History* 19 (1986): 511–19.

68. "Noon Hour Gossip," *Reo Spirit*, May 1924, 23.

69. Cy Rath, Employment Division, "Statistical Data on Average Age of Factory Force, Length of Service, Home Owning and Buying, Nationality," Reo Papers, box 67, folder 35, MSUAHC.

70. Ed Koster, "Reo Spirit?" *Reo Spirit,* April 1916, 2, Reo Papers, box 52, folder 56; Cy Rath to Mr. Lauzun, factory superintendent, Oct. 24, 1918, Re: Harry F. Marion 1577, Foreman Gardner, Personnel, Reo Papers, box 67, folder 54, MSUAHC.

71. "The Real Reo Spirit," *Reo Spirit,* April 1916, 3, Reo Papers, box 52, folder 56, MSUAHC.

72. "What's Wrong?" ibid., Dec. 1916, 21, Reo Papers, box 52, folder 56, MSUAHC.

73. "The Blues," ibid., July 1924, 18, Reo Papers, box 53, folder 4, MSUAHC.

74. "Noon Hour Gossip," ibid., April 1920, 23, Reo Papers, box 53, folder 2, MSUAHC.

75. "Labor Turnover," ibid., Dec. 1919, 3, Reo Papers, box 53, folder 1, MSUAHC.

76. "Club House Activities for 1919," ibid., Jan. 1920, 2, Reo Papers, box 52, folder 2; "Club House Activities for 1927," submitted by Arthur Sinclair, Reo Papers, box 52, folder 13, MSUAHC.

77. Cy Rath to H. H. Jackson, warden, Michigan State Prison, Jackson, Feb. 23, 1933, Reo Papers, box 52, folder 21; "16th Annual Reo Bowling League Banquet," *Reo Spirit,* April 1933, 10, Reo Papers, box 53, folder 5, MSUAHC.

## Chapter Three

*Epigraphs:* Edgar A. Guest, "A Real Man," in Edgar A. Guest, *A Heap O' Livin'* (Chicago: Reilly and Lee Co., 1916), 181. *Lansing State Journal,* Jan. 1, 1931, 12.

1. See *Lansing State Journal,* Sept. 1, 1924, for the most complete account of this event, although the first five pages of that particular newspaper are missing from the microfilm version and no hard copy has been located. This has been an ongoing mystery during my years of research for this book. One is tempted to wonder what incriminating photos might have appeared on the first few pages of this edition of the paper.

2. "Editorial, Recapitulation of 1937," *Lansing State Journal,* Jan. 1, 1938, 6.

3. See Lizabeth Cohen, *Making a New Deal: Industrial Workers in Chicago, 1919–1939* (New York: Cambridge University Press, 1990); Elizabeth Faue, *Community of Suffering and Struggle: Women, Men, and the Labor Movement in Minneapolis, 1915–1945* (Chapel Hill: University of North Carolina Press, 1991); Gary Gerstle, *Working-Class Americanism: The Politics of Labor in a Textile City, 1914–1960* (New York: Cambridge University Press, 1989); Ronald Edsforth, *Class Conflict and Cultural Consensus: The Making of a Mass Consumer Society in Flint, Michigan* (New Brunswick: Rutgers University Press, 1987).

4. See Cohen, Faue, and Edsforth, cited in note 3 above, as well as Rick Halpern, *Down on the Killing Floor: Black and White Workers in Chicago's Packinghouses, 1904–1954* (Urbana: University of Illinois Press, 1997).

5. See Sidney Fine, *Automobile under the Blue Eagle: Labor, Management, and the Automobile Manufacturing* Code (Ann Arbor: University of Michigan Press, 1963); Walter Galenson, *The CIO Challenge to the AFL: A History of the American Labor Movement, 1935–1941* (Cambridge: Harvard University Press, 1960); Roger Keeran, *The Communist Party and the Auto Workers Unions* (Bloomington: Indiana University Press, 1980); Nelson Lichtenstein, *The Most Dangerous Man in Detroit: Walter Reuther and the Fate of American Labor* (New York: Basic Books, 1995).

6. On communists as organizers in the auto unions, see Keeran, *Communist Party.*

7. Among the few works that do are Steve Babson, *Building the Union: Skilled Workers and Anglo-Gaelic Immigrants in the Rise of the UAW* (New Brunswick: Rutgers University Press, 1991); John G. Kruchko, *The Birth of a Union Local: The History of Local 674, Norwood, Ohio, 1933–1940* (Ithaca: New York State School of Industrial and Labor Relations, Cornell University, August 1972); and Peter Friedlander, *The Emergence of a UAW Local, 1936–1939: A Study in Class and Culture* (Pittsburgh: University of Pittsburgh Press, 1975).

8. Layton Aves, interview by author and Shirley Bradley, Lansing, Aug. 8, 1995. We interviewed Layton Aves after we interviewed his brother, so he was prepared for us and began his interview with this revelation about the Klan and the UAW-CIO.

9. The term is from Nancy MacLean, *Behind the Mask of Chivalry: The Making of the Second Ku Klux Klan* (New York: Oxford University Press, 1994), xiii.

10. "Introduction to the K.K.K. Papers," Sept. 15, 1993, ed. Calvin Enders Collection, box 1, Clark Historical Library, Central Michigan University (hereafter Clark). The best recent works on the Klan in the 1920s are MacLean, *Behind the Mast of Chivalry*, and Leonard J. Moore, *Citizen Klansmen: The Ku Klux Klan in Indiana, 1921–1928* (Chapel Hill: University of North Carolina, 1991). This chapter owes a great deal to Nancy MacLean's work.

11. "Lansing Klansmen Meet in Secret Grove North of City," *Lansing State Journal*, July 17, 1922, 1.

12. "Concert Crowds See Klan Cross," ibid., Aug. 24, 1923, 2; "Lansing Sees Ku Klux Klan," *Cheboygen Daily Tribune*, Aug. 24, 1923, 1.

13. "Klan to Meet in the Auditorium," *Lansing State Journal*, Sept. 20, 1923; the meeting at Prudden was reported in *Fiery Cross*, Oct. 5, 1923, "Newspaper Clippings," Enders Papers, box 2, Clark; women's meeting reported in *Fiery Cross*, Jan. 4, 1924, 1, ibid., Clark; "Women of the Klan Meet," *Lansing State Journal*, May 5, 1924, 1.

14. "Klansmen Visit Lansing Church," *Lansing State Journal*, March 31, 1924, 1; "First Public Concert Sponsored by Klan, Fills Concert Twice" ibid., May 22, 1924, 1; "Fourth Finds City Deserted, Thousands of Cars Went Southbound to Jackson for Huge Konklave," ibid., July 4, 1924, 1; "Klan Asks Ban of Aggie Game," ibid., June 5, 1924, 1; "Big Turn Out of Klan Last Night" ibid., May 15, 1924, 1; "Klan Holds Public Initiation in City," ibid., June 28, 1924, 1.

15. Advertisement in *Gratiot County Nighthawk*, Alma, Michigan, Aug. 1928, 3.

16. *Michigan Kourier*, vol. 3, no. 40, Aug. 8, 1924, 3, Bentley Library, University of Michigan.

17. This rendering is consistent with recent works that describe the "normalcy" of the revived Klan of the 1920s. See MacLean, *Behind the Mask of Chivalry*, and Kathleen M. Blee, *Women of the Klan: Racism and Gender in the 1920s* (Berkeley and Los Angeles: University of California Press, 1991).

18. Terry Schultz, "Klan's '24 March in City a 'Monster' Event," *Lansing State Journal*, Dec. 7, 1980, B1, B8. I would like to thank Connie Hutchins of the *Lansing State Journal* for helping me track down the writer of this article and for other help with this chapter. Terry Schultz told me that this article was based on interviews she did in Windsor Township in the 1980s with people who remembered the Klan rally in Lansing. Schultz's article is the only written account of the event I have been able to find.

19. Ibid.

20. Ibid. The only evidence I could find of Klan violence was in connection to a Lansing Catholic school in 1924, in a pamphlet entitled "St. Mary Cathedral" (Lansing, 1980), 19, box: Religion, folder: St. Mary's, LLHC. "The KKK made a bid to elect their members to every office in 1924. The pressure put on Catholics was fierce. The Klan threatened to burn down the Catholic school which had been built in 1902. One evening they marched around the parish buildings carrying lighted torches and wearing their long white robes. Friar O'Rafferty supported by his parishioners and two prominent Protestant clergymen held a counter demonstration. The parade assembled at the Michigan Central Depot. The participants, mostly Blacks and Catholics, greeted Bishop Gallagher and marched to Prudden Auditorium for a rally." This was written by Father George C. Michalek of the Lansing Diocese.

21. "Ku Klux Klan Plans Local Temple," *Lansing State Journal*, Aug. 21, 1924, 1. See also ibid., Sept. 1, 1924, 10.

22. "Estimate Near 50,000 at Mammoth Klan Meet Here," ibid., Sept. 2, 1924, 3.

23. Michael G. Hodges, "The Ku Klux Klan as a Political Influence in Michigan in the 1920s," master's thesis, Central Michigan University, 1997. I would like to thank Michael Hodges for sending me a copy of his excellent thesis. See also "Meetings of Wayne County School Campaign, Oct. 29, 1922," *Michigan Lutheran Schools Committee Records, 1921–1926*, Bentley Library, University of Michigan; Frank B. Woodford, *Alex J. Groesbeck: Portrait of a Public Man* (Detroit: Wayne State University Press, 1962) 224–25.

24. See Woodford, *Alex J. Groesbeck*, 225; "Schism Splits Ranks of Klan," *Detroit Free Press*, Sept. 1, 1924, 7; "School Vote Splits Klan," *Detroit Free Press*, Sept. 2, 1924, 11.

25. Woodford, *Alex J. Groesbeck*, 227.

26. Norman Fredric Weaver, "The Knights of the Ku Klux Klan in Wisconsin, Indiana, Ohio, and Michigan," Ph.D. diss., University of Wisconsin, 1954, 278. In Ingham County, Perry got 16,315 out of 30,400 possible votes. The runner-up was Groesbeck, with 9,241. Three of the four Klansmen running in the county elections won. Weaver's account is different from many other accounts of the Klan in Michigan, which often identify Detroit and Flint as the Klan strongholds. See also *Michigan Official Directory and Legislative Manual* (Lansing: State of Michigan, 1925–1926), 191.

27. "Biggest Perry Vote in State Polled in Ingham," *Lansing State Journal*, Sept. 10, 1924, 1; Homer K. Powell, "History of Plymouth Methodist Protestant Church, Adrian, Michigan," 20–21, manuscript, n.d., Lenawee County Historical Society. I would like to thank Charles Lindquist, the curator at the Lenawee County Historical Society, for his valiant detective work.

28. "Perry Evasive on Speech before Klan," *Adrian Daily Telegram*, March 1, 1924, 1.

29. "Perry Denies Klan Support," *Lansing State Journal*, Aug. 16, 1924, 1; "Dr. Perry in Outline of Platform Says He Is Not Klan Member," *Adrian Daily Telegram*, Aug. 16, 1924, 1.

30. "Dr Perry in Outline of Platform," *Adrian Daily Telegram*, Aug. 16, 1924; "Biggest Perry Vote in State Polled in Ingham," *Lansing State Journal*, Sept. 10, 1924.

31. Frederic Perry to Ransom E. Olds, Dec. 7, 1910, R. E. Olds Collection, box 1, folder 7, MSUAHC.

32. "Perry Speaks to Big Crowd at Reo Plant," *Lansing Capital News*, Aug. 26, 1924, 1; "Perry Tells Ideas before Reo Crowd," *Lansing State Journal*, Aug. 26, 1924, 1.

33. See attachments to MLSC letter, Dec. 12, 1924, "School Amendment Returns, 1924 by County."

34. "State Knights Templar Gathering," *Lansing State Journal,* May 30, 1921, 1.

35. "Templar Hosts a Parade, Stirs City," ibid., May 31, 1921, 1.

36. *Official Proceedings of the City Council, City of Lansing,* June 28, 1926, LLHC. This commission, which was the idea of the special committee on city advertising, published the pamphlet entitled "Lansing's Advantages," boosting what the city elites believed distinguished the capital city at the height of its industrial might.

37. Allen Bennett Forsberg, "Lansing's Advantages," *Lansing State Journal,* Jan. 1, 1927, insert, 7, 8, 11–12.

38. Justin L. Kestenbaum, *Out of a Wilderness: An Illustrated History of Greater Lansing* (Woodland Hills, Calif.: Windsor Publications, 1981), 100.

39. Sallie M. Manassah, David A. Thomas, and James F. Wallington, *Lansing: Capital, Campus, and Cars* (East Lansing: Contemporary Image, 1986), 55.

40. Ibid., 54; clipping from *Lansing Capital News,* May 26, 1932, in R. E. Olds Papers, box 14, folder 2, MSUAHC.

41. "Reo Sales Set Mark in 1927," *Lansing State Journal,* Jan. 2, 1928, 13.

42. See Cy Rath, "Personnel Data—Reo Motor Car Company, Man Hours–Wage–Production–Man Power–Costs: Eighteen Year Period from 1920 to 1937, Inc. (Factory Payroll Only)," Jan. 10, 1938, Reo Papers, box 73, folder 53, MSUAHC.

43. "Wage Adjustments and Reductions—Reo Motor Car Company," no author, n.d., but this was certainly written by Cy Rath in the summer of 1932, Reo Papers, box 73, folder 41, MSUAHC; Rath, "Notice to Division Superintendents," May 27, 1932, ibid., box 67, folder 52.

44. See, for example, Alfred E. Brose, "Trend of Industrial and Municipal Recreation in the Lansing Community," master's thesis, Michigan State University, 1934, 53.

45. Susan Stein-Roggenbuck, "Negotiating Relief: The Development of Social Welfare Programs in Depression-Era Michigan," Ph.D. diss., Michigan State University, 1999; James J. Lorence, *Organizing the Unemployed: Community and Union Activists in the Industrial Heartland* (Albany: SUNY Press, 1996).

46. "City's First Communist Rally Held in Guise of Jobless Meet," *Lansing State Journal,* May 27, 1931, 1.

47. "Governor Tells Masons Radicalism Is Banned," ibid., 3.

48. See Friedlander, *Emergence of a UAW Local,* 131.

49. Fine, *Automobile under the Blue Eagle,* 147.

50. Peter Fagan, socialist publisher of the pro-labor weekly *News of Lansing,* provided early leadership but was replaced by the Lansing Trades and Labor Council. See ibid., 41, and Papers of UAW Local 650, box 1, folder 1, Archives of Labor History and Urban Affairs, Walter Reuther Library, Wayne State University, Detroit (hereafter Local 650/Reuther).

51. Undated notes of meeting held July 13, 1933, Federation of Automotive Workers of Lansing, Reo Papers, box 67, folder 54, MSUAHC. Thanks to Harry Emmons and the papers he shared with me from the employment division, I have other examples of company spies in these early organizing efforts. Most of these are reports written by Cy Rath to highly placed individuals in the firm. Rath obviously had a stooge in the meetings who reported to him. These examples include "Highlights on meet-

ing at Prudden Auditorium, Friday Evening," Aug. 11, 1933; reports dated, March 5, 8, 12, 14, 15, 1934; report to R. A. DeVlieg, works manager, April 27, 1934 (this report described the meeting at which the Reo union decided to affiliate with the AFL); "Minutes of Meeting Held at the Executive Office of the Reo Motor Car Company on Jan. 23, 1935," signed by John Miller and three other members of the employees committee (this and the next few memos report on the formation of the Reo employees association, the company union, and Lester Washburn's efforts to lure its members into the independent union, much to the company's chagrin); memo from Cy Rath to L. P. Smith, general superintendent, June 28, 1935 and June 15, 1936; Cy Rath to George Smith, Nov. 16, 1936; and additional reports on Nov. 23, 1936, and Dec. 7, 1936. Cy Rath even had a report of the UAW National Convention of 1936, "Highlights of the Convention of United Automobile Workers of America," May 7, 1936.

52. Cy Rath, "A Report on Discrimination Claims of Five Employees of Export Shipping Dept.," June 15, 1934, Reo Papers, box 53, folder 18, MSUAHC; Cy Rath to Reo Labor Board, June 20, 1934, ibid., box 53, folder 18.

53. Lester Washburn told Kenneth Germanson that he was born in Pellston, although in Washburn's testimony before the U.S. Senate Select Committee on Improper Activities in the Labor Management Field at a hearing on Aug. 1, 1957, he told Senator John Kennedy that he was born in Muskegon, Michigan. All other aspects of his narrative regarding his early life are consistent.

54. Lester Washburn remembers being hired in the fall of 1927, but the personnel records at Reo show that he was hired as a carpenter for the first time on Feb. 14, 1927. See "Personnel Records of Employees in Export Shipping," n.d., but probably compiled in late 1934 or early 1935, Reo Papers, box 53, folder 18, MSUAHC.

55. The exact date of his layoff was Nov. 3, 1930. He was rehired on July 14, 1931, laid off again on Sept. 9, 1931, and rehired on July 17, 1933.

56. Lester Washburn, interview by Ken Germanson, Milwaukee, May 30, 1986.

57. "Minutes, Aug. 29, 1933–May 6, 1938," Local 650/Reuther, box 1, folder 1. Washburn was elected in May 1934. Washburn, interview, May 30, 1986; "Lester Washburn," *United Auto Worker,* May 1936, 2.

58. Washburn, interview, May 30, 1986.

59. Ibid.

60. Lester Washburn, interview by Ken Germanson, May 27, 1988.

61. Washburn, interview, May 30, 1986.

62. See Keeran, *Communist Party,* 143.

63. "Lester Washburn," *United Automobile Worker,* May 1936, 2–3.

64. "Local Union Leader: Typical Auto Worker," *News of Lansing,* Jan. 22, 1937, 8.

65. Clipping from the *Detroit Record,* Feb. 20, 1939, Homer Martin Papers, box 1, Reuther Library.

66. Ted Morgan, *A Covert Life: Jay Lovestone, Communist, Anti-Communist, and Spymaster* (New York: Random House, 1999), 124–33.

67. See Fine, *Automobile under the Blue Eagle*; Galenson, *CIO Challenge to the AFL*; Lichtenstein, *Most Dangerous Man in Detroit*; Henry Kraus, *Heroes of Unwritten Story: The UAW, 1934–1939* (Urbana: University of Illinois Press, 1993).

68. There was never any doubt in my mind that Lester Washburn was sympathetic to the goals of the Lovestonites. All of his writings and oral histories reveal a powerful

anticommunist and antisocialist slant. Because so many players in this drama assumed he was a Lovestonite or accused him of being one, establishing this link directly has been next to impossible. There is evidence linking him with the Lovestonites from Ben Fisher, who reported to the Socialist Party on auto union activities in Detroit during this period. See Fisher, "Auto Report," Detroit, May 9, 1938 ("The only C.P.O. board member, Washburn, is pursuing a reactionary policy in every sense"), Daniel Bell Papers, box 39, folder 3, Tamiment Library, New York University. In addition, the Maurice Sugar papers also contain information linking Washburn to the CPO and the Lovestonites. See "Confidential Report of the Socialist Party on the Inner Situation in the Auto Union," June 7, 1938, 3, Maurice Sugar Papers, box 41, folder 27, Reuther; "Answer to Charges and Miscellaneous, Special List," 2, Maurice Sugar Papers, box 42, folder 13, Reuther; "Bill of Particulars and Charges (handwritten notes), Maurice Sugar Papers, box 42, folder 12, Reuther; "List of Board Members and Officers," box 43, folder 23, Reuther; memo to Mr. Lewis from Richard Frankensteen, July 11, 1938, Victor Reuther Papers, box 4, folder 27, Reuther. Perhaps the most damaging piece of evidence was a pamphlet written and disseminated by the unity faction entitled "An Appeal to the Members of the UAW," Aug. 1938, Victor Reuther Papers, box 4, folder 34, Reuther.

69. Nelson Lichtenstein, in an e-mail message to me dated April 30, 2000, shared this from his interview with Strachan.

70. Articles on Washburn and Reo appeared fairly regularly in *Workers Age*. See "Auto Workers Force Rehiring," Oct. 17, 1936; "Lansing Auto Union Exposes Company Spy," Jan. 9, 1937, 2; "1500 Reo Men in Sit Down," March 20, 1937, 1; "Reo Strike 100% Solid," March 27, 1937; "Lansing Labor Shows Power," June 19, 1937, 1; "Lansing Union Raps Murphy's Attack on Labor Holiday," July 17, 1937, 6; "UAW Blocks 'Unity' Split," Dec. 25, 1937, 1; "MI CIO to Act for Jobless," Jan. 1, 1938, 1; "Lansing UAW in Plea for Unity" (reprinted from *Lansing Auto Worker*) April 19, 1939, 2, all in *Workers Age*.

71. Washburn, interview, May 30, 1986.

72. Ibid. Washburn described how both factions would try to preempt his authority in local battles.

73. Ibid.

74. "Reo Company Union Falls Down," *Lansing Industrial News*, March 22, 1935, 1; "Auto Unions Vote for Merger," ibid., May 29, 1936, 1; "Special Meeting," Jan. 31, 1936, Local 650/Reuther, box 1, folder 1; "Reo Company Union Dies Natural Death," *Lansing Auto Worker*, March 10, 1937, 4.

75. "Reo Men Negotiate Rates with Company," *Lansing Industrial News*, May 24, 1935, 1.

76. Editorial, "Will the International Be Industrial?" ibid., Aug. 23, 1935, 2; "Reo Local Meets Friday; Eyes Industrial Union," ibid., March 20, 1936, 1.

77. This amalgamated union included the Reo local as well as the local for Fisher Body, Oldsmobile, Motor Wheel, and a number of other small shops. See "Minutes of Union," Sept. 25, 1936, Local 650/Reuther, box 1, folder 1.

78. Galenson, *CIO Challenge to the AFL*, 132.

79. Duane S. Hawkins, secretary of the Lansing District Auto Council, to Homer Martin, July 30, 1936, Martin Papers, box 1, Reuther.

80. "Group Age and Average Age of Reo Factory Employees: Nov. 25, 1937," Reo Papers, box 67, folder 37, MSUAHC; also see "United States Bureau of Labor Statis-

tics Reports, cooperating with Michigan Department of Labor and Industry, Lansing," compiled by Cy Rath, ibid., box 53, folders 17–19.

81. Glenn A. Niemeyer, *The Automotive Career of Ransom E. Olds* (East Lansing: Bureau of Business and Economic Research, Graduate School of Business Administration, Michigan State University, 1963), 124–69.

82. Union minutes for Aug. 30 and Aug. 31, 1936, Local 650/Reuther, box 1, folder 1.

83. "Excerpt from Confidential Report dated Tuesday June 18th," June 22, 1936, probably by Cy Rath; memo from Cy Rath to Louis P. Smith, June 15, 1936, both in Emmons Papers, in author's possession.

84. "Reo Locks Out Union Workers," *Lansing Industrial News*, Sept. 18, 1936, 1; "Official Statement of Reo Local No. 53," ibid., Sept. 18, 1936, 1; "Auto Union to Negotiate with Reo Co.," ibid., Sept. 25, 1936, 1.

85. "End of Dispute at Reo Is Seen," ibid., Oct. 9, 1936, 1; "Auto Workers Seek Wage Increase," ibid., Nov. 20, 1936, 1; "Lansing Local Wins Big Point," *United Automobile Worker*, Nov. 1936, 7.

86. "Auto Workers Flock to Union," *Lansing Industrial Worker*, Dec. 11, 1936, 1.

87. "Auto Workers Seek Wage Increase," *Lansing Industrial News*, Nov. 20, 1936, 1.

88. "Reo Company Union May Join UAW," ibid., Dec. 4, 1936, 1; "One More Company Union Turns against Papa," *United Automobile Worker*, Dec. 1936, 12.

89. See "Reo and UAW Near Settlement," *Lansing Industrial News*, Dec. 18, 1936, 1; minutes of Reo local, Dec. 15, 23, 30, 1936, Feb. 19, 26, 1937, Local 650/Reuther, box 1, folder 1.

90. "Reo Flashes," *Lansing Auto Worker*, Feb. 24, 1937, 4.

91. "Fall In! A Statement by the Lansing Automobile Council," *Lansing Industrial News*, Nov. 22, 1935, 1.

92. "What Is a Union Man?" *Lansing Auto Worker*, Jan. 19, 1937, 3.

93. "Join the United, Prelate Advises," ibid., Jan. 26, 1937, 3; Washburn, interview, May 30, 1986.

94. "Reo Company Union," *Lansing Auto Worker*, March 10, 1937, 1–2.

95. Washburn, interview, May 30, 1986.

96. "Reo Union Stands Solid as New Strikes Rumored," *Lansing Industrial News*, March 12, 1937, 1.

97. "Management Declares Plant Closed, to Pay Sit-Downers and Wait," and "Reo President Reveals Stand of Corporation," *Lansing State Journal*, March 11, 1937, 1; "Reo Union Stands Solid as New Strikes Rumored," *Lansing Industrial News*, March 12, 1937, 1; "Reo Strike Is Nation's Model Demonstration," *Lansing Auto Worker*, March 17, 1937, 1.

98. Washburn, interview, May 30, 1986.

99. Otto Aves, interview by author and Shirley Bradley, Lansing, Jan. 4, 1993; Wayne Nunheimer, interview by author and Shirley Bradley, Lansing, June 18, 1992; Janetzkes, interview; Marvin Grinstern, interview by author and Shirley Bradley, Lansing, Dec. 3, 1992.

100. "Reo Union Stands Solid as New Strikes Rumored," *Lansing Industrial News*, March 12, 1937, 1.

101. See "Emergency Brigade Women Whip up Food Problem," "Motor Plant Brigade Likes Their Work," "Farmers Bring Food," "Strikers Get Contributions,"

"Discipline in the Plant Strict," and other stories that appeared in the "Reo Extra" of the *Lansing Auto Worker,* March 17, 1937.

102. "Reo Strike Is Nation's Model Demonstration," *Lansing Auto Worker,* March 17, 1937, 1

103. Ibid.

104. Ibid.

105. *General Correspondence of the Mayor, 1929–1937,* City of Lansing, mayor's office, box 3, SAM. The twenty-five men who provided their years of tenure at Reo had an average of more than eighteen years of service at the company.

106. J. E. Graham to Max Templeton, March 24, 1937; Sidney R. Brummet to Max Templeton, March 24, 1937; H. E. Nickels to Max Templeton, March 24, 1937, all in *General Correspondence of the Mayor, 1929–1937.* One of those who wrote to the mayor during this troubled time was one of the Leyrer sons, Robert Leyrer.

107. "Reo Peace Parley Not Due to Resume before Monday," *Lansing Industrial News,* March 26, 1937, 1; Sidney Fine, *Frank Murphy: The New Deal Years* (Chicago: University of Chicago Press, 1979), 340.

108. Washburn, interview, May 30, 1986.

109. "Reo Worker Reviews Strike," *Lansing Auto Worker,* April 14, 1937, 2.

110. "Reo Victory Spurs Lansing Workers," ibid., 1.

111. "Capital City Wrecking Company," *Lansing State Journal,* Jan. 1, 1937, 14.

112. Albert A. Blum and Ira Spar, "The Lansing Labor Holiday," *Michigan History* 49 (March 1965): 1. Washburn corresponded with Blum and Spar. Washburn, interview, May 30, 1986.

113. Ibid.

114. Ibid.

115. "Labor Holiday," *Lansing Industrial News,* June 11, 1937, 9.

116. Washburn, interview, May 30, 1986.

117. "Local in Lansing a Progressive Force," *United Automobile Worker,* Nov. 27, 1937, 7.

118. See "Templar Conclave Crowd to Set Goal," *Lansing State Journal,* June 3, 1937, 19; "Templar Hosts Mobilization Here Monday," ibid., June 6, 1937, 1; "Knights Close Conclave," ibid., June 10, 1937, 1.

119. "Lansing UAW Lashes 'Law, Order' League," *United Automobile Worker,* June 26, 1937, 2.

120. "Local in Lansing a Progressive Force," ibid., Nov. 27, 1937, 7.

121. Ibid.; Minutes of Joint Council Meetings, Local #182," April 9, 1938, Local 650/Reuther, box 1, folder 2l; minutes of executive board meetings, Local #182, Oct. 2 and Oct. 9, 1937, Local 650/Reuther, box 1, folder 3.

122. "Begin Sport Shows," *United Automobile Worker,* Nov. 13, 1937, 8.

123. "UAW across the Nation: Lansing," ibid., Jan. 22, 1938, 7.

124. "Lansing Meet Demands Halt on Evictions," ibid., March 5, 1938, 3; "Lansing Fights for Jobless," ibid., March 5, 1938, 7; minutes of the executive board meetings, Local #182, Jan. 14, 1939, Local 650/Reuther, box 1, folder 3.

125. Minutes of joint council meetings, Local #182, Feb. 26, 1938, ibid., box 1, folder 2.

126. "Washburn Trial Set for July 1," *Lansing Industrial News,* June 11, 1937, 1; Washburn, interview, May 30, 1986.

127. "Holiday Here Held a Mistake by UAW Chief," *Lansing State Journal*, July 9, 1937, 1; "Lansing Strike a Mistake—Martin," *New York Times*, July 9, 1937.

128. "Report of Lester Washburn, President of Local 182-UAW at Joint Council Meeting of Dec. 18, 1937," Jay Lovestone Papers, Box 567, Hoover Institution on War, Revolution, and Peace, Stanford University (hereafter Lovestone Papers).

129. "News of the UAW Local Unions," *United Automobile Worker*, March 25, 1939, 5, 7.

130. "Lansing UAW in Plea for Unity" (reprinted from the *Lansing Auto Worker*), *Workers Age*, April 19, 1939, 2.

131. See "Minutes of Union Meeting, Local #182," Aug. 7 and 21, 1936, Local 650/Reuther, box 1, folder 1. Bill Munger was president, and both Hack and Washburn were elected shop stewards; "News of the UAW Local Unions," *United Automobile Worker*, April 8, 1939, 5.

132. Labor-Management Committee meeting, June 28, 1939, Reo Papers, box 67, folder 54, MSUAHC; minutes of the Bargaining Committee, June, 28, 1939, Local 650/Reuther, box 1, folder 4.

133. Labor-Management Committee meeting, Dec. 13, 1939, Reo Papers, box 67, folder 54, MSUAHC.

134. "Nearly 500 Now Employed at Reo," *Lansing Industrial News*, Dec. 22, 1939, 1; "Col. Glover New Reo President," ibid., Jan. 5, 1940, 1; minutes of the Bargaining Committee, Dec. 13, 1939, Local 650/Reuther, box 1, folder 4; Labor-Management Bargaining Committee, Jan. 10, 1940, Reo Papers, box 67, folder 55, MSUAHC.

135. "Reo Company Signs Union Shop Contract with Local 650," *United Automobile Worker*, May 1, 1940, 1.

136. "First New Reo Comes Off the Line," *Lansing Industrial News*, May 24, 1940, 1.

## Chapter Four

1. Glenn A. Niemeyer, *The Automotive Career of Ransom E. Olds* (East Lansing: Bureau of Business and Economic Research, Graduate School of Business Administration, Michigan State University, 1963).

2. Nelson Lichtenstein, *Labor's War at Home: The CIO in World War II* (New York: Cambridge University Press, 1982), 81; Nelson Lichtenstein, *The Most Dangerous Man in Detroit: Walter Reuther and the Fate of American Labor* (New York: Basic Books, 1995); Howell John Harris, *The Right to Manage: Industrial Relations Policies of American Business in the 1940s* (Madison: University of Wisconsin Press, 1982); Alan Clive, *State of War: Michigan in World War II* (Ann Arbor: University of Michigan Press, 1979).

3. *Exhibit H: Agreement and Schedule Relating to Compensation Paid By Reo Motors, Inc.*, to the Reconstruction Finance Corporation, Jan. 29, 1941, Reo Papers, box 145, folder 28, MSUAHC; Jesse Burkhead, *Reconstruction Finance Corporation Loans* (Washington D.C.: U.S. Government Printing Office, 1942), 11.

4. McKim, secretary at Reo, to H. Paul Engle, senior inspector, U.S. Department of Labor, Wage and Hour Division, Detroit, Dec. 30, 1941, Reo Papers, box 7, folder 65, MSUAHC.

5. See minutes of Labor-Management meeting, June 28, 1939, Reo Papers, box 67, folder 54; minutes of Labor-Management meeting, Jan. 10, 1940, Reo Papers, box 67,

folder 55; memo to Reo supervisors on agreement with bargaining committee, Jan. 24, 1940, Reo Papers, box 67, folder 55, MSUAHC.

6. Peter B. Evans, Dietrich Rueschemeyer, and Theda Skocpol, eds., *Bringing the State Back In* (New York: Cambridge University Press, 1985); Lichtenstein, *Labor's War At Home*; Christopher Tomlins, *The State and the Unions: Labor Relations, Law, and the Organized Labor Movement in America, 1880–1960* (New York: Cambridge University Press, 1985).

7. *Lansing State Journal*, Jan. 1, 1942, Jan. 1, 1943, Jan. 1, 1944.

8. The percent of nonwhites in the city by 1950 was still 3.3 percent (see Table 7 in Appendix).

9. James B. Atleson, *Labor and the Wartime State: Labor Relations and Law during World War II* (Urbana: University of Illinois Press, 1998); see also Lichtenstein, *Labor's War at Home, and* Clive, *State of War.*

10. Henry Hund to Andrew Stevenson, Oct. 3, 1941, Reo Papers, box 122, folder 24, MSUAHC.

11. Richard Reisinger, regional director, region 2, to Leo Deacon, recording secretary, Local 650, Sept., 9, 1940, Local 650/Reuther, box 3; Richard Reisinger, truck division, UAW-CIO, to W. O. Scholz, president, UAW Local 650, Oct. 8, 1940, ibid., box 2; Reisinger to W. W. Knight Jr., assistant director, tank, truck and tractor section, Advisory Commission to the Council of National Defense, Nov. 1, 1940, ibid., box 3.

12. W. O. Scholz to Morris L. Cooke, National Defense Committee, Jan. 15, 1941, ibid., box 2; Allen S. Haywood, director of CIO/Washington, to Morris L. Cooke, office production management, March 12, 1941, ibid., box 1.

13. "Reo Receives Orders for US Army Trucks," *Lansing Industrial News*, Sept. 27, 1940, 3; "Reo Is Turning Out New Style Coaches," ibid., Aug. 29, 1941, 11.

14. Notification from War Department Headquarters-Holabird Quartermaster Depot, Baltimore, Sept. 24, 1940, Reo Papers, box 126, folder 88, MSUAHC.

15. *Present Employment* (n.d., but probably late 1941), Reo Papers, box 6, folder 20, MSUAHC; memo from John Tooker to A. R. Kenny, Reo's comptroller, Lansing, Jan. 8, 1943, ibid., box 121, folder 87; materials related to acceptance of bid from navy department, department of ordnance, on 20 M/M Projectiles, Mark IV (1941), ibid., box 50, folders 38–39.

16. A. R. Kenny to Thomas F. Staley Jr., Captain, Air Corps, and Chief Price Adjustment Section, War Department, Army Air Forces, Material Center, Office of the Air Force's resident representative, Detroit, Jan. 21, 1943; George F. Yoran, purchasing officer, Bureau of Supplies and Accounts to Navy Department, to Reo Motors, Oct. 23, 1941; memo from Henry Hund to major administrators (Reo), June 15, 1942, Reo Papers, box 123, folder 30, MSUAHC.

17. A. R. Kenny to Thomas F. Staley, Jan. 21, 1943, ibid., box 123, folder 30.

18. "National Defense Program Priorities," loose sheet, undated but probably from late 1941, ibid., box 6, folder 20; "Present Employment," loose sheet, undated but probably from late 1941, ibid.

19. John Clark had been a Reo representative overseas before taking the post in the capital. John Tooker, born in Lansing and on the administrative staff at Reo since

1924, came from the Lansing plant, where he had been the head of the navy department. Personnel security questionnaire, John Tooker, Sept. 22, 1948, ibid., box 54, folder 12.

20. See John T. Clark file, ibid., box 49, folder 47.

21. *How To Win the Army-Navy Production Award*, issued jointly by the under secretary of War and the under secretary of the Navy, Sept. 7, 1942, ibid., box 123, folder 30.

22. Confidential memo from John Clark to John Tooker, Nov. 18, 1942, ibid., box 127, folder 72; John Clark to Ernie Stephan, New York Branch, Nov. 13, 1942, ibid., box 128, folder 1; John Clark to Henry Hund, Dec. 4, 1942 (on how to improve Reo preference ratings so that the company could purchase machine tools to fill contracts). Clark wrote, "I am attaching hereto a copy of the Acceleration of Aircraft Program Requirements, which was directed to all builders of machine tools together with the preference list and etc. I borrowed this from a certain party in the Navy and I must return same to him in tact within a very short space of time. This is not suppose [*sic*] to be available to us and it was only with the goodness of the heart of this party that I could obtain this that you may read it and then I would appreciate your returning it to me that I may in turn take it back and place it where it belongs. This is highly restricted and I do not want to see anyone get into trouble for it would be difficult for us in the future." Ibid., box 127, folder 61.

23. "Reo in the Fight for Freedom," dated either 1945 or 1946, ibid., Scrapbook 265. In conjunction with Timken Axle of Detroit, Reo boasted of the 200 navy aircraft salvage trucks, 2,318 air force truck tractor units and firefighters, 700 tank transports, 22,204 2.5-ton $6 \times 6$ trucks for ordnance, 438 5-ton navy stake trucks, 594 1.5-ton navy dump trucks, 594 1.5-ton navy stake trucks, 743 3-ton navy stake trucks, 300 5-ton navy dump trucks, and 875 3-ton navy dump trucks it produced in addition to the bomb and rocket fuse programs and all of the subcontracting during the war.

24. A. R. Kenny to Thomas F. Staley Jr., Jan. 21, 1943, ibid., box 123, folder 30.

25. H. E. Hund to R. L. Vaniman, director, automotive division, War Production Board, July 23, 1943, ibid., box 50, folder 80; D. C. Streeter, Reo general sales manager, to Reo distributors, July 23, 1943, ibid., box 50, folder 79; telegram from J. Joseph Whelan, War Production Board, to Reo Motors, Dec. 2, 1943, ibid., box 50, folder 81; typed draft for the 1944 Annual Report, ibid., box 5, folder 77.

26. "*Ordnance Department: Industry Integration Committees,*" Aug. 1942, Appendix 1, 10, ibid., box 125, folder 47.

27. The other truck companies were Autocar, Available Truck, Brockway, Chevrolet, Chrysler, Corbitt, Diamond T, Fargo, Federal, Four Wheel Drive, Hug, International Harvester, Kenilworth, Mack, Studebaker, Ward LaFrance, White, Willys-Overland, and Yellow Truck. Henry Hund received a formal invitation to join an industry advisory committee through the War Production Board and he accepted. Henry Hund to Barry T. Leithead, director of the industry advisory board committees, War Production Board, June 17, 1943, ibid., box 49, folder 50; *Automotive Council for War Production: Bulletin #116*, Aug. 28, 1943, ibid., box 50, folder 48.

28. John Tooker to Lt. Comdr. Arthur Langfield, navy department, office of inspector of naval material, Detroit, Dec. 14, 1942, ibid., box 125, folder 47.

29. Reo, in fact, hosted a large Rocket Fuse manufacturers' meeting late in the war. The other manufacturers were Brown and Bigelow, Pollak, Parker Pen, National Fireworks, Hunter, and Easy Washing Machine. Office memo, Jan. 1, 1945, ibid., box 126, folder 29.

30. See invoices dated March 6, 1942 for 3.5-inch model RA 6 spindle gridley automatic screw machines purchased from National Acme, Detroit, ibid., box 121, folder 94; C. R. Jones to John Clark, March 31, 1943, and response from Clark to Jones, April 12, 1943, ibid., box 50, folder 51.

31. See, for example, the production schedule for Contract #NXS (A) 38418, which was for 100 model 25 tractors made for the navy bureau of aeronautics. For this one job, Reo needed 100 gas engines from Continental Motors, 100 rear and front axles from Timken, 100 transmissions from Clark Transportation, 100 radiators from Modine Manufacturing, 1,000 wheels and tires from Dayton, 100 fuel pumps from A. C. Spark Plugs, 100 generators from Delco Remy, 100 starting motors from Delco Remy, and 100 governors from King Seely. Ibid., box 123, folder 5; M. J. McComb, purchasing follow-up, to John Clark, May 25, 1943, ibid., box 50, folder 34.

32. *Automotive Council for War Production Newsletter: Military Vehicles Bulletin #145*, Oct. 29, 1943, ibid., box 50, folder 48.

33. Departmental communication to all employees, Nov. 17, 1942, ibid., box 121, folder 75.

34. Memo from John Tooker to A. R. Kenny, Jan. 8, 1943, ibid., box 121, folder 87.

35. Marvin Grinstern, interview by author and Shirley Bradley, Lansing, Dec. 3, 1992.

36. Democratic Senator Prentiss Brown, who was also chairman of Detroit Edison and on the Army Ordnance Committee, recounted the story of a vessel in San Francisco Bay experiencing pump failure. "Second Annual Meeting of the Michigan Post of the Army Ordnance Association at Detroit Michigan," May 16, 1945, Reo Papers, box 122, folder 2, MSUAHC.

37. See "Foreign Born Employees on Payroll as of June 15, 1940," ibid., box 67, folder 36, and "Age and Physical Condition Reports for all Departments conducted, Oct., 1940," ibid., box 67, folder 37.

38. Minutes of the meetings of the Labor-Management Bargaining Committee exist for May 3, June 10, 1938; June 29, July 5, 12, 19, 26, Aug. 9, 16, 21, 23, 30, Sept. 6, 13, 27, Oct. 4, 11, 12, 18, 25, Nov. 1, 8, 15, 22, 29, Dec. 6, 13, 20, 1939; Jan. 10, 17, 24, 31, Feb. 7, 14, 22, 28, March 6, 13, 20, May 22, 23, June 26, Sept. 4, 11, 26, Oct. 3, 16, 24, 30, Nov. 7, 14, 27, Dec. 4, 11, 18, 27, 1940; Feb. 21, March 4, 14, 24, April 4, July 3, 14, Aug. 8, Sept. 9, 22, Nov. 14, 21, 1941; May 11, 25, 1942; Feb. 17, June 14, July 26, Dec. 8, 1943. Ibid., box 67, folder 57, and Local 650/Reuther, box 1, folders 4–6.

39. Minutes of Joint Bargaining Committee meeting, March 4, 1941, Local 650/Reuther, box 1, folder 5.

40. Minutes of Joint Bargaining Committee meeting, July 3, 1941, ibid.

41. Minutes of Reo Management-Union Bargaining Committee weeting, July 11, 1941, Reo Papers, box 67, folder 57, MSUAHC.

42. Minutes of Management-Union Bargaining Committee meeting, Jan. 12, 1944, ibid., box 67, folder 59.

43. In 1943 there were 3,307 employees at Reo, 898 of whom were female. Of these, 74 women worked as drill press operators, 57 as miscellaneous machine tool operators, 7 as milling machine operators, 1 at the turret lathe hand screw, 1 as hand arc welder, 3 in inspections, 3 as policewomen, 1 as power shear operator, and 125 in a variety of office jobs. I assume that the remaining 626 women employed at Reo were involved in the fuse operation. U.S. Department of Labor, Bureau of Labor Statistics, Division of Wage Analysis, *Survey of Occupational Wage Rates at Reo*, Dec. 15, 1943, ibid., box 53, folder 29; research department, UAW-CIO, Detroit, April 1942, *Reo Motor Car, Lansing Michigan, Local #650*, Local 650/Reuther, box 19, folder "Joint Time Study, 1945."

44. Memo from R. W. Huxtable, purchasing, to Charlie Parr, safety, Oct. 28, 1941, Reo Papers, box 51, folder 37, MSUAHC.

45. Memo from E. D. Stinebower, factory manager, to Mr. Kopsche, in charge of .700 Project, April 13, 1942, ibid., box 51, folder 88.

46. Memo from R. A. Smith to Ernie Stinebower, Sept. 2, 1942, ibid., box 51, folder 86.

47. Memo from E. D. Stinebower to John Tooker, Feb. 20, 1943, ibid., box 122, folder 69; A. R. Kenny to Thomas F. Staley, Jan. 21, 1943, 10, ibid., box 123, folder 30.

48. "Reo Personnel Department," labor turnover reports, 1944, ibid., box 67, folder 1; labor turnover report, 1945, ibid., box 67, folder 15.

49. "*Special Notice!!!* A dancing party at Fort Custer Saturday, April 29th, 1944," ibid., box 52, folder 15.

50. Memo from Charles Parr, plant protection department, to John Tooker, Feb. 4, 1943, ibid., box 123, folder 30.

51. Memo from Charles Parr to E. D. Stinebower re: Venereal Cases, June 28, 1944, ibid., box 67, folder 43.

52. Charles Parr to E. D. Stinebower on complaint dated May 31, 1943, ibid., box 51, folder 61.

53. Statement of Doris White, May 31, 1943, ibid.

54. Memo, "Statement of Leon Maffitt (Colored Sweeper) Clock #36-303," May 31, 1943, ibid.; memo from Charles Parr to Stinebower, May 31, 1943, ibid.

55. One of my informants, Eileen Nortman, who worked at Reo as a single recent high school graduate during World War II, stated that having women in the shop was disruptive for some of the men. When asked, "What kinds of things did you see going on?" Nortman responded, "Oh, these men that are married play around with these other girls. . . . I'd say probably 10 or 15 percent." When asked, "Was it mutual or were they bothering these girls?" she replied, "Oh, I think it was mutual. . . . Because there wasn't very many men around, you know." Eileen Nortman, interview by author and Shirley Bradley, Jan. 28, 1993, East Lansing.

56. "Employees Who Have Been on Our Payroll since Feb. 28, 1943: Age Given as of March 1st, 1945," Reo Papers, box 5, folder 78, MSUAHC.

57. Memo from Al Zimmer to Henry E. Hund, April 5, 1945, ibid., box 121, folder 129.

58. Martin Glaberman, *Wartime Strikes: The Struggle against the No-Strike Pledge during World War II* (Detroit: Bewick, 1980); Atleson, *Labor and the Wartime State*; Harris, *The Right to Manage*; Clive, *State of War*; and Lichtenstein, *Labor's War at Home*.

59. Since most of this information about these actions comes from the company as it was preparing testimony for later NLRB cases, some of the data reflect the company's own hopes for the outcome of the case. The biases involved notwithstanding, this is probably a fairly accurate listing of the ongoing disruptions in the plant and in the navy division. As already described, the navy division had most of the female workers and was also at the front lines in defense contracts. The majority of these actions never appeared in any general accounting of the wartime wildcat strikes (that I have been able to find), so the proliferation of these sorts of local, spontaneous, short-term actions at Reo suggests that wartime turbulence generally might have been even worse than "official" accountings might indicate. This uncertainty accounts for my lack of precision in counting the number of strikes.

60. State of Michigan, Department of Labor and Industry, #A 255, District 9, Feb. 5, 1943, *Correction Order,* Reo Papers, box 53, folder 45, MSUAHC; *Reo Motors, Inc. vs. George W. Dean, Chairman of the Commissioners of Labor and Industry for the State of Michigan,* Herbert J. Rushton, Michigan attorney general, Victor C. Anderson, prosecuting attorney for Ingham County, Bill of Complaint (draft), 1943, ibid., box 53, folder 29.

61. In the matter of Reo Motors, Inc., and International Union, UAW Local 650 CIO, National War Labor Board (hereafter NWLB), Region XI, Detroit, Case No. 111-12357-D, 7, ibid., box 69, folder 44.

62. Minutes of Management-Union Bargaining Committee meeting, May 12, 1944, ibid., box 67, folder 59; "Grievance, May 2, 1944" (no title or number), ibid.; grievance report—May 4, 1944, ibid.; Minutes of Management-Union Bargaining Committee meeting, May 10, 1944, ibid., box 67, folder 60; Sheet dated May 19, 1944, on vote for fixed or rotating shifts, ibid.; Minutes of Management-Union Bargaining Committee meeting, June 3, 1944, ibid.; "Grievance #483" June 21, 1944, ibid.

63. Del MacWilliams, industrial engineer, UAW-CIO, to Glenn D. Mullett, president, UAW Local 650, April 5, 1944, Local 650/Reuther, box 4.

64. Memos from Carl F. Ogden to Russell Smith, May 23 and June 20, 1944; memo from Russell Smith to Carl Ogden, June 20, 1944; *Application for Approval of a Wage or Salary Rate Adjustment of Schedule,* Form NWLB 10, NWLB, filed June 23, 1944; Harry A. Reifin, supervising inspector, U.S. Department of Labor, Wage-Hour and Public Contracts Division, to Russell A. Smith, Reo Motors, June 29, 1944, Reo Papers, box 53, folder 42, MSUAHC. Statement by Wayne Keeney, Feb. 8, 1947, Local 650/Reuther, box 22, folder "Strike, 1946."

65. *Group Piece Work on Automatics (Gridleys) (New Brittans)* report by Walter Foust, July 28, 1944, Reo Papers, box 67, folder 61, MSUAHC; memo from Walter Foust to Mr. Schwartz, Mr. Logan, Mr. Owens, Mr. Shutes, Mr. Kier, Mr. Grable, Mr. Butler, July 29, 1944, ibid.

66. Minutes of Management-Union Bargaining Committee meeting, July 31, 1944, ibid.

67. Russell Smith to Wage and Hour Division, U.S. Department of Treasury, July 5, 1944; Russell Smith to NWLB, Region XI, Aug. 3, 1944, in the matter of Reo Motors and UAW-CIO Reo Local, Case No: 11-13061, NWLB Region XI, *Ruling of the Wage Stabilization Director,* Philip Arnow, received by Reo, Aug. 4, 1944. All in Reo Papers, box 53, folder 42, MSUAHC.

68. Minutes of Management-Union Bargaining Committee meeting, Aug. 8, 1944, ibid., box 67, folder 61, MSUAHC.

69. Reo and UAW Local 650 to NWLB, Appeals and Review Committee, Aug. 9, 1944; Elizabeth Posner, review division, Office for Emergency Management, NWLB, Detroit, to Russell Smith, Reo, and Glen Mullett, UAW Local 650, Aug. 11, 1944, ibid., box 53, folder 42.

70. Reo and UAW Local 650 to Elizabeth Posner, Aug. 16, 1944; John M. Maguire, Chief, Review Division, NWLB, to Russell Smith, Sept. 8, 1944; memo from Russell Smith to Carl Ogden, Sept. 12, 1944; memo from Russell Smith to E. D. Stinebower, Sept. 20, 1944; Reo and UAW Local 650 to John M. Maguire, Sept. 21, 1944, all ibid., box 53, folder 42.

71. See Table 4 in the Appendix, and A. W. Zimmer, "Automatic Piece Work—One Man, Two Machines," Jan. 4, 1945, Reo Papers, box 69, folder 41, MSUAHC.

72. "Meeting in Mr. Hund's office regarding stoppage of work in Inert Assembly Department," Sept. 25, 1944, ibid., box 67, folder 62.

73. See Reo office memo, Oct. 13, 1944, ibid., box 67, folder 62; Zimmer, "Automatic Piece Work."

74. Grievance report #6292, Oct. 17, 1944, signed by G. H. Manley, Reo Papers, box 53, folder 42, MSUAHC.

75. See grievance reports and "Work Stoppage 10/18 & 19, 1944," ibid., box 67, folder 58.

76. W. E. Foust to Glenn Mullett, Oct. 19, 1944, ibid., box 53, folder 42.

77. Russell Smith to F. J. Holt, Oct. 19, 1944; Reo, Inc., and UAW Local 650 to NWLB Region XI, Appeals and Review Committee, Oct. 19, 1944, ibid., box 53, folder 42.

78. Manley, "Work Stoppage, 10/18 and 19, 1944," and Walter Foust, "Work Stoppage, 10/18 and 19, 1944," ibid., box 67, folder 58.

79. Henry Hund to Russell Smith, Oct. 19, 1944, 2:55 P.M., and draft of press release dated Oct. 10, 1944, ibid., box 53, folder 42.

80. "Reo Division Strike against WLB Ends," *Lansing State Journal,* Oct. 20, 1944, 9.

81. The testimony and grievances filed after the discharges are in Reo Papers, box 67, folder 58; Walter Foust to Al Zimmer, Oct. 28, 1944, revealed great hostility between these two and Wayne Keeney and Bernie Bennett. Keeney was described as having brought all of the navy division stewards into Foust's office to "straighten him out" on how they were going to conduct their union business. See also Minutes of the meeting of the Management-Union Bargaining Committee, Nov. 6, 1944, ibid., box 67, folder 63, and Henry Hund to Jack Holt, Nov. 9, 1944, ibid., box 67, folder 63.

82. Henry Hund to Employees of Reo Motors, Inc., Nov. 10, 1944, ibid., box 67, folder 63; file on Bernie Bennett, ibid., box 67, folder 40; Walter Foust to Henry Hund, Jan. 9, 1945, ibid., box 67, folder 65; statement by Lewis Fisher, Feb. 1, 1944; memo from V. R. Gresso to E. D. Stinebower, Feb. 1, 1944, both ibid., box 67, folder 43.

83. John M. Maguire to Russell Smith, Oct. 24, 1944; Glenn Mullett and Russell Smith to John M. Macguire, NWLB, Oct. 30, 1944; "In the Matter of Reo Motors, Inc. and Local 650 UAW-CIO," board ruling, Nov. 10, 1944, Docket No: 11-13061; memo from Russell Smith to Carl Ogden, Nov. 11, 1944, all ibid., box 53, folder 42.

84. Michigan State Police Record #100745, ibid., box 68, folder 24; personal information, Wayne Keeney, ibid., box 54, folder 5. Since these papers are from the Michigan State Police, I have pursued the Michigan State Police records to find out more about Keeney and others involved in the 1946 strike. The MSP Red Files, from which this material most certainly comes, is sealed until 2020 (unless it is a file on oneself, in which case it can be retrieved under the Freedom of Information Act).

85. See materials prepared for NLRB hearing, 1949, "General—Labor Relations Background," ibid., box 54, folder 4.

86. Special management-union meeting held on Aug. 17, 1945, on termination of contracts, Local 650/Reuther, box 9.

87. Minutes of the Management-Union Bargaining Committee meeting, May 5, 1946, Reo Papers, box 68, folder 3, MSUAHC. In the negotiations on May 16, 1946, Nader made clear that hiring of veterans over women who were unable to do the work was an important option. Ibid., box 68, folder 6; minutes of membership meeting, Oct. 22, 1946, Local 650/Reuther, box 6; Don Falor, sub-regional director, I-C, to Joe Tuma, international union's fair employment practices division, Jan. 13, 1947, Local 650/ Reuther, box 20.

88. "Annual Report to Stockholders for the year ending Dec. 31, 1945," and "Annual Report to Stockholders for the year ending Dec. 31, 1946" both in Reo Papers, box 11, folder 5, MSUAHC.

89. "Meeting Regarding Company Policy," Oct. 16, 1945, Local 650/Reuther, box 7.

90. "Oral Minutes," piecework rate for export boxing, Jan. 8, 1946; "Telephone Call from Ray Reed, 10:45 A.M.," Jan. 29, 1946; Reo Bargaining Committee agenda, grievance #7501, Feb. 11, 1946; Reo Bargaining Committee agenda, grievance #9280, Jan. 15, 1946, all in Reo Papers, box 68, folder 25, MSUAHC; minutes of the Management-Union Bargaining Committee meeting, Jan. 15, 1946 (on grievance #9280); minutes of Management-Union Bargaining Committee meeting, Feb. 12, 1946 (on grievance #7501), Local 650/Reuther, box 7.

91. Raymond Reed, "They Did It Again: Reo Agrees to Raises for Skilled Tradesmen," *Lansing Labor News*, Feb. 14, 1946, 1. This article appeared while the GM strike was raging!

92. There are records of contract negotiations for these dates up to the difficulties in 1946 and beyond in the Local 650/Reuther, box 9 and 10: March 15, 19, 1946; April 5, 8, 10, 12, 15, 17, 19, 22, 25, 26, 29, 1946; May 1, 2, 3, 6, 8, 9, 10, 13, 14, 16, 17, 20, 21, 24, 27, 28, 1946; June 3, 4, 6, 7, 13, 14, 17, 18, 20, 25, 1946; July 2, 3, 9, 16, 26, 1946; Aug. 1, 2, 1946; May 20, 1947; June 4, 6, 13, 16, 18, 20, 23, 27, 30, 1947; July, 1, 2, 3, 24, 30, 1947; Aug. 5, 8, 11, 21, 1947; May 7, 12, 13, 17, 19, 21, 24, 26, 1948; June 3, 7, 9, 11, 14, 16, 18, 21, 23, 25, 28, 29, 30, 1948; July 1, 1948; Dec. 29, 1949; Jan. 20, 26, 1950; Feb. 3, 6, 10, 16, 23, 1950. Many of these materials and some additional ones are found in Reo Papers, box 68, folders 1–25, MSUAHC.

93. Contract negotiations, June 20, 1946, Reo Papers, box 68, folder 12, MSUAHC.

94. Contract negotiations, July 9, 1946, 10, ibid., box 68, folder 13.

95. "Meeting—Joint Time Study—Band Saw," June 17, 1946, 9, ibid., box 68, folder 11.

96. Contract negotiations, June 13, 1946, 10, ibid., box 68, folder 10.

97. See Martin Halperin, *UAW Politics in the Cold War Era* (Albany: SUNY Press, 1988), 71–93.

98. Contract negotiations, June 18, 1946, 6–11, Reo Papers, box 68, folder 11, MSUAHC.

99. J. H. Wishart, research director, UAW, to Wayne Keeney, June 25, 28, and July 8, 1946; Leonard Woodcock to Wayne Keeney, July 1, 1946, Local 650/Reuther, box 5.

100. Contract negotiations, July 3, 1946, Reo Papers, box 68, folder 13, MSUAHC.

101. "To Our Plant Employees," June 19, 1946, ibid., box 68, folder 11; quotation from "To Our Plant Employees," June 21, 1946, ibid., box 68, folder 12.

102. Contract negotiations, July 3, 1946, ibid., box 68, folder 12.

103. Contract negotiations, July 9, 1946, 1, ibid., box 68, folder 13.

104. "Memorandum to Employees," July 12, 1946, ibid.

105. Western Union Telegram, July 13, 1946, Local 650/Reuther, box 2.

106. Roosa's appearance at this unsettled moment suggests the presence of other political currents. Company materials prepared for an NLRB hearing years later described Roosa as a veteran and a new employee at Reo. Before the war he had been the president of an AFL local, "and when he quit the company on Nov. 4 [in the midst of all of the strike turmoil] he stated he was going to work for Washburn as an AFL organizer in Illinois. Rumors have linked his name with AFL activities in connection with the company." If the AFL and perhaps Washburn himself, who was by now the president of the UAW-AFL, were attempting to (re)capture Reo, they were doing so by positioning themselves as the more militant of the two factions. This strategy almost eerily evokes the political terrain of the late 1930s, where the AFL anticommunist champion of the rank and file (not the left- and international-leaning CIO) provided the strongest stance against management. "Contract-Wage Negotiations—1946," Reo Papers, box 54, folder 4, MSUAHC; James Kilroy, *Industrial Worker,* Feb. 22, 1947, ibid., folder 8, Exhibit XXIV-M. There is no evidence that the rank-and-file movement in the UAW had any impact on these events at Reo. While there is some evidence that auto plants in Lansing were aware of the movement, no one from Reo appears to have been in the leadership of the movement. See "GM Officials Get Ballots in No-Strike Referendum," *Rank and Filer,* Feb. 1945, 1, AFL-CIO Unbound Newspaper Collection, Reuther Library, box 16, folder 22. On the rank-and-file caucus, see Martin Glaberman, *Wartime Strikes: The Struggle against the No-Strike Pledge in the UAW during World War II* (Detroit: Bewick, 1980).

107. "Investigation Relative to Rate History, Grievance #7920, 9583, 10351," n.d., Reo Papers, box 68, folder 26, MSUAHC; Contract negotiations, July 26, 1946, 4 and 5, ibid., folder 14.

108. "Report of Meeting Regarding Export Department 22," July 22, 1946, ibid., box 68, folder 14.

109. "Cab Line—Background," ibid., box 54, folder 4.

110. "Special Meeting to discuss certain protests against the Company," July 16, 1946, 8:55 A.M., Local 650/Reuther, box 6.

111. Contract negotiations, Aug. 1, 1946, Reo Papers, box 68, folder 14, MSUAHC; "Supplemental Agreement between Reo Motors, Inc. and the International Union, United Automobile, Aircraft, Agricultural Implement Workers of American, CIO and

Local 650 UAW-CIO," Aug. 1, 1946, ibid.; "Reo Labor Agreement," Local 650/Reuther, box 11, folder "1946."

112. "Minutes of Meeting on Piecework Plan," Sept. 5, 1946, Reo Papers, box 68, folder 16, MSUAHC.

113. "Minutes of Meeting on Piecework Plan," Sept. 11, 1946, ibid., folder 17.

114. "Cab Line—Background," ibid., box 54, folder 4.

115. Memo from Al Zimmer, Sept. 16, 1946, ibid., box 68, folder 19.

116. "Local Union 650, UAW-CIO vs. Reo Motors, Inc.: Facts of Unfair Labor Practices Committed by Reo Motors, on and after Sept. 16, 1946," Local 650/Reuther, box 20; "Meeting—Work Stoppage," Oct. 23, 1946, Reo Papers, box 68, folder 24, MSUAHC.

117. Exhibits XIX 1a, XIX 4a, and XIX 12, Reo Papers, box 54, folder 7, MSUAHC.

118. Carlisle Carver, "Reo Closed by Outlaw Walk Out," *Lansing State Journal*, Sept. 17, 1946, 1.

119. After the end of Prohibition, while there were still dry towns like East Lansing, the sale and consumption of liquor was allowed in Lansing. Many union officials described spending off hours in the bars around the plant meeting with the members.

120. "Reo Strike End Sought," *Lansing State Journal*, Sept. 18, 1946, 1; "Local Union 650, UAW-CIO vs. Reo Motors, Inc. Lansing, Michigan," Facts of Unfair Labor Practices Committed by Reo Motors, Inc., on and after Sept. 16, 1946, Local 650/Reuther, box 20.

121. Telegraph, Sept. 18, 1946, 8:05 P.M., from Keeney to Byrne, Reo Papers, box 68, folder 19, MSUAHC; "Telephone conversation between Gerald Byrne and Wayne Keeney—Sept. 18, 1946—5:22–5:25 P.M.," Exhibit XXI-A, ibid., box 54, folder 8. That the transcript of this and other phone conversations appeared in Reo's NLRB exhibits does corroborate the *Industrial Worker*'s allegation that the union's phone lines were tapped and my suspicions that the Michigan state police "Red Squad" was involved.

122. Carlisle Carver, "Reo Union Votes End of Strike," *Lansing State Journal*, Sept. 19, 1946, 1; Walter Reuther to the membership of Reo Local 650, UAW-CIO, Sept. 18, 1946, Local 650/Reuther, box 22, folder "Strike, 1946."

123. Card No. X317468, "Vets at Reo Fight for Unionism," *Industrial Worker*, 1; Exhibit XXIV-E, Reo Papers, box 54, folder 8, MSUAHC.

124. "Keeney Says Reo Using Tactics of Dictators," *Lansing Labor News*, Oct. 3, 1946, and "Local Union 650, UAW-CIO vs. Reo Motors, Inc.: Facts of Unfair Labor Practices Committed by Reo Motors on and after Sept. 16, 1946," Local 650/Reuther, boxes 20 and 22, folder "Strike, 1946."

125. Henry Hund to Jack Holt, UAW regional director, Sept. 19, 1946; Exhibit XXIII-A, Reo Papers, box 54, folder 8; "Handwritten testimony for NLRB case, Exhibit, XXIII-B," phone call between Holt and Hund, Sept. 19, 1946, P.M., ibid., box 68, folder 20.

126. William J. Dowling, "From a Canned Reo Worker," May 31, 1947, *Industrial Worker*, June 14, 1947, 2.

127. "Kilroy Likes It in Cleveland," ibid., Feb. 22, 1947, Exhibit XXIV-M, Reo Papers, box 54, folder 8, MSUAHC.

128. "Letter to the Editor," n.d., *Industrial Worker*, Exhibit XXIV-L, Reo Papers, box 54, folder 8, MSUAHC.

129. "Minutes of Membership Meeting," Oct. 22, 1946, Local 650/Reuther, box 6; "Minutes of Management-Union Bargaining Committee Meeting," Nov. 12, 1946, ibid., box 7; Willian H. Oliver, co-director, UAW-CIO Unfair Practices and Anti-Discrimination Department, to Lester Palmer, chairman, Local 650, Fair Practices Committee, Jan. 2, 1947, ibid., box 20; "Special Meeting, Jan. 7, 1947, 2:45 P.M. Discrimination and Fair Practice Committee," ibid., box 20; Don Falor to Joe Tuma, Jan. 13, 1947, ibid., box 20; Katie Hornbeck, Alfreda Wiechert, Wilma Knudsen, Katie Montgomery, Wayne Keeney and Lester Palmer to Al Salter, Jan. 20, 1947, ibid., box 20; Lester Palmer to Al Salter, Jan. 21, 1947, ibid., box 20; Lester Palmer to Al Salter, Feb. 21, 1947, ibid., box 2.

130. Committee for revival of Unionism at Reo to members of UAW Local 650, Feb. 15, 1947, ibid., box 20; "Down with Communistic Practices . . ." n.d., but probably just before March 1947 election, ibid., box 5; Leo Cherne, "How to Spot a Communist," *Look* magazine, March 4, 1947, 21.

131. "Declaration of Principles," and "An Open Letter to Members of Local No. 650, UAW-CIO," Reo Papers, box 68, folder 29, MSUAHC.

132. See *Lansing Labor News*, March 6, 1947; "Letter to Members," March 4, 1947, Local 650/Reuther, box 20.

133. See *Industrial Worker*, Jan. 11, 1947, 4: "Says Kilroy: If you like lots of rules Work at Reo"; "Kilroy Says . . ." ibid., March 22, 1947, 3; "Kilroy's Column: Piecework and Rate Cuts and Good Union Practices," April 12, 1947, 3; "Kilroy's Column," May 10, 1947, 3.

134. Gerald Byrne to Ernest Miller, chairman of the Management-Union Bargaining Committee, June 4, 1947, Reo Papers, box 68, folder 31, MSUAHC.

135. "Minutes of Management-Union Bargaining Committee," July 1, 1947, 2, Local 650/Reuther, box 10; Dollie Beadle, recording secretary, Local 650, to Walter Reuther, July 25, 1947, ibid., box 2; "Reo's Stalling Revives Strike Threat," *Lansing Labor News*, Aug. 7, 1947, 1; "Reo Beats Taft-Hartley Law by 15 Minutes," *Lansing Labor News*, Aug. 28, 1947, 2. On Taft-Hartley, see Howell John Harris, *The Right to Manage*.

136. Russell Smith to James J. Bambrick, National Industrial Conference Board, July 26, 1948, Reo Papers, box 155, folder 56, MSUAHC.

137. "Reo Motors Names New Top Officials," *New York Times*, Nov. 5, 1948, 39; "Minutes of the Executive Board Meeting," Feb. 23, 1948, Local 650/Reuther, box 6.

138. Sherer, who had been in charge of defense work at Reo during World War II, knew how to work the bureaucracy to his company's benefit. By 1953 Sherer was one of the vice presidents of the Michigan Post of the American Ordnance Association (a membership society of American citizens dedicated to industrial preparedness for the national defense of the United States) and received its journal, *The Common Defense*. He participated in the Automotive Parts Manufacturing Association (Detroit), the American Management Association, the Aero Club of Michigan, and the Automobile Manufacturers Association, all organizations involved in what Dwight D. Eisenhower would later call the military-industrial complex. See assorted letters and materials in Sherer's papers, Reo Papers, box 1, folders 1–34, MSUAHC.

139. "Reo Repays RFC in Full," *Lansing State Journal*, Sept. 28, 1951, Reo Papers, box 146, folder 32, MSUAHC; "Reo Obtains $9 Million Defense Loan," *Lansing State Journal*, Sept. 27, 1951, ibid., box 147, folder 26; *Amendment to V. Loan Agreement*, May

27, 1952, ibid., folder 39; *Summary of Provisions of RFC Loan and Assignment of Responsibility*, April 19, 1949, ibid., box 146, folder 29.

140. These figures are from a restricted document compiled for the National Production Authority of the Department of Commerce dated Aug. 13, 1951. Max Horton, assistant director, Michigan Unemployment Compensation Commission, to Reo Motors, Aug. 2, 1951; *Report of Actual and Estimated Impact of Defense Mobilization on the Automotive Industry*, Reo Motors, Aug. 13, 1951, ibid., box 124, folder 21.

141. *Annual Reports* for 1951 and 1952, ibid., box 11, folder 6.

142. *Administrative Histories of US Civilian Agencies: Korean War, A Guide to Microfilm Collections* (Woodbridge Conn.: Research Publications, Inc., 1979); "USNPA: Motor Vehicles: History of Motor Vehicles Division of the NPA," (Washington, D.C.: The Authority, June 1953), Korea, Reel 9, #127.

143. R. C. Orrison to John Tooker, Nov. 15, 1952, Reo Papers, box 50, folder 1, MSUAHC.

144. The "Calamity Jane" was a "completely self-contained unit for emergency disaster service. Equipment to be carried includes portable power generators, hoists, first aid materials, ladders of varying sizes, scores of different tools, ropes and many other items." Reo ultimately made fifty-five of these trucks, which were obviously designed to operate after a nuclear attack. In addition to manufacturing the Calamity Jane for the Civil Defense Agency, representatives from Reo participated in the conference on arctic engine oils sponsored by the Aberdeen Proving Grounds, and meetings of the standardized engine program sponsored by the Army Corps of Engineers. Orrison to V. L. Couch, Oct. 20, 1952, ibid., box 50, folder 2; press release from J. Robert Conroy Associates, May 12, 1952, ibid., box 50, folder 5; "Automotive Division Development and Proof Services: Aberdeen Proving Ground, Maryland, Conference on Arctic Engine Oils," April 18, 1951, ibid., box 122, folder 94; minutes of meeting of engine standardization program, U.S. Army Corps of Engineers, Feb. 20 and 21, 1951, ibid., box 123, folder 23; memo from R. D. Jacobs III to W. M. Walworth, Nov. 5, 1953, ibid., box 2, folder 28, MSUAHC. Reo was also involved in a program to produce rockets and was awarded a research and development contract involving 500 man hours per month for the T-131 rocket. J. R. Needham, Reo (Washington), to John Tooker, May 28, 1951, ibid., box 122, folder 1; B. R. Lewis, Lt. Colonel, Office of the Chief of Ordnance, Department of the Army, to Joseph Sherer, May 2, 1952, ibid., box 2, folder 36; memo from W. M. Walworth to Joseph Sherer, Jan. 8, 1953, ibid., box 4, folder 30. Management and engineers seemed keen on developing this program, which would require creating a large staff of rocket technicians. Several hundred of these experimental rockets were shipped to a variety of arsenals during 1953. Memo from George Kramer to Joseph Sherer, March 20, 1953, ibid., box 2, folder 35. George Kramer, "Subject: General Meeting Reference T-131 Rocket, May 21, 1951," ibid., box 122, folder 1.

145. For example, Henry Busch of the union described how "we were supposed to have some Army and Navy men come through Monday and check the plant and Friday they pulled that coach line off and put them sweeping and paid them $1.215. That isn't right. If a pieceworker is pulled off his assigned job when there is work to be performed and he is put sweeping, he should get his average piece work earnings for doing it." Busch's statement also reveals the many masters in the plant when

defense contracts were being filled. Contract negotiations, June 16, 1948, 12, ibid., box 68, folder 51.

146. See Lichtenstein, *Most Dangerous Man in Detroit*, chap. 13.

147. See contract negotiations, June 28, 1948, 9–13, Reo Papers, box 68, folder 53, MSUAHC; contract negotiations, Nov. 11, 1949, 1, and Dec. 29, 1949, 6, ibid., folder 61.

148. George Hill, chairman, bargaining committee Local 650, and Roy Price, International Rep I-C, to Gerald Byrne, Dec. 30, 1949, Local 650/Reuther, box 5.

149. Contract negotiations, Feb. 10, 1950, ibid., box 10; George Hill and Roy Price to Gerald Byrne, Feb. 14, 1950, ibid., box 5.

150. Contract negotiations, Jan. 26, 1950, ibid., box 10.

151. Contract negotiations, Feb. 23, 1950, ibid., box 10.

152. George Hill to Byrne, May 22, 1950, Reo Papers, box 68, folder 63, MSUAHC; contract negotiations, June 15, 1950, 12, ibid., folder 72; contract negotiations, July 18, 1950, 1–6, ibid., box 69, folder 3; contract negotiations, July 26, 1950, ibid., folder 4.

153. "Grievance #77—Discharge," Feb. 9, 1951, ibid., box 68, folder 8.

154. Minutes of executive board meeting, June 13, 1951, Local 650/Reuther, box 6. This meeting also revealed that there were internal divisions within the membership over the pension plan. The chairman of the bargaining committee, Ralph Barnes, reported that there was a "concerted plan by the younger employees of Reo to turn down any pension plan in favor of a straight hourly raise." "Reo Motors Strike Over: Wildcat Walkout Monday Slowed Production but Workers All Returned," *Lansing State Journal*, July 24, 1951, 4; minutes of membership meeting, July 27, 1951, Local 650/Reuther, box 6.

155. "Special Membership meeting, Aug. 4, 1951," Local 650/Reuther, box 6; letter from Raymond W. Reed, president, Local 650, Aug. 6, 1951, ibid., box 11; Lloyd Utter, director, Industrial Health and Safety Division, UAW compensation department, to Raymond Reed, April 2, 1953, re: Plant Safety Inspection, ibid., box 5.

156. Pension negotiations, Aug. 17, 20, 21, 23, and 24, 1951, ibid., box 12; minutes of special meeting of executive board, Aug. 21, 1951, ibid., box 6.

157. "Special Meeting of Executive Board," Aug. 25, 1951, ibid., box 6; "To Our Plant Employees!" Aug. 25, 1951, signed by Joseph Sherer, ibid., box 3; "Reo Talks Fail; 2,500 in Walkout," *Lansing State Journal*, Aug. 25, 1951, 1.

158. Pension meeting, Sept. 5, 1951, Local 650/Reuther, box 12; "Reo Parley Hits Snag," *Lansing State Journal*, Sept. 6, 1951, 2; "Report Strikers Seek Other Jobs," *Lansing State Journal*, Sept. 7, 1951, 16; minutes of special executive board meeting, Sept. 11, 1951, Local 650/Reuther, box 6.

159. Special meeting, Sept. 19, 1951, Local 650/Reuther, box 6; "Pack Ends Reo Strike," *Lansing State Journal*, Sept. 20, 1951, 1; "Pension Agreement, Retirement Income Plan Agreed Sept. 19, 1951," 7, Local 650/Reuther, box 12.

160. "Office Employees Vote UAW in Diamond Reo," *Lansing Labor News*, July 27, 1967, 1 (the vote was 183 for the UAW and 107 against).

161. "Agreement," April 1956, Local 650/Reuther, box 12.

162. "Reo News," *Lansing Labor News*, July 23, 1953, 5.

163. A. H. Gibbons, "News from Reo," ibid., April, 28, 1955, 6; letter from H. W. Forseman in "Reo Items," ibid., May 25, 1961, 8.

## Chapter Five

1. Memo to fall festival advisory board, Sept. 18 and 19, 1953; Ardythe Pappin and Clare Loudenslager to fellow Reoites, June 26, 1953, Reo Papers, box 52, folder 15, MSUAHC; "Fall Fair Issue," *Reo Items*, 1953, ibid., folder 55.

2. Gerald Byrne to Joseph Sherer, Sept. 28, 1953, ibid., box 30, folder 26.

3. Although recent books like Sanford M. Jacoby's *Modern Manors: Welfare Capitalism since the New Deal* (Princeton: Princeton University Press, 1997), and Elizabeth Fones-Wolfe's *Selling Free Enterprise: The Business Assault on Labor and Liberalism* (Urbana: University of Illinois Press, 1994) have now established the persistence of welfare capitalism and an aggressive ideological stance on the part of the business community during the immediate postwar period on the national level, it is important to recognize that these postwar labor-management relations were also a product of company and community history. Reo's management was aware of recent campaigns by the National Association of Manufactures and other business organizations to "sell free enterprise" and establish new paternalistic relationships with employees that served ideological ends while preempting loyalty to unions. Reo's management also knew the history and demographics of the company and its workforce. Jacoby's *Modern Manors* describes only large nonunion firms.

4. Editorial, "Spring Has Come Again to America," *Reo Items*, April, 1948, 2, Reo Papers, box 52, folder 52, MSUAHC.

5. Justin L. Kestenbaum, *Out of a Wilderness: An Illustrated History of Greater Lansing* (Woodland Hills, Calif.: Windsor Publications 1981); Sallie M. Manassah, David A. Thomas, and James F. Wallington, *Lansing: Capital, Campus, and Cars* (East Lansing: Contemporary Image, 1986).

6. Birt Darling, *City in the Forest: The Story of Lansing* (New York: Stratford House, 1950), vii–viii; Kestenbaum, *Out of a Wilderness*, 114.

7. *Reo Items*, Nov. 1948, cover and p. 1, Reo Papers, box 52, folder 52, MSUAHC.

8. Elaine Tyler May, *Homeward Bound: American Families in the Cold War Era* (New York: Basic Books, 1988). The power of this domestic ideology to transcend the racial divide has been challenged by Joanne Meyerowitz, ed., *Not June Cleaver: Women and Gender in Postwar America, 1945–1960* (Philadelphia: Temple University Press, 1994).

9. For example, Fern Placeway took stenographic records of most of the labor-management bargaining negotiations; Ardythe Pappin was the company nurse. Two women I interviewed, Marjorie Koehler and Mabel McQueen, were in the girls' club and worked for individuals in personnel.

10. Annual report of the Reo girls' club, Nov. 1952–Nov. 1953, Reo Papers, box 52, folder 15, MSUAHC.

11. "Reo Girls Reorganize Club," *Reo Items*, June 1949, 4, ibid., folder 53; Reo girls' club constitution and by-laws, Oct. 12, 1953, ibid., folder 15.

12. Memo from Agnes Moist, chairman of Reo girls' club, members only, n.d., ibid., folder 15.

13. Doris Dow, interview by author and Shirley Bradley, Lansing, Feb. 19, 1992.

14. I owe a great intellectual debt here to Angel Kwolek-Folland's *Engendering Business: Men and Women in the Corporate Office, 1870–1930* (Baltimore: Johns Hopkins

University Press, 1994). See in particular chapter 5, "The Family Way: Corporate Domesticity, Kinship, and Leisure."

15. Mable McQueen, interview by author and Shirley Bradley, Dimondale, June 16, 1992.

16. Marjorie Koehler, interview by author and Shirley Bradley, Dimondale, June 16, 1992.

17. Memo to salaried employees from Gerald Byrne, March 31, 1952, Reo Papers, box 27, folder 101, MSUAHC.

18. I have never located any picture of the room but have relied on oral histories to reconstruct the interior.

19. Lewis Garcia, interview by author and Shirley Bradley, Lansing, Jan. 28, 1992.

20. Vivern Haight, interview by author and Shirley Bradley, Webberville, Feb. 4, 1993.

21. Calvin Chamberlain, interview by author and Shirley Bradley, Lansing, June 11, 1992.

22. "800 Reoites Enjoy Thanksgiving Feather Party," *Reo Items*, Dec. 1952, 2–3, Reo Papers, box 52, folder 54, MSUAHC; *Reo Items*, Jan. 1949, 2, ibid., folder 53.

23. Garcia, interview; folder on steering gear club, ibid., box 53, folder 14; Byrd Stelle, president of the industrial executives club of the YMCA, to J. S. Sherer, April 16, 1954, ibid., box 1, folder 22.

24. "A.T.A. Convention," newsletter, Nov. 10, 1953, ibid., box 156, folder 16.

25. *Reo Gold Comet Record Buster,* Jan. 7, 1954, 2, ibid., folder 24; *Reo Gold Comet Record Buster,* Jan. 18, 1954, 2, ibid., folder 24.

26. See Barbara Ehrenreich, *The Hearts of Men: American Dreams and the Flight from Commitment* (Garden City, N.Y.: Anchor, 1983), on the ways sex became a form of leisure for middle-class men in the 1950s.

27. "Who's Who at Reo: Gerald W. Byrne," *Reo Items*, Dec. 1952, Reo Papers, box 52, folder 54, MSUAHC.

28. The Lansing Country Club opened in 1908 and offered access to the game to Lansing's elites. Virtually all the important men of Reo belonged to the club and participated in the expanding range of sporting and social activities. Members included R. E. Olds, Wallace Olds, Donald Bates, Charles Davis (of the Chamber of Commerce) Richard Scott, James Dervin, Russell Smith, John Tooker, Frank McKim, Joseph Sherer (even though he didn't live in Lansing) and Zenon Hansen, to name a few. See "The Country Club of Lansing: Rules and Regulations, 1924"; "Country Club Social Program for Sept., 1924," yearbooks of the Country Club of Lansing, LLHC.

29. Bowling documents can be found in Reo Papers, box 52, folder 6, MSUAHC.

30. Gerald Byrne, "Projected Planning: Personnel and Labor Relations," 1948, ibid., box 27, folder 99; memo from Al Zimmer to Sherer, May 26, 1953, ibid., box 4, folder 39; memo from Gerald Byrne to Zimmer, Campell, Murray, Dier, Schwartz, Griese, Loudenslager, Jack, Greene, and Hamelink, April, 8, 1953, ibid., box 4, folder 39.

31. "Bulletin," n.d., but probably 1953, ibid., box 24, folder 21.

32. "When Opinions Differ. . . ." *Reo Items*, Dec. 1952, 18, ibid., box 52, folder 54.

33. James C. Scott, *Domination and the Arts of Resistance: Hidden Transcripts* (New Haven: Yale University Press, 1990); on work culture, see Susan Porter Benson, *Counter*

*Cultures: Saleswomen, Managers, and Customers in American Department Stores, 1890–1940* (Urbana: University of Illinois Press, 1986); Barbara Melosh, *"The Physician's Hand": Work, Culture, and Conflict in American Nursing* (Philadelphia: Temple University Press, 1982); and David Montgomery, *The Fall of the House of Labor: The Workplace, the State, and American Labor Activism, 1865–1925* (New York: Cambridge University Press, 1987).

34. Raymond Fuller, interview by author and Shirley Bradley, March 19, 1992 at his farm in Mulliken, Michigan.

35. Stephen Meyer, "Work, Play, Power: Masculine Culture on the Automotive Shop Floor, 1930–1960," in *Boys and Their Toys?: Masculinity, Class, and Technology in America*, ed. Roger Horowitz, 26–30 (New York: Routledge, 2001); "In the Matter of Reo Local 650, UAW-CIO and Reo Motors, Inc. Grievance No. 54," Local 650/Reuther, box 20.

36. "The Hunter," in Edgar A. Guest, *A Heap O' Livin'* (Chicago: Reilly and Lee Company, 1916), 59.

37. For a longer version of this section, see Lisa M. Fine, "Rights of Men, Rites of Passage: Hunting and Masculinity at Reo Motors of Lansing, Michigan, 1945–1975," *Journal of Social History* 33 (summer 2000): 805–23.

38. Piecework negotiations, Oct. 12, 1948, Reo Papers, box 68, folder 59, MSUAHC.

39. "Hunters Wreck Council Meet; Date is Moved," *Lansing Labor News*, Nov. 5, 1953, 1.

40. "1955 Vacation Procedure for Hourly Rated Employees, April 26, 1955," Reo Papers, box 27, folder 104, MSUAHC; "Minutes of the Management-Union Bargaining Committee meeting, Nov. 6, 1945," Local 650/Reuther, box 7; "Minutes of the Management-Union Bargaining Committee meeting, Oct. 21, 1947," Local 650/Reuther, box 8; "Minutes of the Executive Board meeting, Nov. 12, 1952," Local 650/Reuther, box 6.

41. "Grievance, William Earl Bailey," Nov. 24, 1944, Reo Papers, box 54, folder 1, MSUAHC; "Grievance #10386—Otto J. Bell," minutes of the Management-Union Bargaining Committee meeting, Dec. 11, 1946, Local 650/Reuther, box 7; "Office Memo, Nov. 16, 1943," from Charles Parr, plant protection, to E. D. Stinebower, Reo Papers, box 51, folder 6, MSUAHC.

42. "Memorandum to all Reo Deer Hunting Employees" from Byron F. Field, personnel manager, Nov. 9, 1942, Reo Papers, box 51, folder 26, MSUAHC; "Memorandum to All Superintendents and Foreman" from Gerald Byrne, Oct. 31, 1951, ibid., box 27, folder 28; "Memorandum to All Superintendents, Department Heads and Foremen" from Gerald Byrne, Oct. 16, 1953, ibid., box 27, folder 29.

43. "Reo Items," *Lansing Labor News*, Oct. 25, 1957, 6.

44. Otto Aves, interview by author and Shirley Bradley, Lansing, Jan. 4, 1993; Layton Aves, interview by author and Shirley Bradley, Lansing, Aug. 8, 1995.

45. Peter Stearns, *Be A Man! Males in Modern Society* (New York: Holmes and Meier, 1979), 18.

46. See, for example, Michael Kimmel, *Manhood in America: A Cultural History* (New York: Free Press, 1996).

47. E. Anthony Rotundo, *American Manhood: Transformations in Masculinity from the Revolution to the Modern Era* (New York: Basic Books, 1993), has a few pages on hunting. Other works that contain little on hunting are Ely Chinoy, *Automobile Workers and*

*the American Dream*, 2d ed., ed. Ruth Milkman (Urbana: University of Illinois Press, 1992), David Halle, *America's Working Man: Work, Home, and Politics among Blue-Collar Property Owners* (Chicago: University of Chicago Press, 1984), and Kathryn Grover, *Hard at Play: Leisure in America, 1840–1940* (Amherst: University of Massachusetts Press, 1992). David D. Gilmore, *Manhood in the Making: Cultural Concepts of Masculinity* (New Haven: Yale University Press, 1990), 113–17, and E. E. LeMasters, *Blue-Collar Aristocrats: Life-Styles at a Working-Class Tavern* (Madison: University of Wisconsin Press, 1975), 132–36, have short but good sections on hunting.

48. Roy Rosenzweig, *Eight Hours for What We Will: Workers and Leisure in an Industrial City, 1870–1920* (New York: Cambridge University Press, 1983); Kathy Peiss, *Cheap Amusements: Working Women and Leisure in Turn-of-the-Century New York* (Philadelphia: Temple University Press, 1986).

49. Lizabeth Cohen, *Making a New Deal: Industrial Workers in Chicago, 1919–1939* (New York: Cambridge University Press, 1990); Ronald Edsforth, *Class Conflict and Cultural Consensus: The Making of a Mass Consumer Society in Flint, Michigan* (New Brunswick: Rutgers University Press, 1987); Lipsitz, *Rainbow at Midnight*.

50. See Stuart Marks, *Southern Hunting in Black and White: Nature, History, and Rituals in a Carolina Community* (Princeton: Princeton University Press, 1991). I would also like to thank Peter Rachleff and Kevin Boyle for insights on this point.

51. Although I do not think it is accurate to understand hunting by twentieth-century Michigan autoworkers as a form of resistance, the literature on workers' resistance to state hegemony is helpful. E. P. Thompson has shown how game laws reveal political tensions brought about by changing conditions of capitalism. Similarly, James Scott has examined poaching as a way for subordinate classes in Europe to exercise their understanding of traditional rights to the forest and its game. Poaching was not a safety valve that weakened "real" resistance; rather, it was a reassertion of rights taken away by the state. See E. P. Thompson, *Whigs and Hunters: The Origin of the Black Act* (New York: Pantheon Books, 1975), and Scott, *Domination and the Arts of Resistance*, 188–92. This way of conceptualizing hunting was presented in two recent books on hunting, Louis Warren's *The Hunter's Game: Poachers and Conservationists in Twentieth-Century America* (New Haven: Yale University Press, 1997), and Nicolas W. Proctor's *Bathed in Blood: Hunting and Mastery in the Old South* (Charlottesville: University of Virginia Press, 2002).

Proctor provides a nuanced account of how the different races and classes in the Old South enacted masculinity through hunting. Warren documents the twentieth-century idea of public lands and game as a common good controlled by the state. This conception of "public" resources allowed conservationists to "deflect local charges that poor people were being shunted from the hunting grounds to make them a playground where the rich could recreate." Warren shows that "disputes over what constituted proper hunting were clashes over rival masculine ideals." For example, "killing female deer or songbirds might have been considered unmanly, even cowardly, in [upper-class] sporting circles, but for many locals it was a part of life" (Warren, *The Hunter's Game*, 12, 14).

52. Proctor, *Bathed in Blood*.

53. Ed Langenau, "100 Years of Deer Management in Michigan," Michigan Department of Natural Resources, Wildlife Division Report No. 3213 (1994) (I would like to thank Dr. R. Ben Peyton of the MSU Department of Fisheries and Wildlife for

sharing this pamphlet with me); Richard Briley, "Outline of Fur and Game History" manuscript, 1940, 6, *Department of Natural Resources—Game Division: Michigan Writers' Project, 1941–1943*, SAM.

54. See Briley, "Outline," and S. E. Sangster, "Tentative Outline for Proposed History of Michigan Fish and Game," 1940, 2, *Department of Natural Resources—Game Division: Michigan Writers' Project, 1941–1943*, SAM.

55. Aldo Leopold, *Report on a Game Survey of North Central State for the Sporting Arms and Ammunition Manufacturing Institute* (Madison: Democrat Printing Co., 1931), 198, 244–46, 131–33.

56. Harry R. Gaines, "History of MUCC," *Michigan-Out-Of-Doors*, Jan. 1947, 12.

57. Chinoy, *Autoworkers and the American Dream*, 86–96.

58. Many more may have been related by marriage. "In the Harvest Field," *Reo Spirit*, Aug. 1919, 22–23. The average monthly total of all employees for 1919 was 4,475, so this was hardly an exodus, constituting only about 2 percent of the workforce. Annual report of the Labor Department—Feb. 1, 1919–Feb. 1, 1920, Feb. 10, 1920, Reo Papers, box 66, folder 4, MSUAHC.

59. Glen Green, interview by author and Shirley Bradley, Lansing, Dec. 22, 1992.

60. We interviewed Herbert Heinz in his home in Dansville on March 16, 1993, and Raymond Fuller in his home in Mulliken on March 19, 1992.

61. "Many of the farmer members of the Reo family are quite worried lately about the harvest of wheat and oats. Rain in excessive quantity has damaged grain very seriously" ("Reo News," *Lansing Labor News*, Aug. 7, 1952, 3). "What's with these farmers, Harvey? They plow all night and come in and drag all day" ("Reo Items," April 18, 1958, 4). On April 25, 1958, Ray Fuller was referred to as the "Mullican [*sic*] Sodbuster" on p. 6.

62. Theodore Roosevelt, *Outdoor Pastimes of an American Hunter* (New York: Charles Scribner's Sons, 1905), 228. See also Roosevelt's essay "The American Boy," in *The Strenuous Life* (New York: Century Co., 1903), 156–57.

63. "Sport and National Security," *Michigan Sportsman*, Aug. 1919, Dept. of Natural Resources—Game Division: Michigan Writers' Project, 1941–1943, folder 9, "Excerpts from Publications," SAM.

64. "Hunting," *Reo Spirit*, Dec. 1918, 4.

65. "The Reo National Rifle Club," ibid., April 1916, 13.

66. Memo from Arlo A. Emery, Lt. Col. J.A.G.D. officer in charge, Detroit District, Michigan Military Area, to assistant chief of staff, G-2 Sixth Corps Area, Chicago, April 3, 1942, *Records of the Michigan State Police: Intelligence and Security Bureau, 1942–1947*. Even though it is impossible to verify the spy report, I have confirmed that the number of hunters was roughly correct, and, according to the oral history of Carl Swanson, on deposit at the Reuther Library, Swanson was a hunter and did do civil defense work. See Carl Swanson, interview by Jack W. Skeels, Oral History Project, University of Michigan–Wayne State University, Institute of Labor and Industrial Relations, Aug. 8, 1960, 30 and 46, Reuther Library.

67. Gomer Reeves, "If You Have a Son," *Sportsmen's Voice*, June 1948, 6.

68. "Reo Items," *Lansing Labor News*, Dec. 13, 1957, 6.

69. "Hit Hunting Bill for Wealthy," ibid., May 31, 1957, 5; "Special Hunting Privileges for the Rich Hit by Scholle," *Michigan CIO News*, May 16, 1957, 3.

70. See, for example, "Play Space for Millions," *Lansing Industrial News*, Oct. 4, 1946, 3; "Welcome Sign For Hunters," *Lansing Labor News*, Oct. 20, 1966, 9.

71. "This Bear Made Him Late for Picket Duty," *Lansing Labor News*, Oct. 17, 1958, 4; "Deer Hunters Looking Forward to Mackinac Bridge," ibid., Nov. 7, 1958, 1.

72. "Deer Herd Controversy Grows," *Michigan CIO News*, Dec. 1954, 7; Mort Neff, "Inequity in Hunting Laws," ibid., Sept. 7, 1955, 6.

73. "Local Sportsman," *Lansing Labor News*, Nov. 6, 1969, 12; "Reo News," ibid., July 11, 1968, 8; Fred Parks, "Local 650 Sportsman's Club Column," ibid., May 1, 1969, 5.

74. Newsletter from J. M. Struble, advertising department, to sales personnel, Nov. 30, 1953, and Aug. 4, 1954, Reo Papers, box 156, folders 16 and 30, MSUAHC.

75. "White Division," *Lansing Labor News*, Oct. 10, 1963, 16.

76. "Diamond Reo News," ibid., April 18, 1968, 11, and May 16, 1968, 14.

77. "Diamond Reo News," ibid., Jan. 23, 1969, 6; Fred Parks, "Local 650 Sportsman's Club" ibid., May 1, 1969, 5.

78. Ehrenreich, *Hearts of Men.*

79. Susan Jeffords, *The Remasculinization of America: Gender and the Vietnam War* (Bloomington: Indiana University Press, 1989).

80. Joshua B. Freeman, "Hardhats: Construction Workers, Manliness, and the 1970 Pro-War Demonstrations," *Journal of Social History* 26 (summer 1993): 725–44.

81. "Reo Items," *Lansing Labor News*, Sept. 13, 1957, 2.

82. Or, as Elliot Gorn puts it, "most workers did not spend their free time reading the *Rights of Man*, toasting Tom Paine, and struggling to resist oppression. Probably more hours were consumed at cockfights than at union meetings during the nineteenth century. Radicals there were, of course, and they have been studied brilliantly. But if historians are to understand working-class people, they must look closely at their folklore and recreations, their pastimes and sports, for it has been in leisure more than in politics or in labor that many men and women have found the deepest sense of meaning and wholeness." Gorn, *The Manly Art: Bare-Knuckle Prize Fighting in America* (Ithaca: Cornell University Press, 1986), 14.

## Chapter Six

1. Fred Parks, "White," *Lansing Labor News*, Nov. 4, 1965, 8.

2. See Homer C. Hawkins and Richard W. Thomas, *Blacks and Chicanos in Urban Michigan* (N.p.: Michigan Department of State, Michigan History Division, 1979).

3. *Lansing Labor News*, Oct. 10, 1975, 2.

4. Daniel Bell, *The Coming of Post-Industrial Society: A Venture in Social Forecasting* (New York: Basic Books, 1973). Two useful but very different works are David Harvey, *The Condition of Postmodernity* (Cambridge: Blackwell, 1989), and Nelson Lichtenstein, *State of the Union: A Century of American Labor* (Princeton: Princeton University Press, 2002).

5. The first chapter of Barry Bluestone and Bennett Harrison's *The Deindustrialization of America: Plant Closings, Community Abandonment, and the Dismantling of Basic Industry* (Basic Books: 1982) is entitled "Capital vs. Community."

6. The two ends of the ideological spectrum in the debate over the causes of plant closings, and role of government, and the effects of mobile capital are Bluestone and

Harrison, *The Deindustrialization of America,* and Richard B. McKenzie, *Plant Closings: Public or Private Choices?* (Washington, D.C.: Cato Institute, 1984). McKenzie has written several dozen works on a variety of economic issues, including plant closings.

7. An incomplete list might include the pamphlet by Gilda Hass and Plant Closures Project, *Plant Closures: Myths, Realities, and Responses* (Boston: South End Press, 1985); Charles Craypo and Bruce Nissen, *Grand Designs: The Impact of Corporate Strategies on Workers, Unions, and Communities* (Ithaca: ILR Press, 1993); Carolyn C. Perrucci, Robert Perrucci, Dena B. Targ, and Harry R. Targ, *Plant Closings: International Context and Social Costs* (New York: Aldine De Gruyter, 1988); Jefferson Cowie, *Capital Moves: RCA's Seventy-Year Quest for Cheap Labor* (Ithaca: Cornell University Press, 1999). Cowie's book is the best new work on this subject.

8. Two excellent works—Thomas Sugrue, *The Origins of the Urban Crisis: Race and Inequality in Postwar Detroit* (Princeton: Princeton University Press, 1996), and Ruth Milkman, *Farewell to the Factory: Auto Workers in the Late Twentieth Century* (Berkeley and Los Angeles: University of California Press, 1997)—identify different periods as key. And Stephen Cohen and John Zysman, in *Manufacturing Matters: The Myth of the Post-Industrial Economy* (New York: Basic Books, 1987), argue that "we are experiencing a transition not from an industrial economy to a service economy, but from one kind of industrial economy to another" (xiii).

9. Tim Martin, "Plans Would Secure 'Car Capital' Status," *Lansing State Journal,* May 17, 1999, 1; see also Jefferson Cowie and Joseph Heathcott, eds., *Beyond the Ruins: The Meanings of Deindustrialization* (Ithaca: Cornell University Press, 2003).

10. Joseph S. Sherer Jr., "Reo's Future as I See It," talk, n.d., probably mid-1953, Reo Papers, box 1, folder 29, MSUAHC.

11. See "Let a Power Mower Do It," *Business Week,* March 22, 1953, 33; "Reo Motors Shows New Products to Be Made When War Work Ends," *New York Times,* Jan. 29, 1953. See also "Reynolds and Company, Stock Department: Daily Statement," *Reo Motors, Incorporated,* May 1, 1952, and July 23, 1952, Reo Papers, box 3, folder 11, MSUAHC.

12. Frank Drob, value line investment survey, to Joseph Sherer, April 15, 1953, and response from Sherer to Drob, May 17, 1953, Reo Papers, box 1, folder 50, MSUAHC.

13. Clipping of *New York Times* article dated Sept. 11, 1953, ibid., box 122, folder 9.

14. In 1953 Reo was apparently a serious competitor for a rocket project and needed only to establish a rocket research department to get the contract. This would have positioned the company to compete for more high-tech and aerospace contracts, but apparently the department was never established. See memo from W. M. Walworth to Joseph Sherer, Jan. 8, 1953, ibid., box 4, folder 30; memo from George Kramer to Joseph Sherer, March 20, 1953, ibid., box 2, folder 35; memo from George Kramer to Al Zimmer, Aug. 26, 1953, ibid., box 2, folder 35.

15. Dollie Beadle, "Reo News," *Lansing Labor News,* April 22, 1954, and May 13, 1954; "Reo Local Awaits Plant Sale Verdict," ibid., July 1, 1954, 1.

16. Ed Wright, "Small Press," ibid., April 15, 1954, 2.

17. *Automotive Industries News Letter,* Nov. 1, 1954, 1, Reo Papers, box 1, folder 5, MSUAHC.

18. Walter Mintz, "The Reo Story: Its Recent Sale Is a Puzzling Piece of Corporate Finance," *Barron's,* Oct. 10, 1955, 9.

19. For example, when Tooker became president, Colonel W. A. Call, the office chief of Ordnance, Department of the Army, wrote to congratulate his friend from the Pentagon. He signed off, "Love to the Family." Dec. 9, 1954, Reo Papers, box 1, folder 46, MSUAHC.

20. Supplemental Agreement between Reo Motors, Inc. and Local 650 UAW for April 1956, Local 650/Reuther, box 12, folder "Misc. Agreements."

21. "Reo Items," *Lansing Labor News*, July 12, 1957, 2.

22. "White Motor: 'A' for Agility," *Forbes*, Dec. 1, 1961, 19; Seymour Melman, ed., *The Defense Economy: Conversion of Industry and Occupations to Civilian Needs* (New York: Praeger, 1970), 400.

23. "White Motor" *Forbes*, Dec. 1, 1961, 21.

24. Zenon C. R. Hansen, *Legend of the Bulldog* (New York: Newcomen Society, 1974), 32. Hansen went on to head Mack Trucks. See also "Heavy Duty, High Gear Merger," *Business Week*, Oct. 5, 1963, 94; "White Molds the Parts," *Business Week*, Oct. 16, 1965, 159.

25. "White Motor Unit Sold to Industrialist; Price Said to Be $15 Million," *Wall Street Journal*, July 16, 1971, 26.

26. "Knudsen Returns in a White Truck," *Business Week*, May 1, 1971, 22.

27. "White Motor Unit Sold to Industrialist," *Wall Street Journal*, July 16, 1971, 26.

28. "White Motor to Merge," *New York Times*, Aug. 18, 1970, 47; "US Will Oppose White Motor Tie," ibid., Jan. 27, 1971, 41; "White Motor's Merger Plan is Abandoned Following Preliminary Order Against Tie," *Wall Street Journal*, Feb. 26, 1971, 26; *Wall Street Journal*, July 16, 1971, 26.

29. John Bryan, "White Truck Chief Urges Delay of White Consolidated Merger," *Plain Dealer*, Jan. 14, 1971, 1; John Bryan, "White Corporation Orders Peterson Away After He Refuses to Quit," ibid., Jan. 15, 1971, 1; John Bryan, "White Merger Wins Overwhelming Vote," ibid., Jan. 19, 1971, 1; Brian Williams, "US Judge Blocks White Merger Plan," ibid., Feb. 25, 1971, 1; John Bryan, "White Drops Merger," ibid., Feb. 26, 1971, 1.

30. See "White Motor Unit Sold to Industrialist," *Wall Street Journal*, July 16, 1971, 26; "Bunkie Knudsen Redesigns White Motors," *Business Week*, Oct. 30, 1971, 44; "To the Rescue," *Forbes*, Nov. 15, 1972, 30; "How Bunkie Knudsen Took on the Bankers," *Business Week*, Dec. 13, 1976, 72.

31. Ann Markusen, Scott Campbell, Peter Hall, and Sabina Deitrick, *The Rise of the Gunbelt: The Military Remapping of Industrial America* (New York: Oxford University Press, 1991), 25, 238, 12–16, and table 2.1 on p. 13.

32. "Galahad to the Rescue," *Forbes*, Nov. 15, 1972, 30.

33. "White Motor Unit Sold to Industrialist," *Wall Street Journal*, July 16, 1971, 26.

34. There is no critical historical account of this era in Lansing's history. On New Haven, see William Lee Miller, *The Fifteenth Ward and the Great Society: An Encounter with a Modern City* (Boston: Houghton Mifflin, 1966), and R. Allen Hays, *The Federal Government and Urban Housing: Ideology and Change in Public Policy*, 2d ed. (Albany: SUNY Press, 1995).

35. Douglas K. Meyer, "The Changing Negro Residential Patterns in Lansing, MI, 1850–1969," Ph.D. diss., Michigan State University, 1970, 114. See also Rose Toomer Brunson, "A Study of the Migrant Negro Population in Lansing, Michigan,

during and since World War II," master's thesis, Dept. of Social Work, Michigan State University, 1955, which describes a debate of the real estate board of Lansing in 1943 about whether to set aside a neighborhood where black migrants could buy homes. The board could not agree to do so (11).

36. Richard G. Crowe, "The Lansing Housing Problem," *Michigan State Economic Record* (July–Aug. 1971): 3; Homer Chandler Hawkins, "Knowledge of the Social and Emotional Implications of Urban Renewal and the Utility of this Knowledge to the Practice of Social Work," Ph.D. diss., Michigan State University, 1971 (a study of the effects of removal on a sample of African American families who were displaced by the construction of I-496); Lansing City Demonstration Agency, *Mid-Planning Statement: Model Cities Program* (Lansing, Nov. 1969); Meyer, "Changing Negro Residential Patterns in Lansing"; and Brunson, "Study of the Migrant Negro Population in Lansing." Brunson interviewed black residents of census tract 18 in Lansing, a neighborhood where the majority of the black migrants during the 1940s had settled. The total black population of the tract was 2,125, while the total black population of the city was 3,290. While crime and other urban problems were not major problems, the neighborhood was overcrowded. Interstate 496 went directly through tract 18.

37. See articles in the *Lansing State Journal*, June 6, 1966, Aug. 26, 1966, and Oct. 20, 1966.

38. "City Urban Renewal Director Starts Job," *Lansing State Journal*, May 16, 1962; Lloyd Moles, "New Look for Downtown Lansing: Urban Renewal Plans Outlined," ibid., May 17, 1964, C1; Lloyd Moles, "Plan Community Renewal Study," ibid., June 15, 1965, C1; Lloyd Moles, "Downtown Urban Renewal Progresses Toward Goal," ibid., Feb. 14, 1965; Curt Hanes, "Pin Hopes on US Aid," ibid., April 19, 1967.

39. Crowe, "Lansing Housing Problem," 3.

40. Lloyd Moles, "Homes Sought for 592 Low Income Families," *Lansing State Journal*, Aug. 18, 1967, D1; Norm Sinclair, "New Guidelines Explained for Reo Housing Project," ibid., April 11, 1968, F1; Curt Hanes, "Housing Accepted By City," ibid., July 31, 1968, D1.

41. "City Housing Mess Seen Getting Worse," ibid., March 5, 1966; Lloyd Moles, "Rental Homes Scarce in City," ibid., Dec. 11, 1966; Crowe, "Lansing Housing Problem."

42. Lloyd Moles, "700 Riot; Police Chief Hurt," *Lansing State Journal*, June 20, 1964, 1; Mike Jones, "Stagier Tells of Mob Actions," ibid.

43. Lloyd Moles, "Police Curb Rioting Youth," ibid., Aug. 8, 1966, 1; "Lloyd Moles, "Four Shot in Violent Night" ibid., Aug. 9, 1966, 1.

44. Lloyd Moles, "Pact Eases Tension on West Side," ibid., Aug. 10, 1966, 1; Lloyd Moles, "Four Junior High Centers Proposed by Negro Group," ibid., Sept. 1, 1966, E1.

45. Lloyd Moles, "Four Shot in Violent Night," ibid., Aug. 9, 1966, A12.

46. Norm Sinclair, "Boycott Threat Lessened," ibid., March 1, 1968, A1.

47. Clippings from LLHC: Marcia Van Ness, "School Aides, Community Center on Orderly Operation at Sexton," *Lansing State Journal*, Feb. 15, 1970; Judy Brown, "Sexton Meeting Explores Causes of Racial Clash At High School," ibid., Feb. 18, 1970.

48. Curt Hanes, "Council to Get 'Keep Reo' Plan," ibid., July 22, 1968.

49. "White Motor Unit Plans Plant at Lansing, Michigan," *Wall Street Journal*, Oct. 21, 1968, 28.

50. *Official Proceedings of the City Council of the City of Lansing*, Sept. 9, 1968, Sept. 30, 1968; Lloyd J. Moles, "Diamond Reo Area Figures in Third Renewal Project," *Lansing State Journal*, June 26, 1968.

51. See Lloyd Moles, "New Terms on Reo Appraisal Accepted," *Lansing State Journal*, Nov. 10, 1969, 1; and Lloyd Moles, "Lansing Renews Pledge to Aid in Reo Relocation," ibid., Nov. 28, 1969; Lloyd Moles, "Diamond Reo Appraisal Funding Allocated," ibid., Dec. 2, 1969.

52. *Official Proceedings of the City Council of the City of Lansing*, March 24, 1968, April 1, 1969, and Feb. 2, 1970; "Diamond Reo Plant Important to City," editorial, *Lansing State Journal*, July 24, 1968, A8; "White Motors Get Welcome by Clinton," *Lansing State Journal*, Feb. 2, 1970.

53. Lloyd Moles, "Reo Rejects HUD's Offer," *Lansing State Journal*, Sept. 30, 1970, 1. The Romney Papers at the Bentley Library, Ann Arbor, and the HUD papers in the National Archives have not shed any additional light on these events.

54. See Hays, *Federal Government and Urban Housing*.

55. Alvin A. Butkus, "The Silent Tycoon: Who Is Francis L. Cappaert? One of the Richest Men in America," *Dun's*, Jan. 1972, 38–40. It was also reported in the *Lansing Labor News* that Cappaert contributed to Richard Nixon's presidential campaigns in 1968 and 1972. See Lorraine Baldwin, "P & M: Diamond Reo," *Lansing Labor News*, May 18, 1973, 10.

56. See, for example, Fred Parks, "Diamond Reo," *Lansing Labor News*, Jan. 25, 1968, 6. He reported, "we followed the Big Three's pattern with some variation."

57. "Office Employees Vote UAW in Diamond-Reo Election," ibid., July 27, 1967, 1; Les Mitchell, "News from the TOP," ibid., April 4, 1968, 8.

58. Wayne Nunheimer, interview by author and Shirley Bradley, Lansing, June 18, 1992. "We had no bargaining power," said Mr. Nunheimer of Local 650's clout as a union.

59. G. Sanders, White Motors, "Who Are We?" *Lansing Labor News*, Nov. 22, 1962, 7.

60. Jim Richardson, "Off the TOP," ibid., April 17, 1970, 14.

61. Lewis Garcia, interview by author and Shirley Bradley, Lansing, Jan. 28, 1992; Glen Green, interview by author and Shirley Bradley, Lansing, Jan. 22, 1992; Doris Dow, interview by author and Shirley Bradley, Lansing, Feb. 19, 1992; Doris Faustman, interview by author and Shirley Bradley, Williamston, June 23, 1992.

62. Interview with informant A, whose identity I am keeping confidential.

63. Interview with informant B, whose identity I am keeping confidential.

64. Interview with informant C, whose identity I am keeping confidential.

65. "Strike Threat at Reo, for Real," *Lansing Labor News*, Feb. 9, 1973, 1.

66. Marilyn and Calvin Chamberlain, interview by author and Shirley Bradley, Lansing, June 11, 1992. See also Herbert Heinz, interview by author and Shirley Bradley, Dansville, March 16, 1993; Marvin Grinstern, interview by author and Shirley Bradley, Lansing, Dec. 3, 1992.

67. See "President's Comments," *Lansing Labor News*, Dec. 15, 1972, 18; ibid., June 1, 1973, 2.

68. Roger D. Foster, "President's Comments," ibid., Jan. 26, 1973, 2.

69. *Joint Issue* (East Lansing), vol. 4, no. 3 (1973): 3.

70. Lorraine Baldwin, "P and M Unit," *Lansing Labor News*, March 23, 1973, 9.

71. Doris Dow, interview.

72. Chamberlain, interview.

73. Raymond Fuller, interview by author and Shirley Bradley, Mulliken, March 19, 1992.

74. Seventeen of the thirty informants in the Reo Oral History Project worked at Reo until the 1970s.

75. Kathleen M. Blee, "Evidence, Empathy, and Ethics: Lessons from Oral Histories of the Klan," *Journal of American History* 80 (Sept. 1993): 596; John Bodnar, "Power and Memory in Oral History: Workers and Managers at Studebaker," *Journal of American History* 75 (March 1989): 1201; Jane Sherron De Hart, "Oral Sources and Contemporary History: Dispelling Old Assumptions," *Journal of American History* 80 (Sept. 1993): 582; Alessandro Portelli, *The Death of Luigi Trastulli and Other Stories: Form and Meaning in Oral History* (Albany: SUNY Press, 1991).

76. Arthur Frahm, interview by author and Shirley Bradley, Lansing, Feb. 10, 1992; Heinz, interview; Nunheimer, interview.

77. "Graves: Reo Too Run Down to Be National Monument," *Lansing State Journal*, June 25, 1978, B3; "Reo Now a National Monument," ibid., June 16, 1978; Roger Hedges, "US to Review Reo Historic Decision," ibid., June 30, 1978, 1.

78. "Graves: Reo Too Run Down"; "US to Review Reo Decision."

79. "Reo Plant Coming Down for (Pretty) Sure," ibid., Jan. 4, 1979; "Diamond Reo Demolition Commences," ibid., July 23, 1979; "Reo Wrecking Halt Order," ibid., Aug. 13, 1979.

80. Edward O. Welles, "The Shape of Things to Come," *Inc.*, Feb. 1992, 66.

81. Ibid.

## Epilogue

*Epigraph:* Vivern Haight was interviewed on Feb. 4, 1993, in his home in Dansville, Michigan, about thirty miles from Lansing. He was the unofficial manager of the clubhouse, worked in the steering gear room, and organized parties and special events throughout the facility between 1945 and 1975. He had extremely detailed and warm memories of his experiences at Reo but was different from many of our informants in that he did not participate in any of the retiree organizations. He did, however, have a huge garage filled with all sorts of memorabilia, a great deal of it from Reo and his time there.

1. Cappaert apparently stopped contributing to the pension funds as soon as he bought the company. Tim Kenney, "Reo Pension Fund $3 Million in Arrears," *Lansing State Journal*, Feb. 12, 1975; Tim Kenney, "Reo Retirees Gather To Trade Memories," ibid., May 27, 1975; Mark Nixon, "Reo Pension Decision Good, Bad," ibid., March 25, 1976; John Teare, "Diamond Reo Owner's Wealth Examined," ibid., June 11, 1976. In 1978, with the help of the UAW, the Pension Benefit Guaranty Corporation (PBGC) filed a suit in U.S. District Court in Grand Rapids to recover about

$1 million in pension money Cappaert had not paid. This suit was finally settled in 1986 when Cappaert was forced to pay PBGC $1.85 million. Approximately 2,000 former Diamond Reo employees had made claims in bankruptcy courts. See Carolyn K. Washburn, "Ex-Owner of Reo, U.S. Settle Feud," ibid., Feb. 6, 1986. All articles from the clipping files of the Lansing local history room at the main branch of the Lansing Public Library in downtown Lansing.

2. I attended luncheons in 1992, 1993, 1995, and 1999.

3. I am indebted to Alessandro Portelli, *The Death of Luigi Trastulli and Other Stories: Form and Meaning in Oral History* (Albany: SUNY Press, 1991).

4. The committee included Jim Cataline, Doris Dow, Arthur Frahm, Richard G. Heil, Betty Kost, Frank Wiechmann, Ardythe Pappin, Fern Placeway, Edwin Rankin, Bill Turill, and James Neal. All but Betty Kost and James Neal were former employees, but none was a factory worker, a fact revealed by the special thanks the committee gave to the Local 650 retiree organization. I would like to thank Laura Ashlee of the State Historical Preservation Department for assistance in tracking down the documents pertaining to the historical marker.

5. J. R. Connor, "They Call Him 'Reo Joe,'" *Lansing Industrial News*, Oct. 20, 1939, 1.

# Index

Page numbers in italics refer to illustrations and tables.

1939 convention, 92
progressive faction, 91
TOP, 13, 159, 160
unity faction, 91
union shop, 93, 101, 117, 118
unions, 1, 2, 6, 8, 9, 11, 12, 22–24, 27–29,
    63–64, 73, 75, 79, 80, 95, 101, 106, 138.
    *See also* names of unions; strikes
United Automobile, Aircraft, and Vehicle
    Workers of America (UAAVW), 28–29
*United Automobile Worker*, 77, 92
urban renewal, 149, 150, 151, 154–58, 160
U.S. Commerce Department, 164
U.S. Interior Department, 164
U.S. Justice Department, 153, 158

vacation time, 138, 139
Veiller, Laurence, 40
veterans, 103, 108, 111, 114, 115, 116, 118,
    119, *184*
Vietnam War, 146, 149, 151, 161

Wagner Act, 9, 64, 81
Wallace, George, 9
War Department, 96, 98
Washburn, Lester, 12, 74–87, 88, 90, 91–92,
    101, 108, 118
Washington, D.C., 97, 117, 119, 152
welfare capitalism, 41–57, 61, 125, 132, 134,
    220n3

wet/dry battles. *See* Prohibition
White Consolidated, 153, 158
White Motors, 2, 149, 152, 153, 154, 157,
    158, 163
whiteness, 5, 61, 62, 125
Whitney, Floyd, 114
Williams, G. Mennen, 124, 144, 145
Wimmer, Alma, 108
Wobblies. *See* Industrial Workers of the
    World
women of the Ku Klux Klan, 65–66
women workers, 35, 55–57, *56*, 59, *60*,
    100–103, 104–8
Workers Age, 78
Workers Alliance, 91
World War II, 2, 7, 8, 11, 95, 118, 119, 125,
    135, 138, 142, 143, 148, 153, 154, 169;
    demobilization after, 108, 119
World's Columbian Exposition, Chicago, 21
WPA, 90, 141
WREO, 40

Yarnell, Duane, 21
YMCA, 32, 131
Young, Carl, 36, 192n43
YWCA, 32, 57

Zahavi, Gerald, 42
Zimmer, Al, 103, 130, 170

**Lisa M. Fine** is Associate Professor of History at Michigan State University. She is the author of *Souls of the Skyscraper: Female Clerical Workers in Chicago, 1870–1930* (Temple), and co-editor, with Mary Anderson, Kathleen Geissler, and Joyce Ladenson, of *Doing Feminism: Teaching and Research in the Academy*.

Also in the **Critical Perspectives on the Past** series: